IMMIGRATION

Social Issues in American History Series

Immigration
Women's Rights
Civil Rights
Labor Relations

IMMIGRATION

by
L. Edward Purcell

Social Issues in American History Series

Oryx Press
1995

The rare Arabian Oryx is believed to have inspired the myth of the unicorn. This desert antelope became virtually extinct in the early 1960s. At that time several groups of international conservationists arranged to have 9 animals sent to the Phoenix Zoo to be the nucleus of a captive breeding herd. Today the Oryx population is over 800 and nearly 400 have been returned to reserves in the Middle East.

© 1995 by L. Edward Purcell
Published by The Oryx Press
4041 North Central at Indian School Road
Phoenix, Arizona 85012-3397

Published simultaneously in Canada
Printed and Bound in the United States of America

Cover photograph courtesy of the National Park Service,
Statue of Liberty National Monument

∞ The paper used in this publication meets the minimum requirements of American National Standard for Information Science—Permanence of Paper for Printed Library Materials, ANSI Z39.48, 1984.

Library of Congress Cataloging-in-Publication Data
Purcell, L. Edward.
    Immigration / by L. Edward Purcell.
        p.   cm. — (Social issues in American history)
    Includes bibliographical references and index.
    ISBN 0-89774-873-5
    1. United States—Emigration and immigration—History. 2. United States—Emigration and immigration—Government policy. 3. Immigrants—United States. I. Title. II. Series.
JV6450.P87   1994
325.73—dc20
                                                              94-38677
                                                                 CIP

CONTENTS

• • • • • • • • •

P R E F A C E

· · · · · · · · ·

This book is intended to explain to high school and college students, as well as the general public, the historical background of American immigration, especially its social aspects, in order that they may more clearly understand the complex and sometimes controversial issues surrounding immigration today. Knowledge of the long-term context of immigration and the immigrants' ongoing role in the development of the nation is basic to this understanding. The passage in 1994 of California's Proposition 187, which denies social services and public education to illegal immigrants, highlights the importance of understanding immigration issues.

The book's narrative text covers the entire scope of modern American history, beginning with the early European explorers. It includes only a brief glance at the prehistory and history of Native Americans (called "Indians" by the first European immigrants) and comparatively little about the enforced immigration of black African slaves and the subsequent development of African American culture. Readers seeking an introduction to these subjects might consult Alvin M. Josephy, Jr., *The Indian Heritage of America* (New York: Alfred Knopf, 1968), James Axtell, *The European and the Indian* (New York: Oxford University Press, 1981), Lerone Bennett, *Before the Mayflower: A History of Black America*, 6th ed. (New York: Penguin, 1993), and John Hope Franklin, *From Slavery to Freedom: A History of Negro Americans*, 6th ed. (New York: McGraw-Hill, 1993). These topics are too large, important, and complex to deal with extensively in this book. Instead, the text concentrates on the history of voluntary immigration from the late 17th century to the late 20th and also discusses many immigrant groups from Europe, Latin America, and Asia.

The book also includes, at the end of the narrative, a section of brief biographies of people important in the history of immigration, a chronology of immigration, and an extensive listing of books for further reading.

The information and interpretation presented in this book are based on reading many books and articles that deal with specific parts of the story. The possible number of these secondary sources is huge, and only a part of them has been consulted during preparation of this book. Sources of specific quotations are cited in the text.

The story of immigration is often made clear in statistics, all of which are available in either *Historical Statistics of the United States: Colonial Times to 1970*, two vols. (Washington, DC: U.S. Dept. of Commerce, 1975) or various annual volumes in the series titled *Statistical Abstract of the United States* (Washington, DC: Bureau of the Census). Because no one can compile their own figures, almost all citations of statistics in any book or article depend on these reports of official government agencies. The U.S. government began to keep immigration statistics in 1820, and the methods, categories, and accuracy have varied greatly since. In recent decades, the Immigration and Naturalization Service has been responsible for compiling immigration figures, and demographic statistics about ethnic or national groups have been gathered by the Census Bureau.

ACKNOWLEDGMENTS

• • • • • • • • •

M y deep appreciation to the library staffs of the Cowles Library at Drake University, the Grand View College Library, the Des Moines Public Library, the University of Iowa Library (Iowa City), the State Historical Society of Iowa (Des Moines), and the West Des Moines Public Library, whose diligence and professional care made the research for this book possible.

Thanks also go to the staffs of the State Historical Society of Iowa (Des Moines), the Boston Public Library (Print Department), and the State Historical Society of Iowa (Iowa City), the Immigration History Research Center, the Jamestown Settlement, and the National Park Service, Statue of Liberty National Monument, and Ellis Island for assistance in finding the illustrations. An extra special thank you is due to Mary Bennett of the Iowa City branch of the State Historical Society, who provided extraordinarily fine advice and service—it was good to renew a professional relationship from many years ago.

My deepest gratitude goes to my wife, Mary, for her continued support and to my daughter, Sarah, who took time from her historical studies to help find illustrations, to supply bibliographical references, and to read and offer advice on an early draft of the narrative.

INTRODUCTION

• • • • • • • • •

The Scope and Character
of American Immigration

All Americans are immigrants or descendants of immigrants. We may not often think of ourselves this way, but the description is literally and absolutely true, because everyone who has ever lived in America came from some place else. Even the "Native" Americans who greeted the first European settlers during the late 16th and early 17th centuries were descended from people who had immigrated by foot from Asia many thousands of years earlier.

Over the course of American history approximately 60 million people have immigrated here and, with the notable exception of black African slaves, almost all of these millions have moved here voluntarily. They were people who came seeking a change: they were in some way unhappy or uncomfortable or threatened, and they thought America promised a better life for themselves and their children. They were usually correct in this belief, and although they sometimes faced difficulties, immigrants to America have built a richly multicultural and multiethnic nation that is unique in the world.

Eighty years ago, it was popular to describe America as a "melting pot." This phrase expressed the powerful idea that a new kind of person—a new American—would emerge from a mixing and blending of all the distinctive people who immigrated to the United States. The melting pot description also implied that the immigrants' old identities and ways of thinking and living would disappear.

In fact, the United States has never been the melting pot that was expected. Instead, immigrant ethnic groups have maintained their unique identities for generation after generation. Only the oldest American ethnic or national groups, such as the English or the Scotch-Irish, have allowed their sense of specialness to be diluted, perhaps only because their cultures were the ones seen to be dominant and the standard against which arriving peoples were measured.

Reminders, both trivial and significant, of our unique immigrant past are everywhere. Whenever someone enjoys a taco, a plate of pasta, an egg roll, a gyros sandwich, a fiery bite of jerk chicken, or the more subtle flavors of lemon-grass spiced specialties from Southeast Asia, the influence of immigrants is experienced directly through smell and taste. Public events ranging from Italian street fairs in Rhode Island to Hispanic festivals in New Mexico celebrate the healthy persistence of national heritages. Hundreds of thousands of Americans worship each week in churches whose modern forms are derived from immigrant imports, ranging from Eastern European Orthodox Judaism to Swiss Anabaptist Mennonites to Norwegian Lutherans. In these and countless other ways, the immigrant heritage has worked itself into the basic fabric of American life.

There are also many less pleasant aspects of immigration. Lately, issues of illegal aliens and refugees are again major problems of public policy and life. Despite reforms in 1986 and 1990, which were intended to make our immigration laws more rational and humanitarian, the nation seems to many to have lost control of its borders.

Evidence of the importance of immigration issues is everywhere in modern American society. We read stories about it in our newspapers and see nightly reports on the television news. We learn that a flood of Middle Eastern immigrants and aliens seeking political asylum includes terrorists. We see state and local government officials launch campaigns to limit services for some classes of immigrant families. Scarcely a week goes by that we do not hear about the thousands of illegal immigrants pushing across the nation's southern border or attempting to land from tightly packed, rusty Asian ships or rickety Haitian sailboats or fragile Cuban rafts. All of these things encourage opposition to immigration.

Anti-immigration feelings and politics are not new. These arguments and attacks have been heard again and again throughout America's past. The cycle seems closely tied to economic issues: when the nation needs laborers, immigrants of all kinds are welcomed; when jobs are scarce, immigrants are excluded.

There is also a deeply rooted tendency for Americans to blame the most recent immigrant group for problems, probably because the immigrants seem too foreign or strange. When a particular immigrant group feels it has established itself, it considers the next group as less worthy. This cycle, too, goes back to the earliest days of the American experience, and we can trace the change in many immigrant groups from being despised newcomers to becoming smug nativists, people who attack immigrants or "foreigners."

IMMIGRATION TO THE UNITED STATES, 1820–1989

Year	Number	Year	Number	Year	Number	Year	Number	Year	Number
1820–1989	55,457,531	1853	368,645	1888	546,889	1922	309,556	1957	326,867
1820	8,385	1854	427,833	1889	444,427	1923	522,919	1958	253,265
1821–30	143,439	1855	200,877	1890	455,302	1924	706,896	1959	260,686
1821	9,127	1856	200,436	1891–1900	3,687,564	1925	294,314	1960	265,398
1822	6,911	1857	251,306	1891	560,319	1926	304,488	1961–70	3,321,677
1823	6,354	1858	123,126	1892	579,663	1927	335,175	1961	271,344
1824	7,912	1859	121,282	1893	439,730	1928	307,255	1962	283,763
1825	10,199	1860	153,640	1894	285,631	1929	279,678	1963	306,260
1826	10,837	1861–70	2,314,824	1895	258,536	1930	241,700	1964	292,248
1827	18,875	1861	91,918	1896	343,267	1931–40	528,431	1965	296,697
1828	27,382	1862	91,985	1897	230,832	1931	97,139	1966	323,040
1829	22,520	1863	176,282	1898	229,299	1932	35,576	1967	361,972
1830	23,322	1864	193,418	1899	311,715	1933	23,068	1968	454,448
1831–40	599,125	1865	248,120	1900	448,572	1934	29,470	1969	358,579
1831	22,633	1866	318,568	1901–10	8,795,386	1935	34,956	1970	373,326
1832	60,482	1867	315,722	1901	487,918	1936	36,329	1971–80	4,493,314
1833	58,640	1868	138,840	1902	648,743	1937	50,244	1971	370,478
1834	65,365	1869	352,768	1903	857,046	1938	67,895	1972	384,685
1835	45,374	1870	387,203	1904	812,870	1939	82,998	1973	400,063
1836	76,242	1871–80	2,812,191	1905	1,026,499	1940	70,756	1974	394,861
1837	79,340	1871	321,350	1906	1,100,735	1941–50	1,035,039	1975	386,194
1838	38,914	1872	404,806	1907	1,285,349	1941	51,776	1976	398,613
1839	68,069	1873	459,803	1908	782,870	1942	28,781	1976, TQ	103,676
1840	84,066	1874	313,339	1909	751,786	1943	23,725	1977	462,315
1841–50	1,713,251	1875	227,498	1910	1,041,570	1944	28,551	1978	601,442
1841	80,289	1876	169,986	1911–20	5,735,811	1945	38,119	1979	460,348
1842	104,565	1877	141,857	1911	878,587	1946	108,721	1980	530,639
1843	52,496	1878	138,469	1912	838,172	1947	147,292	1981–89	5,801,579
1844	78,615	1879	177,826	1913	1,197,892	1948	170,570	1981	596,600
1845	114,371	1880	457,257	1914	1,218,480	1949	188,317	1982	594,131
1846	154,416	1881–90	5,246,613	1915	326,700	1950	249,187	1983	559,763
1847	234,968	1881	669,431	1916	298,826	1951–60	2,515,479	1984	543,903
1848	226,527	1882	788,992	1917	295,403	1951	205,717	1985	570,009
1849	297,024	1883	603,322	1918	110,618	1952	265,520	1986	601,708
1850	369,980	1884	518,592	1919	141,132	1953	170,434	1987	601,516
1851–60	2,598,214	1885	395,346	1920	430,001	1954	208,177	1988	643,025
1851	379,466	1886	334,203	1921–30	4,107,209	1955	237,790	1989	1,090,924
1852	371,603	1887	490,109	1921	805,228	1956	321,625		

NOTE: The numbers shown are as follows: from 1820–67, figures represent alien passengers arrived at seaports; from 1868–91 and 1895–97, immigrant aliens arrived; from 1892–94 and 1898–1989, immigrant aliens admitted for permanent residence. From 1892–1903, aliens entering by cabin class were not counted as immigrants. Land arrivals were not completely enumerated until 1908.

SOURCE: The U.S. Immigration and Naturalization Service

Moreover, recent world economic and political conditions, as well as changes in American policy have produced an explosion of new immigration. Of the estimated total of over 55 million people who immigrated to America between 1820 and 1990, more than 10 percent (5.8 million) arrived during the 1980s, mostly from Mexico and Asia, relatively new sources. The resulting pressures, fears, adjustments, and developments—while no different than problems experienced throughout history—have produced urgent public concern about immigration.

Despite the impression that current immigration problems are new and that the recent increase in newcomers from Asia and Latin America presents issues unique to the 1980s and 1990s, the historical record shows that the *social process* of immigration has changed little over the nearly four centuries of American life. Although the settings and circumstances have varied sharply, the actual experience of immigrants has been remarkably similar whether the people came ashore at Jamestown in the first years of the 17th century or arrived 10 years ago by plane from a Vietnamese refugee camp in Thailand. We have all experienced a process of adjustment, both the newcomer and those who were here to greet them.

America's immigration experience has had a two-way, double-edged effect: life in the new world changed immigrants (drastically in some cases) and their imported viewpoints, customs, and abilities changed America.

This exchange did not melt immigrants together into some standardized form of American. Instead, it produced a society in which Hmong hill warriors and 10th-generation descendants of British colonists share a nationality. This uniquely American mixture, though uneasy at times, is the product of a long historical process and exists in fact as well as in ideal.

Maldwyn Jones, a perceptive British historian of American immigration, wrote in *American Immigration* (Chicago: University of Chicago, 1992): "The story of American immigration is one of millions of enterprising, courageous folk, most of them humble, nearly all of them unknown by name to history. Coming from a great variety of backgrounds, they nonetheless resembled one another in their willingness to look beyond the horizon and in their readiness to pull up stakes in order to seek a new life."

CHAPTER 1

. . . .

The First Europeans, Native Americans, and the Forced Immigration of Black Africans

It wasn't until nearly a century after Columbus made his landfall in the Caribbean in 1492 that Europeans began to actually colonize today's United States. Initially most Europeans viewed the New World almost purely in terms of potential for exploitation rather than as a place to emigrate.

The explorers from England and France who sailed along the eastern seaboard during the 1500s, staking claims for their countries as they went, were driven by visions of quick and easy wealth. The Spanish *Conquistadors* who conquered and terrorized all of Mexico and Central America were openly greedy. Reports of the fantastic journeys of Cabeza de Vaca and Francisco Coronado though the North American wilderness and desert only heightened the Spanish hunger for gold, slaves, and easy riches.

THE FIRST COLONIAL IMMIGRANTS

In 1598, the Spanish finally sent a group of settlers and colonists under the command of Juan de Oñate north into present-day New Mexico. Greed was again probably one of the chief motivations of these colonists, and they certainly hoped to exploit the native peoples to produce easy fortunes for themselves. However, they were not merely explorers or travelers; they were immigrants, people who intended to settle in the new land. Modern Santa Fe

Replicas of the three ships that brought the first permanent English immigrants to Virginia in 1607 are moored at the re-created Jamestown Settlement near Williamsburg. (Photo courtesy of Jamestown-Yorktown Foundation)

eventually developed from one of these early settlements. However, this group of Spanish settlers in the Southwest was small; the really serious business of immigration and colonization took place far to the east.

England claimed the eastern coast of America after a voyage sponsored by Sir Walter Raleigh in 1584. Virginia, named by Raleigh after Elizabeth I, the "Virgin Queen," covered a vaguely defined territory between the Spanish territory to the south (in what is now Florida) and French and Dutch claims to the north, in areas explored respectively by Jacques Cartier and Henrik Hudson.

The first English immigrants were members of an experimental colony, set up strictly for exploitation more or less on the Spanish model, who settled on Roanoke Island off the Carolina coast in 1587. All of these colonists had disappeared without a trace by the time a supply ship returned three years later. Because they came ill-prepared for long-term settlement, their fate pointed to the truth that the real future of America lay in immigration for settlement rather than for greed.

In 1607, the first permanent English settlement began when slightly more than a hundred Englishmen (with no women or children) landed in Virginia and built a colony at Jamestown. They acted in the name of a joint-stock company, a form of 17th-century corporation founded to acquire gold, fur, and other precious commodities that were supposedly available for the picking. Though the period produced some charming folklore, such as the romantic story of Captain John Smith and Pocahontas, life was actually very hard for these first English immigrants. In the first two decades, they experienced terrible starvation, social disorientation, and conflict with the native Indians. Though about 8,000 men and women came across the Atlantic to Virginia between 1607 and 1624, only about 1,300 survived.

Slowly, however, a pattern developed that became a successful basis for the English settlement of Virginia and the Chesapeake region. (Virginia became a royal colony in 1624 and Maryland was chartered in 1634, originally as a haven of religious tolerance for Roman Catholics but soon turned into a royal colony.) The southern English colonists admitted that there were no quick riches to be found, but that by diligent work and careful cultivation the fertile soils of the region would produce abundant crops. The primary product was tobacco, a New World plant that became almost as precious as gold in the European marketplace.

A few wealthy landowners came to control the tobacco-based economy of Virginia and the Chesapeake. Because tobacco farming required large numbers of workers and English attempts to enslave the Indians failed, tens of thousands of ordinary lower-class men and women (the first females arrived in 1620) also immigrated. Most came to the English southern colonies as indentured servants. In exchange for passage to Virginia or Maryland and the promise of land at the end of their service, they contracted to give up temporarily most of their economic and legal rights and work for the landowners under terms of a contract (called an indenture) for between four and seven years. These people were eager to escape from England, where economic changes had driven many workers into poverty and where decades of political unrest and revolution had created social chaos. Most of those who immigrated as indentured servants were young and rootless men between the ages of 15 and 24, former farmers or common laborers. A significant number, however, had been craftsmen or small tradesmen in Britain.

They often led harsh and difficult lives during their time as servants. Their tasks on the tobacco farms were hard, and they worked 10 to 12 hours a day, six days a week. They had little recourse against their cruel masters, who could sell or trade them like commodities. Disease killed many and the early death rate may have been as high as 40 percent among white indentured servants. Yet, despite these conditions, thousands upon thousands of young English people accepted the risks—as many as 100,000 may have immigrated to Virginia and Maryland as indentured servants during the 1600s, forming the backbone of the English southern colonies.

To the north of Virginia and Maryland, in the region known as New England (made up of modern-day Massachusetts, Connecticut, New Hampshire, Rhode Island, Vermont, and Maine), English immigrants came to the

New World for reasons at least in part different from either the wealthy landowners or indentured servants of the South. These immigrants sought not just land and wealth, but also freedom from religious and political restriction.

The landing at Plymouth Rock in 1620 of members of a small English sect known as the Pilgrims marked the beginning of what became a great migration. The Pilgrims can be called the first immigrant refugees to land in America. They had been harassed in England because of their extreme religious views and had spent several years in Holland before they decided to make a new beginning in the New World. There were not many of them, however; the population of the colony at Plymouth never grew beyond a few hundred.

The Pilgrims were followed 10 years later by a much larger and better-funded group, the Puritans, who shared some of the Pilgrims's religious beliefs but were on the whole less radical. They were not so much escaping persecution in England as seeking to establish in the New World a model society based on their religious principles.

Many of the Puritans, especially the leaders, were relatively prosperous in England. They formed a joint-stock company (which became the basis for their government in the New World) and in a very clever move, took the company's charter along to America, thereby controlling their own political and economic destiny. The Puritans named their colony Massachusetts Bay and set up their chief town in Boston.

Although there were a few non-Puritans among them, most of the Massachusetts settlers were like-minded families from the same region (East Anglia) who gave the northern colony a different character from that of the English colonies to the south. Lead by men such as John Winthrop, the Puritans sought stability and permanence rather than quick exploitation of the land. Their major efforts were put toward finding ways to establish self-sustaining agriculture. The family-run farm and the villages supporting the farms formed the basis of their society, and there were few indentured servants.

Moreover, the Massachusetts Puritans were religious and social reformers. In the topsy-turvy world of English society during the 17th century, the Puritans had clashed with the king and the aristocracy and especially the established political and religious practices of the Church of England. Puritans who immigrated may have wanted to escape from the constant tensions of life at home, but they also saw an opportunity to put their reform ideas into practice by creating an ideal society in which godly principles guided and controlled life. They felt they were on an "errand in the wilderness" and believed they had a mission, as Winthrop wrote in a famous description, to build "a city upon a hill, the eyes of all people are upon us." (Quoted in Mary Beth Norton, et al., *A People & A Nation* [Boston: Houghton, Mifflin, 1990] 32.)

In only a few years, tens of thousands of Puritans braved the long sea voyage and the often cruel conditions of New England during the first decades after its founding to find religious freedom and a new start. As newcomers occupied most of the good land in the first settlements and as religious dissention (they were often at odds over matters of belief) created spin-offs, the northern colonists spread from Massachusetts Bay to begin new settlements in what became the neighboring colonies of Rhode Island, Connecticut, and New Hampshire.

In an important sense, the settlement of the southern colonies and New England by English immigrants of the 1600s and 1700s established the basic context of American society. English was the dominant language in America; English legal and governmental forms were the norm; and culture was for two centuries copied after English literature, drama, and art. Whether we like to admit it or not, the British immigrants gave us the first model of what Americans thought society should be.

This aspect of British immigration has often been over-emphasized or over-promoted for dubious purposes in the past. During the late 1800s, for example, when large numbers of immigrants were streaming into New York from southern and eastern Europe, looking and sounding very different from the English, the anxieties of many Americans were focused through a celebration of a vaguely defined "Anglo-Saxonism" that all too often had unpleasant racist and nativist overtones.

Nonetheless, the society established by British immigrants of the 17th and 18th centuries produced most of the basic forms of American life, many of them flowing from the American Revolution and decades of political development dominated by descendants of the original English immigrants. Other key elements of American life, such as the widespread use of the English language and English systems of law, education, and business, must be traced directly to the British immigrants.

In the 20th century, the British immigrants and their descendants came to be characterized (and sometimes ridiculed) as WASPs (White Anglo-Saxon Protestants). People of WASP heritage were depicted as somewhat stuffy but ever-powerful movers and shakers of American society.

What is sometimes overlooked is the fact that the British exerted a powerful historical presence by sheer numbers as well as cultural influence. British immigration to America continued at significant levels until late in the 19th century. However, many of these immigrants were virtually invisible to history because they were so indistinguishable from the general American population. Today, more than 40 million Americans claim descent from British immigrant ancestors, and it was not until the mid-1980s that Americans of German heritage surpassed the British as the largest immigrant group.

In short, the distinctively American form of British culture that developed in the United States is—like it or not—the background against which all subsequent immigration took place.

THE NATIVE AMERICANS

The continent to which the English and other immigrant colonists came during the 1600s was not, of course, unpopulated. The Indians, as the Native Americans were called by the Spaniards when they thought they had found the Orient, had lived in the Americas for perhaps as long as 40,000 years. It is not known exactly when humans first walked across a temporarily dry land bridge from Asia to what is now Alaska. However, there is no question that the New World was populated over this route and that these ancient immigrants developed a fantastically complex set of cultures.

Millions of Indians lived in North and South America by the time Columbus made the first European contact. The Indians developed as many as 2,000 separate languages and lived in hundreds of different kinds of cultures, ranging from the extremely complex societies such as the Aztecs of Mexico to the relatively simple lifestyles of California tribes such as the Shasta. Though their cultures were rich and strong and they were well adapted to their environment, almost all the Indians shared two fatal weaknesses when dealing with the European invaders: they had no immunities to even the simplest European diseases and their weapons and war-making technology remained rooted in the stone age.

The full effect of European disease on the Indians will never be known precisely, because estimates of pre-European populations are only informed guesses. However, it is certain that tens of millions of Indians died from the spread of diseases such as small pox and measles. The situations we know most about show only the edge of the experience: of the million or so Indians living on the island of Hispaniola when Columbus landed there in 1492 only 500 remained 50 years later. As many as nine million Indians in Mexico alone may have died from disease during the first hundred years of contact with the Spanish.

Those Indians who survived illness were unable to withstand the military onslaught of the Europeans. Time after time, superior European technology and military organization crushed the Indians' armed resistance. Furthermore, though white propaganda and folklore usually painted the Indian as savage, uncivilized foe, it was the ruthless European policies of extermination and repression that epitomized savagery in the New World. Europeans did not hesitate to use firearms and modern tactics to subdue, enslave, and kill any Indians who stood in their way.

The English who came ashore in Massachusetts during the first half of the 17th century stumbled into a region where disease had already done its deadly work. Germs spread from earlier contacts with European fishermen had nearly depopulated the immediate vicinity of the Pilgrim and Puritan settlements, thus isolating the European immigrants from the more vigorous tribes of the northeast, at least for the time being. The early white settlers could not have survived the first winter—nor many winters thereafter, most likely—without the generous advice and assistance of the local tribesmen who survived the diseases the English brought.

The first encounters of the English in Virginia with the Indians also were lucky. During the European colonists' first miserable years there, the local Indians were led by the highly tolerant Powhatan, who was busy consolidating his own political power and did not see the few whites as a threat. For more than 10 years, conflict between them was relatively low-key and sporadic.

Eventually, however, in both the southern and northern colonies, peace came to an end, and a pattern emerged that remained constant until the late 19th century. As the Europeans expanded farms and settlements inland from the coast, they bumped up against Indian tribes who did not want to give up territory that had been theirs for generations. Neither side understood the other's concept of land and land usage—the Indians had no concept of owning land and the Europeans could not understand any form of using land except settled agriculture—and neither respected the other's right to exist. Sometimes the Indians struck first, sometimes the whites did, but in the end, the Indians were dispossessed and forced to move on, further and further inland. By the last armed conflicts in the 1890s, the natives had been reduced to the tiniest fraction of their former numbers and were generally confined to small enclaves of poverty and social distress.

In Virginia, the first big clash came in 1622, when Powhatan's brother led a surprise attack that killed almost a third of the British settlers. Other battles followed during the next 20 years, until the Indian confederation was decisively defeated. At intervals thereafter, as the need for more and more land drove European immigrant settlers westward, renewed conflicts removed the Indians entirely from east of the Mississippi River.

The story was nearly identical in New England, where the first peaceful relationship of white and Indian was broken when settlers pressed into new territory in the Connecticut Valley. The resulting warfare was even more vicious than in Virginia. During the Pequot War of 1637, for example, the Puritan soldiers of Massachusetts Bay colony annihilated almost the entire Pequot tribe, selling off into slavery the few who had not been hacked, shot, or burned to death. Nearly 40 years later, an Indian confederation under a leader known to the British as King Philip nearly succeeded in wiping out the outlying European settlements before succumbing to the superior force of Puritans. This pattern was repeated over following decades until the Indians were no longer a threat or a barrier.

Thus, the migration of people from Britain and Europe to the New World—a movement that seemed to the immigrants to embody hope and promise and opportunity—was for the native Indians a death sentence. This epic tragedy was one of the most terrible consequences of American immigration.

AFRICAN SLAVES

The greatest historical tragedy of all, called America's original sin by Thomas Jefferson, was the forced immigration of hundreds of thousands of black Africans, brought to America as slaves.

The first 20 black slaves landed at Jamestown from a Dutch ship in 1619. After that the English were relatively slow to import black slaves into Virginia and the Chesapeake colonies, though many thousands were purchased for labor on sugar plantations in the British West Indies. Only when the supply of white indentured servants began to wane in the last decades of the 1600s, did the English colonists of North America turn to Africa for agricultural workers.

During the final quarter of the 17th century, forced immigration of blacks increased sharply. By around 1690 there were more black slaves than white indentured servants in the region that would become Maryland. By 1700 at least a thousand black slaves were brought to Virginia each year. Overall, between the first importations in 1619 and the official end of the slave trade in 1807 (under the laws adopted by the new nation as part of the compromise that resulted in agreement over the Constitution), hundreds of thousands of black Africans arrived. Probably 275,000 black slaves were imported during the 1700s alone when the slave trade was at its peak.

There is some evidence that blacks were initially regarded as only slightly different than white indentured servants, at least in the legal sense. But the English colonists saw the black Africans with racist eyes and were quick to develop a form of slavery based on the color of the Africans' skin. By 1640, there were new laws fixing black slavery for life and imposing harsh rules of behavior on black Americans. It was virtually impossible for black Africans to arrive in America as anything but a slave. The vast majority of modern black Americans are descended from Africans who were enslaved and imported against their wills.

The African slave trade was one of the most vicious episodes in history. Several black states along the West Coast of Africa cooperated with the white European merchants from Britain, Holland, Spain, and Portugal by providing the human merchandise (because few Europeans were brave enough to venture inland to procure their own slaves), but the economic motivation for these Africans to enslave and trade their fellow blacks came directly from Europe.

The great black civilizations of Central Africa of earlier centuries, such as Ghana, Mali, and Songhai, had faded by the beginning of the American slave trade and were vulnerable to exploitation. Once separate African peoples were captured and lumped together, their rich and diverse cultures were obscured in European eyes into a single identity, that of "Black Gold."

The slave trade lacked even the minimum standards of humanity. The European slave traders inflected misery on a massive number of humans, treating them as nothing more than a commodity. People were yoked together like animals at West African slave ports, then packed together below decks. Feeding and hygiene of those in the slave holds were done only to preserve profits, and only feeble attempts were made to provide anything but the barest necessities. Many traders calculated a high death rate among the black passengers as the cost of doing business.

Those black Africans who survived the ghastly trip arrived in a new world filled with disorientation, hard work, and lifelong hopelessness. They were separated from family, friends, society, culture, and home—spewed from the slave hold into places where few understood the language and most were forced into torturous labor, day after day for the rest of their lives. The contrast to other immigrants to America could not have been more stark.

The English colonists of Virginia and the Chesapeake found ample use for black slaves in the tobacco fields, but the institution of slavery in America really escalated only after the founding of new colonies in the Carolinas. The major crop there was rice, which required both the expertise of black slave farmers who had grown rice in Africa and the forced labor of black workers who could withstand diseases such as malaria that were common in the swampy Carolina back country as well as in the hot climates of Africa.

Carolina was founded as one colony in 1669, but split into north and south 60 years later. In South Carolina, the addition of indigo (a plant that produced a valuable natural blue dye) to rice as a staple crop only increased the English colonists' need for slave labor. By around 1710, there were more black Africans than white colonists living in South Carolina, creating the beginnings of a society based on coercion and fear. Until the American Civil War a century and a half later, white slave owners in South Carolina were terrified that their black slaves might rise up and overwhelm them, and this anxiety made the region the stronghold of resistance to reform.

Although there were certainly black slaves held in the New England colonies, the pattern of small-farm agriculture was not well suited to the exploitation of slave labor, so the institution never flourished there. However, the pattern of large-scale slave-based farming was fixed in the southern British colonies by the turn of the 17th century, and little occurred to alter it for generation after generation.

Not all black Africans and their offspring were mere victims, of course. Even in slavery, black African Americans developed social customs, music, religion, and food of their own, and after the Civil War contributed mightily to the general culture and development of the United States. Yet the effects of the forced immigration of African slaves on both the enslaved and the enslavers and the subsequent effects of the racism that the system introduced have never left America.

OTHER EUROPEAN COLONIAL IMMIGRANTS

The English were always the dominant colonial power, but they were by no means the only white immigrants from Europe during the first decades of settlement. For a brief but important span, the Dutch were their chief rivals, and the Swedes made a half-hearted attempt to foster an early Scandinavian presence in the New World.

The Dutch claimed much of what is modern-day New York after Henrik Hudson explored the Hudson River in 1609. Twelve years later, the first Dutch immigrants arrived to begin a colony known as New Netherlands, with its chief settlement at New Amsterdam (modern-day New York City) and an outpost at Fort Orange (modern Albany).

The Dutch immigrants came under the sponsorship of the Dutch West Indian Company, a commercial venture much like the English company that started settlement at Jamestown. William Usselinx, a Dutch entrepreneur and promoter, had badgered the government of Holland to create the company, but he grew impatient with their slow progress and withdrew. The real spark for colonization of New Netherlands came from Peter Minuit, its second governor who is famous in American mythology for his supposed purchase of Manhattan Island from the local Indians for a handful of trinkets.

The ablest and subsequently best-known Dutch official to preside over New Netherlands was Peter Stuyvesant, who was governor during the colony's final years from 1647 to 1664. He was a strong-willed character often at odds with the mixed population of New Amsterdam, a place famed for its cosmopolitan, multicultural make-up, including small numbers of immigrants from many European nations. Stuyvesant also guided the establishment of a Dutch presence in upstate New York, where the West India Company made grants of huge tracts of land to individual "patroons" who were responsible for importing immigrant Dutch farmers to work the land. This feudal system was moderately successful, and by the end of Stuyvesant's reign there were Dutch farming settlements all along the upper reaches of the Hudson Valley—a heritage that inspired 19th-century writer Washington Irving to produce the *Knickerbocker Tales*. Many place names in New York state and New York City such as the Bronx still give evidence of the original Dutch settlement and immigration, although the actual numbers of Dutch immigrants during the 17th century was low.

The Dutch claims to the region were disputed from the beginning by the English, however, and as was common in questions of empire, might made right. An English fleet sailed into the harbor at New Amsterdam in 1664, and aided by a revolt among Stuyvesant's local political foes, took over the colony in the name of the English king's brother, the Duke of York.

Before being engulfed by the English, the Dutch did their part to stifle another European attempt at colonization. The Swedes had ambitions in the New World also, stimulated by the same Peter Minuit who had touched off Dutch settlement. Having switched allegiance, he was the organizer of the first Swedish trading colony in modern-day Delaware.

The Swedish enterprise was never realized on a large scale. In fact, it was probably doomed from the beginning because social and economic conditions in Sweden were good at the time, which meant that very few Swedes wanted to emigrate. The sponsors of New Sweden were forced to recruit whomever they could with whatever results. The colony fell to a Dutch attack led by Stuyvesant and virtually disappeared. The major impact of Swedish immigration did not come for another 200 years.

THE FIRST REFUGEES

There were two distinct refugee groups during the 17th century who represented another aspect of immigration.

The first came from France, where in 1685 Louis XIV revoked the Edict of Nantes, which allowed French Protestants to live peacefully among their Catholic neighbors. The result was the virtual expulsion from France of tens of thousands of Protestants, known as Huguenots.

Many Huguenots were relatively wealthy and well placed in French society. Among their number were merchants, professionals, and skilled craftsmen, many of whom immigrated to America. More than a hundred families came to Massachusetts after 1685 and many others moved to cities such as New York and Charleston, where they were generally successful in starting new careers. For the most part, the Huguenots easily submerged themselves into the dominant British culture of the American colonies, with only a few French names (Paul Revere's family name was originally De Rivoire, which his father anglicized) signalling their origins.

Another small but important refugee group also appeared during the 17th century. The first group of 23 immigrant European Jews moved to New Amsterdam in 1654 from a Dutch colony in Brazil that had fallen to the Portuguese. They were Sephardic Jews whose forbearers had lived in Spain before their expulsion or forced conversion under the Inquisition. A trickle of similar Hispanic Jews found their way to America during the following decades, so that by the time of the American Revolution there were significant colonies of Jews in the major cities of Newport, New York, and

Philadelphia. These educated and generally prosperous people had an impact far beyond their numbers and enjoyed relative freedom from overt persecution in the British colonies, although they were barred from holding public office or voting. The tens of thousands of Germanic Jews and the hundreds of thousands of Ashkenazic Jews who immigrated to America from Eastern Europe at the end of the 19th century in many cases obscured the heritage of these first Jews.

NEW COLONIES

The leavening of small but important groups such as the Huguenots and the Sephardic Jews illustrated the direction immigration would take in the new colonies formed after the surrender of the Dutch. British king Charles II granted a vast region encompassing most of the modern states of New York and New Jersey to his brother, James, Duke of York. The English warships that compelled the Dutch surrender of New Amsterdam acted in the Duke's behalf, and sovereignty of the region passed to him. He retained most of New York state under his own control, but granted the area of New Jersey to two of his friends who set up a proprietary colony and put in place schemes to attract immigrants. One of the characteristics of the new colony was its diverse make-up: more than just Englishmen came to settle.

Even more diverse was the population of Pennsylvania, granted by Charles II in 1681 to William Penn, a wealthy and influential English Quaker. The subsequent Penn proprietary colony welcomed dissenters and immigrants from all over. This attitude plus the attraction of Pennsylvania's fertile farmlands and rapidly growing port at Philadelphia meant a significant inflow of people, including Germans, Irish, Welsh, and Dutch, the latter spilling over from what had been New Netherlands.

By about the end of the 1600s, the nature of immigration to America changed. The century of settlement and enterprise had produced relatively stable conditions in the colonies (life there was no longer always a desperate struggle), and the circumstances in England, the source of most early immigration, changed also. For example, the great burst of immigration by the Puritans to New England had ceased altogether by the mid-1600s when the great Puritan Revolution in England wiped out the need for the Calvinist dissenters to leave, and by the late 1600s the supply of young Englishmen willing to indenture themselves for work on Chesapeake tobacco farms had dried up (the collapse of tobacco prices contributed to the change). In sum, these and other developments meant that new immigrant groups in addition to the English entered the American colonies in large numbers in the 50 or 60 years before the Revolution.

CHAPTER 2

New Immigrants and a New Nation

C hief among the new immigrants of the 18th century were hundreds of thousands of Scotch-Irish, a group that came to form one of the fundamental bases of American population and culture. Indeed, the Scotch-Irish might be accurately depicted as the backbone of American life from the 1770s until the Civil War. Since then, the distinctive nature of their background has been submerged into American culture to a large degree, although the essence of Scotch-Irish culture has been preserved in the rural and mountain regions of the South and Southeast, particularly in Appalachian culture.

Even though no one in the 1700s made the distinction, the Scotch-Irish should not be confused with the native Irish, who sent comparatively few immigrants to America before the mid-19th century. Nor should the Scotch-Irish be mixed up with the few but distinctive Highland Scots who immigrated to the Carolinas after the failed Scottish uprisings of the 1740s.

The Scotch-Irish were Protestant Presbyterian Scots, Lowlanders who had been transplanted by the British government to the northern counties of Ireland during the early 1600s to form a barrier against the unruly Irish Catholics to the south. The modern-day political and religious divisions in Northern Ireland have their origins in the same developments.

The Scotch-Irish emigrated to America for several reasons, the most important being economic. Conditions turned bad for most of them in Northern Ireland (also called Ulster) around the turn of the 18th century when land rents went up sharply and it became increasingly difficult for small farmers to support a family. Since the Scotch-Irish were Calvinist Presbyterians they also suffered under new British laws that deprived non–Church of England "dissenters" of political rights.

The first wave of Scotch-Irish began in 1717 and was followed by four more bursts at regular intervals over the next six decades. This fairly steady flow in the years before the American Revolution almost ceased after it. No one is certain exactly how many Scotch-Irish came during this time, but the numbers certainly exceeded a quarter million. There was a good deal of encouraging communication between recent immigrants and those still in Ulster during the middle years of the migration, and ship owners recruited immigrants as well, two factors that probably increased the numbers crossing the sea.

At first, the Scotch-Irish came to New England, establishing farms on the western frontier of Massachusetts and Connecticut and acting as a buffer against the Indians—a role characteristic of the group throughout history. The amount of land in New England was limited, however, and the Scotch-Irish were not warmly received by the older colonists, so within a few years the bulk of the Scotch-Irish turned south and west to Pennsylvania. As the years went on, another shift funneled large numbers of Scotch-Irish immigrant settlers down the Great Valley of the Appalachian Mountains toward new lands in the western regions of the Carolinas (many newcomers also landed directly in Charleston).

Some of the Scotch-Irish emigrated under the organizing hands of their Presbyterian ministers, with entire congregations moving together, but for many the only way to finance emigration was to indenture themselves. Once they worked off their obligation, they looked for land, which they typically found on the western borders of the colonies. By the 1770s, thousands of Scotch-Irish families were farming areas that were regarded by old-line colonists as back country. They became, in fact as well as image, the prototypes of the American frontiersmen. Since they had been displaced in England, they had no strong allegiance to an "old country" and were in the opinion of many historians the first immigrant group to strongly identify itself as essentially American. They participated significantly on the patriot side in the American Revolution and enjoyed great success in national politics—at least 11 presidents between James K. Polk and Woodrow Wilson descended from the Scotch-Irish.

Yet, perhaps because they had to struggle so hard to exist on marginal lands and because they lacked the educational or social polish of immigrants from England, the Scotch-Irish have seldom been portrayed in a flattering way. Travelers on the American frontier often reported on the eccentricities of these isolated people, and repeated political conflicts with colonial governments over land and taxes created the impression that they were uncouth and undisciplined. The 20th-century stereotype of the "hillbilly" developed directly from these 18th-century beginnings.

It is probably safe to assert that, outside the rural South, most modern Americans descended from the Scotch-Irish seldom recognize their own heritage, because it has become buried so deeply in the American past.

THE FIRST GERMANS

More Americans alive today—about 18 percent of the population—claim German ancestry than any other national heritage. The forbearers of these people came to America in two distinct waves. The first began in 1683, when the *Concord* sailed into Philadelphia with several German families seeking new homes in Pennsylvania. They came under the leadership of Francis Pastorius, an immigration recruiter who had arranged for the purchase of land from William Penn. This first contingent established Germantown, only a few miles from Philadelphia.

These early Germans, who as Quakers and Mennonites were religious dissenters, were the first of many people willing to leave the fragmented German states (there was no unified Germany until 1871 when the high tide of German immigration had already passed) where repressive governments and frequent wars made life miserable for ordinary folk. Other Germans followed, settling in Pennsylvania, where their English-speaking neighbors referred to them as "Dutch," misunderstanding that when they called themselves "Deutsch," they meant German. Thus, these German immigrants became known as the "Pennsylvania Dutch," a linguistic confusion that has persisted into the 20th century.

In 1710, British colonial officials recruited a large group from the Rhineland of Germany to settle in the Mohawk Valley of New York to increase the production of forest-grown naval stores such as mast timbers and pine pitch for the Royal Navy. The Palatinate Germans (as the Rhinelanders were called in America) had many disagreements with the government over the terms of settlement and land, so they moved into their own settlements in the western part of the colony, braving Indian attacks in exchange for rich lands and freedom from government directives.

Several other colonization schemes in the first decades of the 18th century resulted in enclaves of Germans in places such as New Bern, North Carolina, but the majority of the first wave of German immigrants probably came on their own.

Many of them were too poor to afford passage, so they became what were called "redemptioners," a variation on the indentured servitude of the previous century. After immigrants from Germany reached the port cities in Europe and England, they pledged themselves to the ship masters or the shipping companies in exchange for passage to America. When they landed in American ports, they were sold off (or "redeemed") to the highest bidders. This system led to hideous abuses because the shippers had little incentive to provide a comfortable or healthy passage once a pledge had been made and many who bought the services of the immigrants were wicked masters. However, the terms of service were relatively short and tens of thousands of Germans financed their journeys in such a fashion.

The large migration of Germans was stimulated initially by the long War of Spanish Succession that disrupted life in Europe from 1702 to 1713. The Rhineland region was particularly hard hit, and thousands of Rhinelanders left, going first to Great Britain and then to America. There are no accurate figures, but historians believe that Palatinate Germans and people from southern Germany arrived in increasingly large numbers each year from around 1717 to 1756, when a new war between France and Britain, involving North America, halted travel.

There were also several groups of religious refugees among the Germans. The largest group consisted of Anabaptists who had developed apart from the mainline Reformation churches, such as the Mennonites and Amish who eventually created a distinctive region in Lancaster County Pennsylvania. The Moravians, another splinter sect, also immigrated during this period and had an impact on the frontier of Pennsylvania and Ohio. The great majority of German immigrants to America, however, were members of the German Lutheran or German Reformed churches. Their religion set them apart from the older Anglo-Americans, but only to a slight degree.

The Germans were by far the largest non-British and non-English speaking group in America, and they usually brought with them a full-blown culture and set of social habits that were considerably at odds with the Scotch-Irish or the old-line English. To many older Americans, the Germans seemed obsessed with hard work and insistent on orderliness and regularity—characteristics that sharply contrasted with the easy-going habits of the Scotch-Irish. The Germans also imported a great national literature and a love of fine music.

Because they stood out from earlier immigrants, the 18th-century Germans were the first large immigrant group to suffer from the fear and suspicion of those who had been here before and demanded that they assimilate into an existing culture. Because the Germans resisted changing their customs or their language just to accommodate a new land, some Americans saw them as a threat. In fact, Benjamin Franklin complained that Pennsylvania was in danger of too many German immigrants and their potential to inundate everyone else. He wrote in 1751: "Why should the Palatinate Boors be suffered into our Settlements, and by herding together establish their Language and Manners to the Exclusion of ours? Why should Pennsylvania, founded by the English, become a Colony of Aliens, who will shortly be so numerous as to Germanize us instead of our Anglifying them, and will never adopt our Language or Customs . . . ." (Leonard W. Labarce, ed., *The Papers of Benjamin Franklin*, vol. 4 [New Haven: Yale University Press], 234.)

THE AMERICAN REVOLUTION

When in the spring of 1775 armed hostilities broke out between British soldiers and American farmers at Lexington and Concord, Massachusetts, there were between two-and-a-half and three-million people living in the 13 colonies, the result of 168 years of immigration. By far the largest segment of the colonial population was British, with the New England colonies nearly all English, although there were thousands of Scotch-Irish. The southern colonies of Maryland, Virginia, the two Carolinas, and Georgia were dominated by descendants of English immigrants, with huge numbers of black African or African American slaves (a majority of the population in Virginia and South Carolina) and significant numbers of Scotch-Irish clustered in the back country and along the western edges of settlement. The Middle Colonies of Pennsylvania, New Jersey, and New York had by far the most diverse population with many Germans and Scotch-Irish settled on the rich farmlands and an interesting mixture of other immigrant groups.

Despite the ethnic mix of the colonies, the War of the Revolution began as a dispute between two English elites: one ruling in Britain and the other in the colonies. Many historians since have seen the conflicts between Americans—for example the earlier armed warfare, known as the Regulator movement, between backcountry Scotch-Irish settlers and coastal English officials in Carolina—as being just as important and divisive as the conflict between colonies and mother country.

Whether or not this analysis is correct, soon after the war began most non-English immigrant groups supported the patriot side. Although there were tens of thousands (perhaps more) Loyalist Americans who maintained allegiance to the British crown, most were of English heritage. At the end of the eight years of conflict, thousands and thousands of Loyalists re-emigrated to Canada or Great Britain, but virtually all were English. Scotch-Irish or German farmers did not feel much loyalty to the King, and they certainly didn't want to leave their homes in America just because the British lost the war.

In fact, non-English immigrant groups formed much of the Continental Army's regular forces and the state militias that together fought the British Army. While it is true that the southern states and parts of the New York and New Jersey back country were experiencing virtual civil war between local factions, there were never enough Loyalists in any colony to give the British a significant military advantage.

The most notable exception were the Highland Scot enclaves in the south, where several thousand Jacobites (Highlanders who were loyal to the deposed royal house of Stuart and had unsuccessfully fought the English to restore Bonny Prince Charlie to the throne) had immigrated after their defeat in the late 1740s. The Highlanders turned out to feel more loyalty to any monarchy, even the English king who had defeated them, than to any upstart revolutionary American government. After a crushing defeat at Moore's Creek Bridge early in the war, however, the Scots were never a military factor in the conflict.

The events of the American Revolution had an interesting effect on the some of the fears of patriot English Americans. For example, many patriots worried about the loyalty of the Pennsylvania Germans, especially because so many lived near the American revolutionary capital of Philadelphia. Their initial fears proved groundless, but when Great Britain purchased the services of German mercenaries (known as "Hessians" even though they came from several German states in addition to Hesse), the patriots' previous anxieties were resurrected. In the end, however, many Hessian mercenaries realized an unexpected fate. Many thousands of them were captured by the revolutionaries—most taken at Trenton or Saratoga—and marched through Pennsylvania under light guard and encouraged to "escape" into the German-speaking settlements. Thousands took advantage of the opportunity and became immigrants under unique circumstances.

Overall, the effect of the Revolution was to draw the diverse ethnic and national groups together. After all, the goal of the revolt was to create a new American nation out of what had previously been British colonies. All of this fostered a sense of American identity acknowledged early in the conflict by patriot leaders, who welcomed the contributions of the non-English among the patriots.

Despite differences, there were many factors pulling everyone in America together. Almost all colonists were Protestants, for example, because Roman Catholics were specifically excluded almost everywhere in the American colonies. Even though German or Dutch was spoken in many places, the predominate language was English, a fact that united rather than divided. And, ultimately, all the colonies had similar forms of government, education, and business—based on the British models, but altered significantly by the American experience.

With the British surrender at Yorktown in 1781 and the peace treaty two years later, the new nation was born, one that would be characterized by ethnic diversity and generation after generation of renewal through immigration.

IMMIGRATION AND THE NEW NATION

Wars have traditionally had significant effects on immigration, halting or slowing immigration during the conflict, then stimulating immigration immediately after or during intervals of peace. Into the 20th century, the reason that war stopped immigration was simple: travel by sea from Europe was dangerous during wartime. This was certainly true during the Revolution. Throughout much of the war, the British held the important American port cities, such as New York, Charlestown, Newport, and Philadelphia, and the Royal Navy almost always controlled the sea lanes and approaches to the few good ports in American hands.

Immigration did, however, resume after the war, but for several decades— until after the War of 1812—the flow of newcomers was relatively slow, due more to circumstances in Europe. Several European nations set new restrictions on emigration of their subjects and citizens, and the long period of international warfare that began in the 1790s with the French Revolution and stretched until the mid 'teens and the final defeat of Napoleon (the Anglo-American conflict of 1812–1815 was a sidelight to the larger struggle), made travel almost impossible for a long period. It was difficult to get permission to leave Europe, it was difficult to travel overland or upriver to a seaport, and it was nearly impossible to cross the Atlantic.

The overall rates of immigration between the end of the Revolution and the end of the War of 1812 varied considerably from year to year, with the largest numbers arriving during the 1790s and the fewest during the last years when naval warfare shut down the sea lanes entirely. Most historians believe that the total for the roughly three decades from 1783 to 1815 was about a quarter million.

Probably the bulk of the immigrants during this time were Scotch-Irish and English, two groups who for at least the first years of the period were less affected by Continental warfare. Emigration from the German states, however, virtually ceased after the mid-1780s. In 1788, the British government banned emigration of skilled artisans from Ireland, a method of protecting the infant British industrial development. A further brake on Scotch-Irish emigration came in 1803 with the British Passenger Act that limited the number of passengers that ship captains could pack into their vessels, cutting the numbers of poor immigrants.

Despite the relatively low level of immigration activity during this period, it turned out to be an important time for the development of American attitudes and policies. The great burst of nationalistic sentiment brought on by the Revolution included a central idea in the way America viewed immigration: America was a haven and an asylum for the oppressed. Many Americans, including several of the so-called Founding Fathers, saw the logic of extending the liberties and freedoms hard-won during the war to all

European peoples who suffered from oppressive regimes and ancient monarchies. The widespread expression of this idea was relatively short-lived during the first years of the new nation, but it nonetheless became a staple of America's self-image. It was given perhaps most prominence a century later by Emma Lazarus's widely quoted verse about sending to America huddled masses who yearned to be free (see page 72). The idea has cropped up again and again throughout American history, even during periods when official national policy was to restrict immigration and reject refugees.

From 1781 to 1789, the former British colonies formed a new American nation, joined loosely by a central government under the Articles of Confederation, a unifying structure that proved to be relatively weak and ineffective against a wide range of issues and problems. Immigration policy for the new nation was one of the least-pressing concerns during the first few years of independence, so little was done or discussed during the Confederation. In fact, the Articles said only that the rights of free citizens should be available in all states.

When the Constitution of the United States was written and ratified, it made no specific reference to immigration, strong evidence that the issue was not a pressing one for Americans at the time. Almost every other aspect of life and government was debated during the ratification struggle, except immigration.

The new Constitution did, however, deal with the question of naturalization (the process whereby foreigners may become citizens) and the rights of the foreign born, two issues closely tied to immigration. The Constitution granted Congress the power to adopt laws about naturalization but set no specific guidelines. The only political or civil prohibitions placed against foreign-born citizens was that they could not hold the office of President and were restricted from becoming members of the House of Representatives until they had been naturalized for seven years, and members of the Senate, for nine years. While these provisions show slight favor to those born in America, the thrust of the Constitution was broad, extending virtually all freedoms to immigrants on an equal basis—with the usual exception, of course, of black slaves and their offspring.

The first naturalization laws passed by the new Congress showed a similar liberality. All "free white persons" could become citizens after only two years in the United States—the least restrictive naturalization policy ever in American history. The provision excluded blacks and white indentured servants, but embraced all others. The law did not pass without considerable debate, with several members of Congress pleading for restrictions on the grounds that foreigners might well be contaminated with aristocratic or monarchical ideas or might not be suited for American citizenship if they had come from an impoverished European underclass. Note that these misgivings became the standard arguments of restrictionists, who insisted that immigrants should be treated cautiously or barred altogether because of dangerous political ideas or economic or cultural shortcomings. In 1790, however, the strong sense of new nationhood and identity reinforced the attractive symbol of America as a refuge. Naturalization—and by extension, immigration—was made simple, easy, and quick.

The initial era of liberal good feeling did not last long, however. Events in Europe during and immediately after the beginning of the French Revolution, combined with a growing political split in the United States, produced a wave against open and easy immigration and naturalization laws. The reasons for the development of the first political parties in America were complex, but the opposing sides came to focus on the ideas of the French Revolution as symbolic of their differences with consequences for national policy. Thomas Jefferson and his followers, eventually known as the Democratic Republicans (the forerunners of the modern Democratic Party), embraced the ideas of French revolutionaries and formed political clubs to celebrate liberty, equality, and fraternity. The Federalists, led by Alexander Hamilton (himself an immigrant from the British West Indies) and John Adams saw the French Revolution as the embodiment of all that was dangerous and evil.

The Federalists were in control of the new Congress when it passed a second naturalization law in 1795, only a half decade after the first. The provisions increased the waiting period for eligibility for citizenship to five years. An influx of highly visible French and English political radicals during the mid-1790s, many of whom became vocal opponents of the Federalists, and a serious undeclared naval war with Revolutionary France, promoted the government to take even stronger measures. The Federalists were also alarmed by what they perceived as a growing political alliance between the Jeffersonian Democratic-Republicans and recently immigrated Scotch-Irish.

In 1797, the Federalists proposed a tax of 20 dollars (a very large sum at the time) on certificates of naturalization. The intent of the law was to keep large numbers of recent immigrants from becoming citizens, thereby denying them the power to vote. The proposal was defeated, but a year later, the Federalist Congress passed yet another new naturalization law that set the waiting period for citizenship at 14 years.

The most famous attack of the Federalists against immigrants was the passage of the Alien Acts in 1798, part of a package of laws that enabled the government to suppress political dissent in the name of national security and to move against noncitizen aliens at will. The Alien Friends Act required aliens to register with the government and allowed the president, John Adams, to deport any alien he deemed dangerous. An even more repressive Alien Enemies Act never went into effect because a formal war with France was narrowly averted by Adams' diplomacy. The Alien Acts were allowed to expire when the Federalists were voted out of office and Jefferson became president in 1801.

National policy reverted to a more liberal stance with the victory of the Democratic-Republicans. A new naturalization act in 1801 revoked the requirements for alien registration and once again set the citizenship waiting period at five years. This marked the end of Congressional tinkering with naturalization, and the five-year waiting period has remained in effect ever since.

CHAPTER 3

Building a Nation Through Immigration

actors in both Europe and the United States surfaced immediately after the end of the Napoleonic wars that set off a long, steady period of immigration, which coincided with the development of America as a strong, prosperous nation. The story of modern immigration begins after 1815 and is closely intertwined with the story of how the United States changed from a small nation of colonists clinging to the eastern seaboard into a transcontinental country of immense power and potential.

MODERN IMMIGRATION BEGINS

Until 1820, all statistics about the numbers of immigrants and their origins are educated guesses (although they are quite likely to be accurate). In 1820, however, the United States began to keep records of arrivals, so despite many discrepancies and demographic inadequacies, there is reasonably good data from then on. However, it should be noted that the U.S. government has used political, not ethnic, definitions to count immigrants; in other words, the nation of origin has been used to designate immigrants whether or not the persons involved were really part of that nation's language and culture. This was not a major problem in 1820, but became one by the end of the 19th century when the policy obscured a great deal about immigration from European empires. Hundreds of thousands of Poles, for example, were counted as Germans or Russians, because Poland had been divided between the two countries.

During the decade between 1820 and 1830, slightly under 152,000 immigrants arrived in America. During the 1830s, the number was just short of 600,000. Immigration jumped during the 1840s to more than 1.7 million,

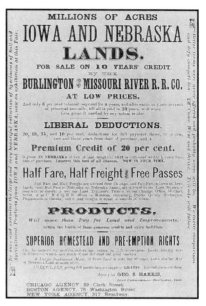

The 1844 naturalization certificate of Thomas Banbury, an emigrant from Great Britain. (Photo courtesy State Historical Society of Iowa, Iowa City)

An advertisement from 1873 for land for sale in the Midwest. The railroads had acquired hundreds of thousands of acres and hoped to sell much of it to European immigrants seeking farms. German and Scandinavian immigrants were particularly targeted for such promotions, which included reduced rates or free travel by rail. (Photo courtesy State Historical Society of Iowa, Iowa City)

and during the 10 years just before the Civil War, 2.6 million arrived. In total, well over 5 million new Americans immigrated between 1815 and 1860, adding to a total population of more than 30 million, nearly 10 times the number at the time of the Revolution.

The classic explanation of immigration is called the "push-pull" theory, which says that elements must be in place at both ends for immigration to occur: elements in the old land must push immigrants to uproot themselves and leave home; other elements in the new land must look so attractive that immigrants are pulled to a new place. During the decades from 1815 to 1860, both sorts of incentives were at work.

First of all, Europe entered a prolonged period of peace. The widespread and awesomely destructive wars of the French Revolution and the Napoleonic Era came to an end and were not repeated in such scale until World War I. There were several small wars, such as in the Crimea in the 1850s, and many violent revolutions and civil skirmishes, but none brought the violence that had pinned people in place during the last years of the 18th century and the first of the 19th. For many years, it was possible to move from the interior of Europe to a sea port and then across the Atlantic. Hamburg, Liverpool, and Le Havre became thriving, bustling points of embarkation.

Most of the immigration came from northern and western Europe, including more than two million Irish and more than a million Germans, who lived in places where particular circumstances calculated to stimulate movement. One of the most important circumstances, and least understood by historians and demographers, was the huge explosion of population in much of Europe and the British Isles. There were simply more and more people every year, with the result that any form of political or economic dislocation triggered mass migration. There was also some political immigration after the great political revolutions of 1830 and 1848, and these immigrants tended to have high profiles in their new lands. The actual numbers of political exiles to America were relatively small, but their influence was relatively large.

There was also a major shift in governmental policy in many European nations when the viewpoint became widespread that excess population was a threat to a nation's prosperity. Countries that had previously restricted emigration began to encourage it, hoping to avoid the liabilities of too many people, especially poor ones. Great Britain, most of the German states, Holland, and Sweden all changed policies and in some cases were only too glad to see people leave.

The rapid industrialization of Britain and western Europe also added immeasurably to the factors pushing immigrants to the New World. The growth of the factory system and numerous advances in scientific farming moved tens to hundreds of thousands of small farmers or renters off the land. People who had lived on small parcels of land following essentially the same patterns of agricultural life familiar for centuries were abruptly forced to give up and leave. The only livelihood they could find was in the new industrial cities, so they came to America.

The allure of land in America was nearly irresistible. The idea of nearly an entire continent for the taking was overwhelmingly attractive to many Europeans who wanted to live rural lives but could not find land in their original countries. The fact that land in the United States was relatively expensive—it cost hundreds of dollars in hard cash to buy even the smallest farm—and often came with difficulties and conditions unfamiliar to Europeans meant little in the face of the romantic attraction of what appeared to be limitless acres rolling out toward the Pacific.

Moreover, a great deal of impetus for Europeans considering a move to the United States came from the thousands of previous immigrants who sent glowing accounts in what became known as "American letters." These letters often motivated many from the writer's former home to seek a new life abroad.

There were also several kinds of promoters at work during most of the first part of the 19th century. Many individual American states actively recruited in Europe with advertising, distribution of literature, and promotional offices. Land agents recruited in Europe as did shipping companies and railroads. All had something to gain by encouraging immigration.

Part of the immigration boom was inspired by the fact that transportation grew increasingly simpler and cheaper. During the first decades of the 19th century, travel across the Atlantic was still slow and uncertain, with sailing ships at the mercy of the seas and the weather. But the cost of transport dropped as shippers, headed to America to pick up loads of timber and cotton to bring back to Europe, sought to fill their vessels and avoid deadhead runs to America. Between the end of the Napoleonic Wars and the 1850s, trans-Atlantic fares dropped by as much as 75 percent. Eventually the the steam-ship made the trip quicker and relatively healthier.

Transportation once the immigrants reached America also improved markedly during the period. Early in the 19th century, water travel was still the cheapest and easiest way to get to the interior. For example, the fare for

Steerage passengers on deck for a breath of air while aboard a steamship in the Atlantic around 1900. Such transportation was cramped and unpleasant but relatively cheap and swift compared with crossing the Atlantic during the age of sail. (Photo courtesy State Historical Society of Iowa, Iowa City. Print courtesy Mary Bennett)

travel from New York City to Detroit by way of the Hudson River, the Erie Canal, and the Great Lakes was as low as eight dollars. By the 1850s, rail transport was common in the northeastern part of the nation, and immigrants took full advantage of it to reach settlements in the growing states of the upper Midwest.

Until very late in the 1800s, the individual states, not the federal government, had responsibility for processing immigrants. Massachusetts and New York shouldered the largest burdens because of the popularity of Boston and New York City as immigrant landing ports. Massachusetts tried to improve conditions for immigrants in the 1840s by collecting a landing fee that was used to set up a hospital. New York, which came to be the busiest port of entry for immigrants from Europe, established a Board of Emigration in 1847 to regulate the influx and processing of newcomers. There were essentially no restrictions on entering the country, but the Board wanted procedures to register immigrants. The New York Board took over Castle Garden on Manhattan Island in 1855, which became the primary receiving point for immigrants to America until it was superseded by the new Federal facility at Ellis Island in 1892.

The immigration reception center at Castle Garden in New York City in the 1880s. Before the Federal government took over and moved operations to Ellis Island, the State of New York ran a huge immigrant processing center at Castle Garden. (Photo courtesy the Ellis Island Immigration Museum)

Immigrants pile their belongings on a wagon for the trip from the docks to the railway station in 1873. This was the stage at which many greenhorn immigrants were swindled and robbed by con artists. (Illustration courtesy State Historical Society of Iowa, Iowa City)

New York made some efforts to protect recent arrivals from the exploiters who found the "greenhorns" (as the immigrants were known) easy victims for fraud and deception. Because many of the arriving immigrants were disoriented, could not understand the language, and knew little of the customs, con men sold them phony rail tickets or offered other services that, of course, never materialized after the immigrants paid cash in advance. The worst abuses came from immigrants' fellow countrymen, who put the greenhorns at ease by speaking their language and assuming the role of friendly guide, then left them stranded and penniless. New York's immigrant registration procedure included a brief indoctrination designed to help the greenhorns avoid the most obvious confidence games.

The patterns of distribution of immigrants during the years before the Civil War followed the path of the nation's development. The growing importance of cities was emphasized by the tendency of many immigrants to choose urban life once in America. Many of the most dynamic American cities such as New York, St. Louis, Cincinnati, Chicago, Cleveland, Detroit, and San Francisco were about half populated by foreign-born immigrants by 1860; others had from one-fourth to one-third immigrant populations.

Of course, there were hundreds of thousands of immigrants who turned toward the farming states of the upper Midwest, especially the prairie lands of

Illinois, Iowa, Wisconsin, and Minnesota. Some groups such as the Scandinavians, skipped over the cities almost entirely in order to reach the fertile soils of the interior.

The one section that few immigrants chose was the South. In general, the newcomers saw the slave societies and slave economies as unattractive: there was little place in southern agriculture for free immigrant labor, and the only available land was taken by well-established Scotch-Irish and other earlier immigrants. The South had few important cities outside the sea coast ports and not much industry to provide jobs for immigrants. By 1861 and the final breach between North and South, only about 13 percent of the nation's foreign born lived in the southern states, and most of these were concentrated in a few port cities.

THE SECOND GERMAN IMMIGRATION

Following the defeat of Napoleon and the restoration of peace in Europe, German immigration to America resumed. From 1815 to past the turn of the 20th century, this tide of people was so large that immigrants of German origin outnumbered all others, with only the Irish coming close. The pattern of German immigration was relatively modest during the 1820s, but rose steadily, peaking in the decade surrounding the Civil War and during the 1880s. Between 1820 and 1920 (a period for which moderately reliable figures are available), more than 5.7 million Germans immigrated to the United States.

Basic changes in the structure of the economy and society in the German states had much to do with impelling people to emigrate. The development of larger and larger cities, the growth of industry, and political changes all helped to create an atmosphere in which the old ways of life were more and more difficult to maintain. The widespread (and largely inexplicable) population growth that affected most of Europe hit Germany also. The result of these changes was to motivate small farmers, merchants, and artisans to find new occupations or new places to live.

The majority of German immigrants to America before the late 1840s came from the southwestern states of Wurtemburg, Bavaria, and Baden, which were heavily agricultural regions. The immigrants included many families that had been forced off the land by debt and poor harvests; the same potato blight that struck farms in Ireland ravaged crops in Germany, but with less human toll. The changes and failures in the German agricultural system prompted many to leave before reaching the crisis stages, so the greatest numbers of immigrant German farmers of this period were not destitute, though they were usually far from prosperous.

The flow of German immigration also included a significant number of reasonably wealthy farmers who lacked faith in the future of the German economy and saw a chance to invest in American lands, and substantial artisans and merchants who simply wanted a change.

One of the most colorful groups to emigrate from Germany, and one that for a long time almost monopolized the attention of historians, was the small but important number of political activists in the failed revolutions of 1848, when the German states were swept by a wave of liberalism that captured the imagination of some of the most talented Germans. When the movement collapsed and repressive conservative regimes regained power, most of the revolutionaries were forced to flee, many of them choosing the United States as their refuge.

These "Forty-Eighters," as they were known, included writers, scholars, editors, doctors, lawyers, and others of similar background and experience. Not surprisingly, they tended to move into positions of leadership among the German communities of their new homeland. Several individuals subsequently had major influence in American life, most notably Carl Schurz, a 19-year-old Bonn student radical in 1848 who escaped Germany and after sojourns in France and England immigrated to the United States in 1852. He made his way to the Midwest and by the outbreak of the Civil War was a successful businessman and one of the most powerful leaders of the new Republican Party. He served as a Union general in the war and subsequently as a diplomat, Secretary of the Interior, and editor of *Harper's Weekly*.

The majority of German immigrants were, of course, less influential than Schurz and other Forty-Eighters, but the tendency of most Germans to preserve their national and ethnic identity gave them a pervasive cultural influence in any of the several German enclaves or German-dominated cities. Unlike the German immigrants of the previous century, who predominately secured farms and populated rural Pennsylvania with "Dutch" settlers, many among the second wave of Germans turned to the growing American cities (although there were significant numbers of 19th-century German immigrant farmers). By the time of the Civil War, places such as Cincinnati, Milwaukee, and St. Louis were heavily German in appearance and style, and New York had a huge German population that lived primarily in a "Little Germany."

Because so many German immigrants came with valuable skills, it is not surprising that they had a major economic impact wherever they went. They set up breweries, packinghouses, saw mills, and machine shops, for example, and usually they prospered. Skilled German workers also found work in businesses owned by native-born Americans and gave a strong boost to the development of industrialism in the United States.

German taverns, beer gardens, *Turnvereins* (social and athletic clubs), bands, orchestras, literary clubs, newspapers, churches, choral groups, and similar cultural organizations were found in every American city that supported a significant German population. German was the language of instruction in many local schools, and German language and customs were fostered through several generations. However, almost all of this elaborate German culture was destroyed virtually overnight during the anti-German hysteria that gripped the country during World War I.

Although by far the great majority of German immigrants during the 19th century came as families or individuals—mostly from the ports of Le Harve or Hamburg after a sometimes difficult overland journey—there were also notable but unsuccessful efforts at group colonizations. Several groups came to Texas, for example, during the years while it was an independent republic, including the founders of New Braunfels in 1845 who were participants in the settlement scheme of several German noblemen. German immigrant families paid the organizers of the New Braunfels colony a set fee in return for transportation, a log house, and a 160-acre Texas farm. The scheme failed, but many Germans came to Texas, nonetheless. Other German immigrant colonists moved to Minnesota, where they began a colony at New Ulm in 1857 that was a model of social planning. The New Ulm Germans formed a land association and set up "Turner" clubs and halls.

Mixed among the hundreds of thousand of German immigrants were many German Jews, who began to come to America in important numbers during the 1820s as part of the general migration from the German states. These Jews had a significant economic and social impact on the long-established but relatively small communities of Sephardic (Hispanic) Jews that had settled in America previously. By the Civil War, there were as many as 150 Jewish communities in the United States and more than 40,000 Jews in New York City alone. Few of these German-Jewish immigrants opted to take up farming, although some moved to rural areas as peddlars and merchants. The greatest numbers settled into the cities of the eastern sea board and began building urban Jewish communities.

THE IRISH

The history of Ireland—"that most distressful nation"—is full of drama and tragedy, but nothing rivals the astounding story of what happened to the Irish during the mid-19th century and how millions of Irish came to live in America.

Although the peak of the drama was the years of the devastating potato famine from 1845 to 1848, immigration historians point out that emigration from Ireland was significant before the famine and continued very strong until the turn of the 20th century: in the 100 years between the first recording of immigrants in 1820 and the passage of immigration restrictions in 1924, well over 4.5 million Irish immigrated to the United States.

In a classic view of the economic and social transformation wrought by immigration, this illustration depicts a shabby, destitute Irish emigrant as he leaves for the United States and then later as a prosperous, well-dressed American contemplating a return visit to Ireland. (Illustration courtesy State Historical Society of Iowa, Iowa City)

However, no matter how important the long-range Irish immigration pattern was, the statistics of the famine years are astounding. At the beginning of the decade of the 1840s, when the economy and agricultural production were still adequate, there were roughly 8.2 million people living in Ireland. Ten years later the population has been reduced to 6.6 million—more than a million and a half people had disappeared. A very large percentage had died from starvation or diseases related to malnutrition; the rest fled. It seems certain that at least a million persons emigrated from Ireland to America in the years surrounding the famine. This is, perhaps, the clearest example of "push" factors in all of immigration history.

The prefamine immigration of the Irish had some of the same background factors but without the tragic urgency and scale. Ireland had nearly doubled in population during the first decades of the 1800s, and repeated division of the small land holdings made producing adequate food supplies more and more difficult. Only the high-nutritional value and low-production cost of the potato allowed the Irish to survive. Moreover, Ireland was subject to the political control of the British, who were seen as oppressors. When added to the fact that transportation across the Atlantic was relatively cheap, these conditions motivated about 300,000 Irish to immigrate to America between 1820 and 1840. Most of the prefamine immigrants were apparently single men who found jobs as laborers in the North and Northeast—jobs on the lowest rungs of the free-market economic ladder but still a step up from their former situations in Ireland.

Another characteristic behavior pattern of the Irish immigrants in the prefamine years was a practice that came to be known as "chain migration." The earliest immigrants found jobs, saved assiduously, and sent passage money (often prepaid tickets) to relatives in the old country. By very hard work and dedication, immigrants financed the passage of entire families in this way. It was difficult and took remarkable courage and perseverance, but it worked. Many other immigrant groups used the technique as well; in fact it is still common practice at the end of the 20th century. However, the Irish were among the first to use it on an important scale.

When the potato crop failed disastrously in 1845 and for several years thereafter, a large percentage of those Irish who managed to survive sailed for America. When they arrived they formed a high-profile immigrant group that was distinctly different. First of all, almost all the Irish immigrants of this period were Roman Catholic. Despite the early attempt of Lord Baltimore to establish a haven for Catholics in Maryland in the 17th century, America was solidly Protestant and erected a wall of prejudice against Catholics. The circumstances of the arrival of the famine refugees, who had almost no capital and were often in ill health, added to Americans' poor opinion of Catholics, and their very large numbers caused anxiety. The Irish "hordes" were the targets of discrimination for decades: they were perceived by many Americans as poor, dirty, uneducated, and practitioners of an alien religion. It was not, perhaps, until the 1960 election of President John Kennedy, a Roman Catholic descendent of prefamine Irish immigrants, who faced anti-Catholic propaganda throughout his career, that the Irish finally shrugged off the effects of discrimination.

The Irish of the famine years (and the decades following) moved more or less in the same patterns as their prefamine predecessors: they remained in the cities of the North and Northeast, seeking employment as construction workers or, as in the case of many Irish immigrant women, as domestic servants. On the whole, the Irish had no interest in moving back onto the land. Even though land in America was relatively rich and plentiful compared to home, very few had the money to buy farms.

During the decades after the end of the famine immigration, the balance of Irish immigrants changed gradually from mainly men to mainly women, although in all cases the average age of Irish immigrants was very young. The Irish immigrant women tended to stay in domestic service jobs or in mill work, but the men gradually moved up the economic ladder during the late 19th century. As the immigrant and second-generation Irish discovered the power of the vote in the American system and as American cities grew and needed people to operate the expanding governments and public services, the Irish virtually took over such occupations as urban firemen and police.

NATIVISM BEFORE THE CIVIL WAR

There is nothing unusual about people viewing newcomers as strange and curious; this is a natural human reaction to someone or something new. Americans have always reacted to immigrants in this way, particularly if the immigrants spoke a language other than English and came from a place where the clothing, customs, and experiences were quite different than those of the United States.

However, this sort of healthy curiosity has frequently given way to nativism, a virulent, often violent, paranoid, and irrational hatred and fear of immigrants. At its least destructive, nativism is the motive for relatively mild government regulation, such as prolonging the waiting period for naturalization. At its worst, nativism edges over into bigotry and something resembling racial hatred, although "race" is seldom involved despite some nativists's tendency to use such labels. (Nativists around the turn of the century confused cultural differences based on national customs and language with true genetic differences between races.)

Until 1924, when nativism finally triumphed in the passage of restrictive laws and regulations, immigration to the United States was open to all (with the exception of the formal exclusion of the Chinese and the informal barring of the Japanese). There were few serious movements to restrict immigration; however, there were several periods in which nativism came to the forefront of American life and politics.

The first important nativist movement was in the 1830s, 1840s, and 1850s, concerned almost entirely with Protestant American fears of Roman Catholicism and the importation of Catholic worship by European immigrants.

The Irish and the German Catholics bore the worst of the nativist outbreak during the period before the Civil War because they were the most prominent Catholic newcomers. There were public protests against Catholics in New York in the early 1830s, with newspapers and Protestant preachers at the forefront. In 1834, a Protestant mob in Boston burned down an Ursuline convent. Ten years later in Philadelphia, a conflict over schools and the use of the Catholic translation of the Bible escalated into full-scale rioting that destroyed blocks of houses in the Irish section of town and resulted in 13 deaths.

By the 1850s, the nation was in a precarious state of unity and balance, with divisions over the issue of slavery producing constant tension and anxiety. Many basic American institutions, such as political parties and religious denominations, seemed in jeopardy and the national consensus that held the nation together began to fail. Against this background, nativists organized on a national scale.

They argued that recent immigrants were wicked slum-dwellers who had imported alien customs and could never adapt to the practices of pure American democracy. These exact arguments have appeared over and over in American history whenever older generations have felt threatened by newcomers. These arguments never seem to lose their power over a certain part of the population who tend to make scapegoats out of newcomers whom they cannot be bothered to understand. One of the most potent recurring arguments has been that immigrants are too uneducated and politically degenerate to ever understand the American system, and therefore they are a threat to the essential American characteristic: democracy.

The nativist political party organized in the 1850s was known as the Know-Nothing Party, because its members were supposedly sworn to secrecy and replied that they "knew nothing" when asked about the organization. It began humbly but grew very rapidly, in part because the other established political parties—the Whigs and the Democrats—were disintegrating over the issue of slavery. The Know Nothings had a single principle, which was to oppose Catholicism and by extension to oppose immigrants.

In 1854, the Know-Nothing Party won astounding victories in Massachusetts, where it captured the entire state government, in Pennsylvania and in Delaware. A year later, the party won in five more states and showed strongly in seven more. Oddly enough, even with electoral success—there were several Know-Nothing members of Congress—the party never was able to actually pass much legislation against Catholics or immigrants. For example, bills to restrict entrance and create a 21-year waiting period for citizenship died before coming to a vote in the House of Representatives.

In Massachusetts, where they had seized full political and governmental power, the Know Nothings did pass a state requirement for a long naturalization waiting period and managed to establish a law restricting state office holders to the native born.

As strong as the Know-Nothing movement seemed in the mid-1850s and as rapidly as it grew, it also dissolved rapidly. The party nominated former President Millard Fillmore as its national candidate in the election of 1856, but he failed to attract support at the polls except in Maryland. The concerns of the nation over sectionalism and slavery came to a head by the end of the decade and the impending crisis of the Civil War left little time or energy for side issues such as immigration. The nativist movement collapsed for the time being.

THE CIVIL WAR AND AFTER

Recent immigrants—most of whom lived in the North and Northeast— played important roles in the great national disaster of the Civil War. The foreign-born flocked to the standard of the Union and joined the northern army in droves. Any questions about their loyalty or commitment to the American ideal were swept away between 1861 and 1865, when immigrant soldiers provided the backbone of many of the regiments in the field. Hundreds of thousands of immigrants, the Germans and Irish most conspicuously, served in the ranks, and there were several all-immigrant units.

After the last gun sounded, America moved into one of the most dynamic periods of growth in its history. During the two decades after the war, the country expanded westward, pulled by the railroads and the Homestead Act, and the great industrial cities of the Northeast and Midwest began the economic developments that eventually made the nation prosperous and powerful.

Immigrants were closely involved in all of these national movements, particularly in the growth of cities and industry. During the late 1860s, total annual immigration climbed back to pre–Civil War levels, and during the early 1870s, twice passed the 400,000 mark, with people coming from more or less the same source countries as before the war. The flows from Germany and Ireland continued, although at a reduced pace from the boom years. A steady stream came from Britain (including the Welsh and the Cornish) and there were smaller but important groups such as the French Canadians and the Dutch.

THE SCANDINAVIANS

The three Scandinavian nations—Sweden, Denmark, and Norway—sent slightly more than two million immigrants to the United States between the early 1800s and early 1900s. The greatest numbers came in the decades from 1870 to 1910, and the majority skipped over the cities of the East and headed directly for the great farm lands of the upper Midwest, where they created a lasting Scandinavian presence.

The relationships among the three Scandinavian nations have been historically complex, with political dominance shifting several times in the modern era: Denmark held all of Norway and Sweden at one time, then Sweden gained the upper hand, with Norway emerging as a more-or-less sovereign nation only in 1814 (complete separation did not come until 1905). The Norwegian and Danish languages are virtually the same, and Swedish speakers can usually understand the other two.

The immigration history of each nationality had its own characteristics, but there were also strong similarities. The majority of Scandinavians came seeking land and farms, and many of them came with enough capital to make landowning a reality. For most of the period of immigration, Scandinavians came as families and settled whenever possible in communities that often

A Scandinavian immigrant family farmstead under construction in Minnesota around the turn of the 20th century. Many Scandinavians were skilled in log technology and built elaborate homes from trees cut on the site. (Photo courtesy Immigration History Research Center, University of Minnesota)

became rural ethnic enclaves. Later in the period, more single immigrants made the journey as conditions changed in the homelands.

The most potent force pushing immigrants from Scandinavia was the widespread and pervasive dislocation of small farmers. During the 19th century, land became extraordinarily hard for the average person to obtain, and the only choice was to change from an agricultural existence or to emigrate. In addition to land hunger and a desire to remain farmers, many Scandinavians were happy to leave behind the overbearing state Lutheran churches of their native lands. While seeking religious freedom was probably not the predominate goal of most Scandinavian immigrants, it was an important reason to emigrate.

Until 1840, the Swedish-Norwegian government officially discouraged emigration with a national law restricting individuals from leaving. However, widespread economic dislocations and a major growth in population forced the withdrawal of these prohibitions. There were simply too many people for the limited supply of land to support, and all controls were dropped by 1860.

Immigration from Sweden before 1840 had consisted of a small scattering of middle-class businessmen and professionals, but shortly before the American Civil War relatively affluent small farmers, usually traveling in groups with families, began to arrive. The pattern continued for 15 years after the war, with the Swedish immigrants moving to the fertile northern prairies of Illinois and Minnesota because of the expansion and promotion of the new western railroads. During the 1880s, more and more Swedish immigrants who had been agricultural workers and probably had never owned land at home arrived. The decade between 1880 and 1890 marked the biggest years of Swedish immigration with nearly 400,000 arriving. By the turn of the 20th century, the character of Swedish arrivals changed again, as rural immigrants gave way to younger single men and women from the Swedish cities.

Not all Swedish immigrants fit the stereotype of midwestern farmers, and there was a significant number of Swedes who settled in industrial cities. Chicago, for example, had a heavily ethnic Swede Town until well into the 1900s.

The smaller numbers of Danish immigrants followed a similar pattern, with the bulk of the first wave coming from the low- to middle-socioeconomic ranks, mostly in family clusters. After the turn of the century, the same shift occurred to younger, unmarried urban immigrants. We know a great deal about the Danish immigrants because the Danish police kept meticulous records of all emigrants from 1869 to 1914, and historians have made a thorough study of the social and economic patterns. Once in America, the Danes were more inclined to disperse than the Swedes or the Norwegians, but about three in 10 Danes ended up in Iowa, Wisconsin, or Minnesota.

The pressure to emigrate created by a lack of land was undoubtedly greatest in Norway, where the 19th-century growth in population dramatically outstripped the small amount of farmland wedged between the coasts, fjords, and mountains: no more than about 4 percent of the land in Norway can be farmed. In addition, the Norwegian Lutheran church seemed particularly oppressive to many lower-class Norwegians—the first boatload of immigrants in 1825 were religious dissenters—and the political domination of Norway by Sweden gave extra motivation to leave.

In all, close to 700,000 Norwegians came to America between 1860 and 1920, which was roughly equivalent to half of the total population of the country in 1845. Most of these immigrants sought the land they had been denied at home, and an absolute majority settled in the midwestern farm states of Wisconsin, Minnesota, and North Dakota, often in rural ethnic clusters.

THE CHINESE

The most unusual immigrant group of the 19th century, and by far the worst received, were the Chinese who came to America between the 1850s and 1882. They were treated differently from all other nationalities: the Chinese were discriminated against, physically attacked, and finally excluded. Their story is one of the unhappiest in American history.

Three Chinese immigrants, probably low-wage workers, stiffly pose during the 1880s. (Photo courtesy State Historical Society of Iowa, Iowa City)

The first Chinese to enter the United States were a handful of students were discriminated against, physically attacked, and finally excluded. Their story is one of the unhappiest in American history. brought to this country in the late 1840s by a missionary. One of them, Yung Wing, graduated from Yale in 1854 and became a naturalized citizen, although his citizenship was later revoked.

Most Chinese, however, immigrated to the United States originally as sojourners—immigrants who intended from the beginning to return to their native lands. They were almost exclusively males who left their families in China and came to improve their economic lot. About 90 percent of the Chinese immigrants to America came from the same region of Canton in South China. Before immigration was cut off in 1882, about 300,000 Chinese found their way to America, most of them to California.

The original attraction was gold in the California mountains, a factor that set off a rush among many immigrants of all nations. Although a large percentage of Chinese became miners, it was a difficult occupation for them because of persecution by other American miners. The white miners took Chinese claims by force, pushing the Chinese miners to less productive diggings, and continually harassed and attacked them. The state of California passed a series of discriminatory laws that reduced the Chinese to second-class status and specifically put them under legal penalties that were borne by no other group.

When the Union Pacific Railroad began construction of the western portion of its line in 1864, thousands of Chinese laborers were hired to build a railroad over the challenging western landscape. They were extremely hard workers, lived in difficult conditions with little or no complaint, and were willing to sacrifice for the sake of wages.

Although often accused by opponents of participating in "coolie" labor systems, which were illegal arrangements used in South America and the Caribbean to import Chinese workers under conditions of near slavery, most Chinese immigrants to California were individuals. There was, however, a thriving system of underground finance that allowed men in China to pledge themselves to pay back transportation loans at high rates. This was a twist on the old indentured servant and redemptioner systems, but in the skewed vision of Chinese opponents, the idea seemed somehow to threaten the American free labor market.

The center of Chinese culture in California was indisputably a small section of San Francisco that was transformed into an all-Chinese enclave known as Chinatown. Other immigrant groups also tended to cluster in city neighborhoods, but none did so with the thoroughness of the Chinese in San Francisco. Virtually all Chinese in the city lived in Chinatown, including both rich and poor, and there was never any significant movement out of the enclave as individual members of the community advanced economically—

the racism of the surrounding natives made it impossible. Ironically, the separation of the Chinese was used as a weapon to attack them for exclusiveness.

Part of American suspicion was directed against what was seen as a sinister "invisible government" among the Chinese community. In truth, the Chinese relied on a system of associations known as the Six Companies, based originally on clan and village affiliations. The Six Companies supplied social services to the Chinese community, particularly newcomers, and acted as spokesmen to the outside world. The Six Companies were often confused in the minds of critics with the so-called tongs, which were completely separate criminal organizations that were also tinged by Chinese domestic revolutionary politics.

The Federal Naturalization Act of 1870 was the forerunner of a series of legal and policy decisions against the Chinese. The Act limited naturalization to whites and people of "African descent," which meant that of all the immigrants to America, only the Chinese were barred from citizenship. In effect, the Chinese were put on notice by this law that they would never be allowed to enter the society of the United States on the same footing as all others.

The economic depression of the 1870s led to even more repressive measures. As has commonly been the case, when times turn bad, a certain segment of Americans express their anxieties by turning on immigrants. As jobs dried up, the cry that cheap Chinese labor was pushing aside "good Americans" gained momentum in California. The idea was a fiction, because the Chinese amounted to less than 10 percent of the state's population and probably contributed much more economically than they withdrew. Facts usually have little effect on such nativist hostility, however.

In 1876, a California state legislative investigation accused the Chinese of failure to satisfactorily assimilate and detailed a long list of supposed moral and intellectual inadequacies that the investigators claimed were Asian racial characteristics. During the same year, out-of-work American laborers, led by an Irish immigrant sailor named Denis Kearney, began regularly to attack Chinese neighborhoods and individual Chinese who were unlucky enough to be on the street. The attacks escalated during the following years and included several full-scale riots and instances of violence in other California towns where Chinese had come to work.

By the late 1870s, the United States government had begun to put diplomatic pressure on China to limit immigration. The efforts continued and intensified until the official treaty between the nations was modified to allow the United States to regulate entry of Chinese immigrants.

The final inequity was carried out in 1882, when the federal Chinese Exclusion Act suspended the immigration of Chinese laborers altogether. Additional laws eventually prohibited all immigration of Chinese workers and put humiliating conditions on the entry of any Chinese national into the United States. These laws marked the first time that the United States had taken action to limit or stop immigration from a foreign land. Until the Chinese Exclusion Act, the very concept of an illegal immigrant was virtually impossible. Afterward, American immigration policy would never quite be the same again, although more than 40 years lapsed before restriction clamped down on European immigrants.

The Exclusion Act also denied naturalization to Chinese in America and refused to allow Chinese to return to America if they left to visit China. The result was a warped sort of Chinese immigrant society in America (the center remained in San Francisco) made up of a large percentage of males who were cut off from their families. This "bachelor" society was characteristic of Chinese immigrant communities for decades.

THE JAPANESE

Although initially fewer in number than the Chinese, Japanese immigrants became the target of similar anti-Asian discrimination and racially based immigration restriction. However, by the time pressure began to build on the West Coast to keep out new Japanese, Japan had become one of the major military powers in the world, after victory over the Russian Empire in 1905. It was dangerous to offend the entire nation by excluding its immigrants.

The earliest Japanese immigrants, about 30,000, had come to Hawaii in the second half of the 1880s as agricultural workers. When Hawaii was annexed by the United States in 1898, the Japanese population shifted to the West Coast mainland. Most of the Japanese of the first generation of immigrants became farmers or agricultural workers, and in some parts of California almost dominated the industry. The influx of new immigrants was mostly male farm workers.

In 1907, the U.S. government was forced to deal with the rising tide of anti-Japanese prejudice in California when the school board of San Francisco tried to segregate Japanese and Japanese American students. The insult to Japanese pride was blatant. President Theodore Roosevelt got the school board to rescind the plan, and in return he negotiated what was known as the Gentleman's Agreement with Japan. In order to avoid further friction, the Japanese imperial government agreed to stop allowing farm workers to emigrate. The agreement halted almost all immigration by Japanese males, but significant numbers of Japanese women immigrated each year until 1924, when new restriction laws barred all Japanese. The 1920 census counted 111,010 Japanese and their descendents in the United States, more than 85 percent of them living in California.

CHAPTER 4

• • • • • • • • •

Millions from Eastern Europe and the Mediterranean

I n the 40 years between 1880 and 1920, a tidal wave of Europeans immigrants entered the United States, so many and so fast that their arrival
affected the course of American history in fundamental and dramatic
ways. The nation has been greatly enriched, but also profoundly altered, by
this great inflow of people.

At the time, many older, native-born Americans felt the masses of
immigrants threatened the very foundations of what they understood as the
nature of America. They reacted with fear, loathing, and bigotry, and by the
mid-1920s they had put in place the restrictive barriers to immigration that
have essentially remained ever since (see Chapter Six).

To the immigrants who poured into the country, however, America was
still the great asylum for the poor and those seeking a new home. Life was
almost always difficult for the first generation of newcomers, but the basic
hopes that fired their decisions to leave home and journey to the New World
were seldom extinguished.

The numbers really are staggering: between 1880 and 1920 slightly under
23.5 million immigrants arrived. During six of these years, the number
exceeded one million annually—1907 was the peak with nearly 1.3 million
in that year alone. The massive arrivals make it easy to understand why so
many American institutions seemed on the verge of being overwhelmed.

Moreover, the sources of the immigration shifted away from those common earlier in the 19th century. The great forces of social and economic
change that had previously stimulated immigration from Ireland, Germany,

Immigrants aboard a trans-Atlantic steamer in 1920 wait to land at Ellis Island. The following year, new laws choked off most immigration from eastern and southern Europe. (Photo courtesy the Boston Public Library, Print Department)

and Scandinavia began to have an impact on people in southern and eastern Europe. Population growth, the reorganization of land ownership, changes in agricultural production, and the industrial revolution all made life difficult and people restless. In addition, Italian laws that had barred emigration were changed, and people in large area of the Austro-Hungarian Empire and the Balkans were freed to emigrate after political changes in the 1870s. The "push" factors were massive and irresistible; the "pull" of economic and social opportunity in America was undiminished for the time being.

For a generation after the end of this burst of arrivals, Americans thought of this period as one of a "new" immigration, drawing a line between the more recent immigrants from southern and eastern Europe and those of the "old" immigration, predominately from northern and western Europe. Older Americans felt the new "hordes" were primarily unskilled male workers who threatened the livelihood of the average American laborer. Moreover, they saw a majority of the new immigrants as economic parasites, often recruited by steamship companies, who planned to stay only temporarily in the United States and would return to their native lands after draining money from the American economy. The older immigrants also accused the new immigrants of avoiding farming (which was still seen as a virtuous occupation), flocking instead to the industrial cities where they formed cliquish ethnic enclaves that were characterized as the most degraded kind of slums. The older immigrants doubted that the "new" immigrants, who were thought to be mostly the poor, uneducated "dregs" of a degenerate Europe, would ever adapt to America and enter the mainstream as defined by the native born.

This last point was reinforced for many nativists by the obvious cultural differences between their ancestors and the new immigrants. The immigrants of the 1880–1920 period came from bewildering places basically unfamiliar to most Americans. They spoke languages seldom heard in the United States, and they dressed, worshipped, and behaved in new ways. There were also subtle but undeniable differences in physical appearance among the Italians, Greeks, and Slavs of the new wave and the British, Irish, Germans, and Scandinavians of the old.

Essentially, however, the differences among the "new" immigrants and the previous immigrants were illusions. When viewed a hundred years or more later, the major differences dissolve. For example, while it was true that during the early part of the period the immigrants from southern and eastern Europe were predominantly single males, this was true of nearly all immigrant groups. As time went by, each group saw more families come after the first members proved they could cross the ocean and find jobs.

More balanced examination of the historical record also reveals that roughly the same percentage of new immigrants were skilled workers. However, certain groups at the turn of the century—mostly the Eastern

Europeans—were dominated during the first stages of immigration by unskilled former peasants or rural villagers.

Although the rate of re-immigration to Europe was relatively high among some specific groups, most notably the Slavic groups from the Balkans—such returns were common among previous immigrants. Many new immigrants subsequently returned to the United States, because moving back and forth became relatively easy in the age of the rapid ocean liner.

The accusations that the new immigrants avoided agriculture and lived by preference in squalid, crowded urban slums is the easiest of all to demolish. The truth was that land in America had become scarce and expensive, and many older groups of native-born Americans were avoiding farming. The nation was urbanizing; soon more people were living in cities than on farms, a trend that has continued. Furthermore, the new immigrants did not choose to live in substandard housing in crowded, unsanitary slums, but that was all that was available and all that most of the newcomers could afford during their earliest years in America.

The basic factor that so skewed the image of the new immigrants was that all the things the new arrivals experienced and exhibited were on a huge scale. Not hundreds or even thousands came in each year but hundreds of thousands—even millions during some years. There was no way for the nation to absorb these masses of people without stress. There simply were not enough decent, affordable places to live or jobs to do, so underemployed newcomers did the best they could.

Today, these groups are part of the American mainstream. Though they still retain in many cases a clear sense of ethnic identity, they are usually no longer viewed as strangers or outsiders. Some of them in turn now make up part of the public that is increasingly critical of the late 20th-century "new" immigration from Latin America and Asia.

THE TRANSPORTATION REVOLUTION

A dramatic change in the speed, cost, and methods of transportation played a major role in allowing the massive immigration of the period. The essential factors were the introduction of fast steamships for transoceanic travel and the extension of steamship lines to what before had been remote ports. By the 1880s, people living in previously isolated regions of eastern Europe could get to steamers with relative ease, so they could leave their homes with America in sight. In short, by the end of the 19th century a trip from Odessa to the United States was as easy as a voyage from northern Germany had been a generation or two earlier.

The conditions of travel improved immensely with the advent of ocean steamers. A trip that had taken a minimum of several weeks (much longer if the voyage was unlucky with weather) aboard a sailing ship was reduced to a matter of days. The new ships were built to accommodate passengers, unlike the earlier timber or cotton transport vessels that filled their primitive cargo holds with immigrants. Even traveling below decks in steamship steerage class was a great deal healthier and more pleasant than in the days of sail. Passage below decks, however, still defined immigration—between 1892 and 1903, for example, people arriving by the more expensive cabin class were not counted officially as immigrants.

When it became apparent that the immigrant trade was destined to expand, several British and European passenger steamship lines organized to give a structure to the lucrative business, developing a sometimes fierce competition in the process. Cunard, Hamburg-Amerika, Holland-America, and several others vied for the hundreds of thousands of would-be travelers. They established extensive networks of ticket agents across Europe and plastered village walls with posters and promotions. Contrary to the belief of many American nativists, however, this form of advertising did little to stimulate emigration but rather was intended to direct business to specific companies.

The passenger lines also further developed the prepaid ticket system, which aided immigrants in bringing over family and friends. The larger European steamship lines had thousands of agents in cities all over America, and it was estimated in 1901 that around half of all immigrants traveled on prepaid tickets or on tickets purchased in the United States.

During the earlier decades of the great immigration, the flow from Europe came from ports all over Europe, but after the turn of the century it was concentrated in Naples, Bremen, Liverpool, and Hamburg.

Several of the passenger companies set up elaborate facilities for handling the crush of would-be travelers. The Hamburg-Amerika line, for example, built a virtual immigrant village, complete with dormitories, dining halls, and health facilities, and developed a standard process for moving immigrants through medical exams and onto the ships.

ELLIS ISLAND

The place in America most often associated with the great flood of immigration in the decades around the turn of the century is Ellis Island in New York Harbor, recently restored as a historical site and monument to the immigrants of that era.

The federal reception center at Ellis Island did not open until 1892. Before that, responsibility for receiving and processing immigrants remained with the state and city of New York, which was the major port of entry for Europeans. Technically, the federal government had assumed legal responsibility in 1875 with a U.S. Supreme Court decision that took away the states' authority, but in fact, the federal government paid New York to continue to handle immigrants at the Castle Garden center.

The burden grew too great for the state, however, so in 1892 Ellis Island became the focal point for immigration processing. By the time it closed as a center over 60 years later, millions of people had passed through. During the peak years, as many as 8,000 immigrants a day were processed by a relatively small staff.

Most immigrants went through the center rapidly, with only a brief pause before boarding the ferry for Manhattan or New Jersey. In theory, each person was given a physical examination, had his or her papers checked, and was interviewed before being passed on or held. In fact, with such a crush of people, processing was cursory much of the time.

If something was wrong—a physical problem or a difficulty with papers for instance—the immigrant was pulled out of line and held on the island until being either admitted after further examination or sent back to Europe. The island had dormitories, dining halls, and a hospital to take care of the detainees.

For those who were rejected (only about 1 percent), Ellis Island was a place of doom and frustration: they were then turned away at the doorstep of their dreams. Among the most important causes for rejection were physical

Ellis Island, in New York Harbor, the major point of arrival for the millions of European immigrants who came to America between 1890 and 1920. The buildings and grounds fell into bad disrepair after the reception center closed in the 1950s, but much of the island was restored as a museum of immigration during the 1980s. (Photo courtesy the Ellis Island Immigration Museum)

afflictions, particularly contagious diseases and eye diseases like trachoma. Even at the height of the inflow there were only eight Public Health Service doctors on the staff, so diagnoses were less than carefully considered. The regulations also called for excluding anyone deemed "likely to become a public charge," so penniless immigrants with no relatives or contacts in America were suspect, especially women and children.

THE ITALIANS

More than four million Italians immigrated to the United States between 1880 and 1920, making them the most concentrated of all immigrant nationalities, outstripping even the Irish of the famine years.

The Italians had been on the move for much of the 19th century, but most of the flow had been to Latin America, with only a comparative few immigrating to the United States before 1880. Economic circumstances for the peasantry of southern Italy—particularly Calabria, Apulia, and the island of Sicily—had seldom been good and got increasingly worse during the last decades of the century, with worn-out soil and harsh system of absentee landlords pushing people to the New World. Beginning with about 12,000 Italians in 1880, the numbers rose steadily to over 100,000 annually in the decade from 1900 to 1910. The high point was in 1914, before World War I cut the flow, when almost 300,000 arrived in that year alone.

While there were notable exceptions, such as the Italians who established a presence in northern California agriculture and those who became midwestern miners, the vast majority of Italian immigrants entered America through New York City and remained there or in nearby cities. Some historians estimate that only about 3 percent of Italian immigrants between 1880 and 1920 landed in ports other than New York Harbor.

The actual demographic statistics show that Italians lived in all parts of cities such as New York, but the indelible image is of powerfully ethnic neighborhoods dominated by Italian businesses and retail stores. Strangers wandering into New York's "Little Italy" or around Providence's Federal Hill district could have been excused for believing everyone living in these sections was Italian. Southern Italian dialects were heard on the streets, the dress of the people was distinctly that of the Italian peasantry, and virtually all the signs were in Italian. In many American cities, Italian immigrants attempted to re-create in their neighborhoods social communities based on the villages or towns they had come from, which reenforced the sense of ethnic urban exclusivity.

Most Italians arrived with little capital or training, so they moved into jobs at the bottom of the economic ladder. Italian males, for example, virtually took over from the Irish the pick and shovel work in construction, and many young Italian women became domestic servants and textile indus-

An urban neighborhood saloon catering to Italian immigrants in 1906 at the height of the
"new" immigration. (Photo courtesy State Historical Society of Iowa, Iowa City)

try workers. Economic necessity forced even the youngest Italian immigrants
into the workforce; only a minority of first-generation Italian children could
take time away from work to attend public schools.

Although they were virtually all Roman Catholics, the Italian immigrants
were relatively loose in their church affiliations—at least when compared to
other immigrant Catholic groups. There was little of the association that
other national groups made between church and ethnic identity, perhaps
because of the fragmented national history of Italy and the tendency of the
immigrants to remember priests and bishops as agents of oppression rather
than as sources of support. Whatever the explanation, Italian immigrants
were noticeably less vigorous in supporting churches and parochial schools
in America than were other European Catholics, preferring instead to focus
on individual festivals that had been important to specific villages or regions
in Italy.

The Italians were also, on the whole, not much involved during their
early years in local politics, mostly because they were completely absorbed
with grinding out an existence in America. It was well into the 20th century
before Italian immigrants or second generation Italian Americans sought
political power in urban areas. On the other hand, several Italian immigrants
were prominent among the ranks of American political radicals during the
first decades of the 1900s. Two obscure Italians, Nicola Sacco and Bartolomeo
Vanzetti, became highly publicized national symbols when they were

arrested, tried, and eventually executed in Massachusetts as much for their political radicalism as for the robbery and murder of which they were officially accused.

The association of Sicilian immigrants with organized crime in America is, of course, one of the most publicized (perhaps even romanticized) aspects of Italian immigrant culture. No matter what the truth is historically—whether the Italian and Sicilian elements have been overemphasized and whether extralegal organizations played a beneficial social welfare role early in the immigrant experience—it is undeniable that figures with Italian names have been prominent in American crime ever since the early years of the century. Many Italian Americans see government attempts to lay the blame for urban criminal activities onto a massive, secret Mafia society as only another example of anti-Italian or nativist prejudice.

THE GREEKS

The earliest known Greek immigrants were 400 indentured servants brought to the colony of New Smyrna near St. Augustine, Florida, in 1768. The colony failed, and the handful of Greeks dispersed into the general population. There was no significant Greek immigration again until the latter decades of the 19th century, when a flood of Greeks joined the other nationalities making up the so-called new immigration from eastern and southern Europe.

The total number of Greek immigrants is difficult to gauge, because ethnic Greeks came from both the nation of Greece, which won independence from the Ottoman Turks in 1821, and the Greek populations that had formed around the Ottoman Empire while the Turks ruled the Greek homeland. The issue is further complicated by the large number who came here primarily to take advantage of economic opportunity and did not intend to stay: at one stage around 1900, the number of returning Greek immigrants equalled nearly half the number arriving.

The best estimates are that Greeks arrived in America at a rate of more than 30,000 a year during the two decades of peak immigration just before 1914, most of them unskilled workers who were fleeing poverty and lack of opportunity at home. These immigrants were attracted strongly to American cities, and overall the Greek population in the United States became one of the most heavily urbanized of all the major European immigrant groups. Historians believe that most turn-of-the-century Greek immigrants associated farming with poverty and therefore avoided agriculture and rural regions when they got to America, although significant numbers settled in Utah as miners.

Many were doubtless attracted to urban centers by stories from previous Greek immigrants of good wages and jobs. In the 1890s, for example, Greek

workers found good employment in the manufacturing cities of Massachusetts and New Hampshire. They recruited more and more countrymen into
the same industries, eventually almost displacing French Canadian workers.
Several counties in these two states still rank among the highest in the
nation in percentage of population with Greek ancestry. Significant numbers of Greek immigrants also moved to Detroit after 1905 to work for the
relatively high wages in the new auto industry and then spread to other
Midwestern industrial cities such as Milwaukee and Cleveland.

The largest number of Greek immigrants settled, however, in New York
City, though few distinct Greek neighborhoods developed during the period.
The second largest urban Greek colony grew in Chicago, where immigrants
concentrated conspicuously in a Greektown near the Loop. During the early
decades of this century, it was not uncommon to see Greek men gathered in
the characteristic Greek coffee shops that served as community social and
information centers, seeking news of jobs and good wages from all over the
country. Although fewer in absolute numbers than in New York, the Greek
immigrants of Chicago formed the highest percentage of Greek-born in any
American city.

Greek immigrants who arrived between 1880 and 1914 brought with
them a strong sense of national identity—despite, or perhaps *because of* the
up-and-down history of Greece as a modern independent state—which was
reinforced by the presence in the United States of the Greek Orthodox
Church. Technically, the Orthodox Church in America was under the
ecclesiastical authority of the Russian Orthodox Church, but the specifically
Greek Orthodox Church was the only acceptable form of religion for the
majority of Greek immigrants. Consequently, whenever a sufficient number
of Greek immigrants congregated in one place, they founded a local Greek
Orthodox parish and usually imported a priest from Greece to conduct the
services and affairs of the church in Greek, with a proper regard for Greek
Orthodox customs.

As many as 40,000 Greek immigrants returned to Greece during 1912 and
1913 to fight in the Balkan Wars between Greece and its neighbors. This sort
of intense involvement in Greek affairs continued during World War I and
the protracted series of conflicts that saw the ouster of the pro-German
Greek king. The confusing role of Greece in World War I brought on a
backlash in the United States against Greeks and, along with the general
postwar wave of nativism, may have prodded some Greek immigrants to
begin loosening ties with the old country.

EASTERN EUROPEANS

The huge area of Europe to the east (and southeast) of Germany and north of
Greece contributed millions of immigrants during the era of peak immigra-

tion, particularly between 1900 and 1924. The more than two dozen nationalities that made up this influx are difficult to separate into discrete strands.
Some of the ethnic groups are tiny, such as the now-obscure Wends who
immigrated to Texas. Others, such as the Poles or the Hungarians, were
numerous and have received more historical scrutiny.

If there were nuggets of accuracy in the smug stereotypes drawn by native-
born Americans about the "new" immigrants, examples are offered by some
of the Eastern Europeans, who were motivated by promises of economic gain,
dominated by large numbers of single males, and who returned home at high
rates. Many of those who permanently settled in America continued to be
more interested in the politics of their homelands than in those of the
United States.

Most of these peoples were subjects of one of the three empires of the
region—Austria-Hungary, Russia, and Germany—and even though they
may have had extensive, even glorious, national histories, at the time of the
great migration to America, almost none were sovereign states. In some
cases, such as Bosnia, the "nationalities" had only recently emerged from yet
a fourth empire, the Muslim Ottoman Turks.

Many of the Eastern Europeans undoubtedly hoped to find good jobs, save
money, and return to buy land at home. In fact, the return rate of many
Eastern European nationalities was relatively high. For the most part, the
Eastern European immigrants were poor village farmers or peasants with few
skills but an abundance of strength and the tenacity to survive difficulties.
Their object was to take advantage of the economic opportunities in America,
which on the whole, they did.

The Eastern European immigrant typically settled in one of the growing
manufacturing cities of the American interior, where the men did the back-
breaking and often dangerous work that built cities like Detroit, Chicago,
Buffalo, Pittsburgh, and Cleveland into the industrial giants of the world
economy. Some groups decided early on favorite locations, while others
moved around to find the best jobs and pay rates.

Separating the distinct ethnic nationalities of Eastern Europe immigrants
is difficult because of the complexity and extent of the mixture. The task is
made even harder because immigration statistics were compiled by country
of origin, not ethnicity, so that almost all of the Eastern Europeans were
recorded not as Poles, Slovenes, or Romanians, but as Austro-Hungarians,
Russians, or Germans.

The truth, of course, was more complicated. The Poles, for example, were
a completely coherent national and ethnic group with an extensive history
as an independent nation dating from the Middle Ages. Unfortunately for
them, their nation had been split up since the late 18th century, and until
after World War I, Poles were subjects of one or the other of the European
empires. Nonetheless, it was easy to identify a Polish immigrant: anyone who

A "Hungarian" immigrant mother and child at Ellis Island in 1912. (Photo courtesy the
Boston Public Library, Print Department)

spoke Polish as his or her first language and who was Catholic. When the
U.S. Census counted foreign-born Polish speakers in America in 1910, it
found more than 400,000 from Russia, 330,000 from Austria-Hungary, and
190,000 from Germany. The best estimates place total Polish immigration
between 1880 and 1920 at two to two and a half million.

The largest single concentration of Poles was in Chicago, with New York in second place, followed by Pittsburgh, Buffalo, Milwaukee, Detroit, and Cleveland—a classic distribution pattern for Eastern European immigrants. The high return rate among Poles was classic also, with estimated re-immigrations as high as 50 percent during some years. Polish identification with the homeland, moreover, remained strong even among those who stayed in America (when the first post-Communist free elections were held in modern Poland after 1989, candidates found it worth their while to campaign among the many qualified Polish voters in Chicago), and much activity in Polish American communities has traditionally centered on domestic Polish politics and national affairs rather than on participation in American politics.

Other illustrative examples among the nationalities and ethnic groups emigrating from Eastern Europe were the Croats and the Slovenes, two neighboring peoples occupying territories south of Austria and east of Italy with borders on the Adriatic Sea. Both the Croats and Slovenes can be classified as "southern" Slavs, which is the meaning of the term "Yugoslav." The nation known as Yugoslavia, which was created from parts of the Austro-Hungarian Empire after World War I, eventually included these two groups and several others—notably the Serbs, the Bosnians, and the Macedonians. The nation was broken up by Nazi invasion during World War II, re-formed as a Communist state after the war, and then disintegrated in the face of ethnic and nationality competition after the collapse of Communism in the early 1990s, creating yet another Balkan crisis for the world to deal with.

The Croats had not been independent since the 11th century. Since then they had been united with Hungary and by the end of the 19th century had become part of the Austro-Hungarian Empire. But despite this centuries-long political submersion and a language virtually indistinguishable from Serbian, the Croats maintained a distinct sense of national-ethnic identity typical of the region.

Because of confusion in the way language groups and national origins were counted by the Immigration Service and the U.S. Census, it is impossible to know exactly how many Croats immigrated to the United States, but some estimates place the number at around a million, which would have made them the largest of the southern Slav groups. The majority probably came between 1890 and 1914.

Most were displaced peasants or small villagers who fled economic depression and sought jobs at what seemed to them to be high wages. The immigrants were predominately male with little or no education and most found work in unskilled jobs in the industrial cities. Roughly half of the Croatian immigrants returned home when they had amassed sufficient funds. The half who stayed brought their families to join them and settled in to

As was the case with this miner, who is shown around 1905, many eastern or southern European immigrants found work in the coal mines of America. (Photo courtesy State Historical Society of Iowa, Des Moines)

become Americans. As with other groups from the region, the immigrant Croats of the first generation maintained a keen interest in the political fortunes of their native land until well after World War II.

Their neighbors immediately to the north, the Slovenes, though also "southern" Slavs, spoke a distinct language and considered themselves entirely separate from the other groups in the region. There had not been an independent Slovenia since the 15th century, when the Slovenes were incorporated into the Austro-Hungarian Empire and scattered among several provinces. Like the Croats, most Slovenes were Roman Catholic.

The Slovenes also were impelled to emigrate by a deteriorating Eastern European economy. By the late 19th century, landholdings had been so subdivided that the growing population could scarcely feed itself on the small, relatively unproductive acreages. To merely survive (much less even dream of prosperity) meant leaving for America.

The usual problems apply in attempting to estimate how many Slovenes actually immigrated between 1880 and 1914 (they were often counted among the Croats, for example), but a reasonable guess is between 250,000 and 300,000. Cleveland came to be the preferred destination for thousands of Slovenes, with many of the immigrants finding first jobs in industry. Other cities attracting Slovenes included Milwaukee and Chicago. There were also significant numbers of Slovene miners in most of the mining regions of the nation.

Even the most careful students of Balkan history are often brought up short by the complexity of the political alignments and realignments in the region in the last century and a half. The Romanians, a group considerably smaller than the Poles, Croats, or Slovenes, illustrates the difficulties. The Romanians had a coherent ethnic identity, based on a shared language (not a Slavic tongue, but a language derived from Latin) and a shared Eastern Orthodox religion. Moreover, at the time of the great migration, Romania was one of the few small independent nations in the region, not part of an empire. The Romanian kingdom had been formed initially in 1859, although significant numbers of ethnic Romanian lived outside its borders—principally in the province of Transylvania—and so were recorded as immigrants from other nations. The estimates are that 85,000 Romanians came to America before World War I and the imposition of immigration restrictions by Congress brought movement to an end.

Immigration by the Romanians echoed the other Eastern Europeans, with increasing small landholdings and bad economic times motivating young men to seek better fortune in America. Persecutions of Orthodox Romanians living under the political control of the Catholic Hungarians also led many to leave their homelands. They had one of the highest of all return rates, however; as many as two-thirds may have gone back to Romania after World War I. Most Romanian immigrants found unskilled jobs in the industrial cities of the American heartland, though there was a marked tendency for them to move around, sometimes four or five times while sojourning in the United States. On the whole, Romanians showed less inclination to form ethnic enclaves and seemed content to live among others.

The Hungarians provide a final example of the immigration from Eastern Europe. This story is likewise full of complexity. The political entity of Hungary was part of the larger Austro-Hungarian Empire, but had achieved considerable autonomy—or at least independent power within the empire— by the late 19th century. As typical of the imperial pattern, there were many ethnic and would-be national groups living within the borders of Hungary. However, the "true" Hungarians were the Magyars, a large, very distinct ethnic group united by a language unrelated to the Slavic tongues of the region and by a national form of the Roman Catholic religion. Unlike most other Eastern European ethnic groups that tended to be spread across political lines, few Magyars lived outside the borders of Hungary.

Beginning in the 1880s, harsh economic conditions pushed a growing migration from Hungary to the United States, but until almost the turn of the century, the majority of the flow was from non-Magyar people who just happened to live within the designated Hungarian borders. These immigrants were counted, nonetheless, as Hungarians by U.S. statistics.

In the late 1890s, however, significant numbers of Magyars began to immigrate, including poverty-stricken rural and village farmers, as well as members of the more prosperous and better-educated parts of society (an unusually high percentage of Magyar immigrants were literate). Perhaps as many as 450,000 arrived between 1900 and World War I, but the return rates were very high—typical of immigration from the region.

There are many indications that the patterns of migration, remigration, and re-remigration were amazingly complex, with immigrants sending money to bring brothers or sisters to America, then returning to Hungary to marry and perhaps returning to America to settle down. The higher rate of literacy for Magyars did little to elevate their initial prospects in the United States, and most took low-paying, unskilled jobs in mining or the industrial cities of the American heartland, such as Cleveland. (The story of Hungarian immigration continued, of course, in later decades as part of the story of European political refugees.)

THE EASTERN EUROPEAN JEWS

The official immigration statistics for the four decades from 1880 to 1920, which list arrivals only by country of origin, disguise a massive migration of Eastern European Jews—primarily from Russia and Poland—that swept into the eastern cities of the United States during that time, inundating the quarter million or so American Jews who were descendants of the previous Sephardic (Hispanic) and German Jewish immigrants.

By counting the number of first- and second-generation Americans who spoke Yiddish (a special dialect of Eastern European Jewry, based on German) or Hebrew as their original language, the U.S. Census came up with some fairly reliable numbers for Jewish immigrants. There were more than two and a half million Jews living in America in 1910. By 1924, when Jewish immigration was virtually ended by the new restrictive laws, there were about four million American Jews, at least three-quarters of them originating from Eastern Europe. This made Eastern European Jews one of the largest of all of the immigrant groups of the period.

While many Jews also elected to leave Eastern Europe for economic reasons, there was an extra motivation that exerted a powerful "push" for Jewish immigration. For decades, Jews in Russia and Poland had been subject to a growing series of legal persecutions and physical attacks. Under the Russian Empire, Jews were allowed to live only in a restricted area of western Russian and eastern Poland, known as the Pale, and to follow only certain trades or businesses. Jews could not farm but had to congregate in small rural villages known as *shtetls*. They had almost no legal rights and were denied access to public education. Moreover, the government periodically encouraged the Jews' neighbors to attack them in fits of violence (called *pogroms*) that destroyed Jewish homes and businesses and claimed the lives of thousands of defenseless Jewish men, women, and children. Taken together, these factors gave the Jews of Russia and Poland (which was part of the Russian Empire) powerful incentives to seek a new life in America. Historians believe that by 1906 as many as 150,000 Eastern European Jews each year reached the United States, almost all of them landing in New York City.

Although they were similar to other immigrant groups in the large percentage of youth among them, the majority of Jewish immigrants had distinctive characteristics. They were highly skilled, for example, with almost 60 percent of them knowing a trade or an industrial skill. They also had a much higher than normal percentage of women among the immigrants (only the Irish had more), and they tended to stay in America once they arrived, with one of the lowest return rates of any group of European immigrants. Of course, there was little to go back to.

Like the Greeks and the Italians, the Jewish immigrants remained in the cities of the eastern seaboard. A very large percentage of Jewish immigrants concentrated in New York. Hundreds of thousands of recent arrivals crowded into one relatively small area of the Lower East Side of New York, transforming it into a virtually complete Jewish world. Not surprisingly, this created a crisis in housing and social services, and slum-like conditions prevailed for many years.

Accurate demographic statistics are hard to come by, but historians believe that as many as a half million immigrant Jews lived in an area on the Lower East Side that was no larger than one and a half square miles, making

A view of Hester Street on New York's Lower East Side taken in 1890. This was the heart of the densely populated immigrant Jewish section. Most of the signs are in either Yiddish or Hebrew. (Photo courtesy the Boston Public Library, Print Department)

it one of the most densely populated places in the nation. Most of these people lived in tightly packed tenement buildings with five or six stories of dark, subdivided apartments with as many as five or six people to a room. Most tenements lacked heat or hot water and had only rudimentary toilets shared by everyone on a floor.

The Eastern European Jews were also distinctive in appearance, language, religion, and customs. Their ways of living had been developed in the isolation of tightly controlled rural villages, where they lived under constant stress and threat, and the result was a unique culture that differed markedly from the Americanized Jews who descended from German and Hispanic immigrants. For example, almost all the new Jews spoke Yiddish. To older Americans, it hardly seemed a language at all and served to set the new immigrants apart.

The greatest contrast, however, was religious. Because the Eastern European Jews had been forced to turn inward in religious matters, they had developed specialized forms of Jewish doctrine and worship that involved intense devotion, even mysticism, and put them at odds with the more relaxed forms of Judaism that had developed among older American Jews.

The fervor of the Eastern European Jews and the intensity with which they imbued daily life with religious practice was new and sometimes unsettling.

When concentrated in an all-Eastern European Jewish enclave such as the Lower East Side of New York City, the new immigrants presented a picture of ethnic solidarity that was hardly matched by any other immigrant group. The streets were crowded with men and women going to work in the garment district (the clothing trades attracted a large number of Jewish immigrants). Everyone spoke Yiddish, the signs were in Hebrew script, and there were a number of basement synagogues.

This concentrated Jewish presence was overwhelming to many older Americans, including many American Jews. It has exerted a powerful hold on the imagination ever since, in part because there have been so many expressive and popular literary and historical accounts of the urban world of the Eastern European Jews by writers such as Mary Antin, Marcus Ravage, Abraham Cahan, Daniel Fuchs, Henry Roth, Bernard Malamud, and Saul Bellow. However, the truth is that the phenomenon of the Jewish urban ghetto was relatively short-lived. By the end of World War I, the economic conditions had improved greatly, and Jews began to move out of the concentrated slum areas and into new sections of the cities. The children of the Jewish immigrants proved to be especially adept at using the public education system as a route for transcending the lot of the early immigrants. Within a generation, many Jewish immigrant families included well-educated and prosperous professionals.

The subsequent impact of the Eastern European Jews on America is impossible to summarize or accurately reduce to a few sentences. Without question, American culture in the 20th century would have become something quite different without the enormous influence of the Jewish population. Can anyone imagine the fine arts or popular culture in America without Jewish artists and cultural entrepreneurs? To cite just one small example, Eastern European immigrant Jews such as Sam Goldwyn and Carl Lammele were particularly attracted to the new motion picture industry and dominated the pioneer generations of both movie making and movie showing.

As time went on and the succeeding generations of Jews separated themselves from the eastern urban immigrant ghettos, they spread more widely into the general population. The obstacles they met, including a persistent strain of nativist American anti-Semitism, have for the most part been overcome in the latter years of the 20th century, and there is scarcely any geographical region or area of activity in American life that has not been successfully penetrated by descendants of the great wave of Eastern European Jewish immigrants.

CHAPTER 5

•••••••••

The Social Process

The social process of immigration involves how immigrants assimilate, how they maintain their ethnic identities, how their religion changes, and how they behave politically. Historians and social scientists now believe that the social process immigrants experienced after arriving in America was remarkably similar from place to place and from decade to decade. Even immigrant experiences that seem widely different on the surface share certain basic characteristics according to this viewpoint. In short, all immigrants bring with them cultural and social patterns from their previous homes, and within a brief span these patterns are altered by exposure to the new environment of America. At the same time, these cultural and social patterns have an impact on America. This two-way effect was as true for an indentured servant in 17th-century Virginia as for a Norwegian farmer in late 19th-century Minnesota. It was also certainly true of the great masses of immigrants who arrived in America between 1880 and 1920.

Furthermore, it is very important—as observers have recently pointed out—to understand that immigrants from the turn or the century were not passive victims who were torn from former lives and thrust into a bewildering new world. On the contrary, all immigrants (save, perhaps, political refugees) were people who had taken active control of their lives.

In short, they chose to emigrate, to leave the old behind and embrace the new. Far from being victims, immigrants at the turn of the century were examples of courage and determination. They not only sought change, but dealt with it well once in their new homes.

At the height of the flood tide of immigration, the English-Jewish playwright Israel Zangwill's 1908 play "The Melting Pot" first popularized the idea that the new immigrants would find themselves in a process by which all alien people would be recast by contact with America and older American groups so that an entirely new kind of person would emerge.

This idea spread quickly as an interpretation of immigration and had considerable charm for older Americans, most of whom wanted the newcomers to change as quickly as possible into something more recognizable than transplanted eastern or southern European peasants or *shtetl* dwellers. It also had some attraction for many immigrants, those who rapidly tired of being on the bottom of the economic ladder and outside the system of social acceptance in America.

The melting pot idea, of course, supposed that immigrants would be transformed into "good" Americans but America would only be affected to a small degree by the culture of the immigrants.

In retrospect, it is clear that the entire concept of a melting pot was erroneous. Immigrants did not dissolve culturally on contact with America, and they did not cease entirely to be Italians or Croatians or Russian Jews, at least in the sense of how they understood the world and how they wanted the world to accept them. Moreover, America was certainly not immune to changes caused by the presence of millions of new people. Even kinsmen and fellow countrymen who had come earlier were unable to resist the changes brought by the new immigrants: German and Sephardic Jews, for example, found the Russian Jews perturbed and unsettled their lives.

That a clash would take place between old and new was, perhaps, inevitable. Older Americans, including many who were themselves relatively recent immigrants or the children or grandchildren of recent immigrants, organized social movements to alleviate some of the economic hardships of the new immigrants and to begin the process of "Americanization," attempting to strip away the alien culture and assimilate the newcomers into the mainstream of traditional American society. Just after the turn of the century, the Americanization movement was spearheaded by urban social workers who saw at close range the effects of immigrant poverty and poor living conditions. The movement soon took on a note of urgency that came from supporters who wanted to enforce social unity on a nation they saw in danger of falling into a chaotic diversity. State agencies as well as volunteer organizations were pressed into this effort, and they attempted to educate the immigrants to the basics of the "American way" from hygiene and to ideology. When America entered World War I, the Americanization effort took on even more importance and became a bulwark of what was all too often overzealous patriotism.

Interestingly, the Americanizers' dreams of assimilation were seldom realized, at least not among the first generation of immigrants. The old ways persisted and could not be suppressed by persuasion and propaganda. People could not and did not give up their identities just because they had decided to move to America. Almost all the immigrant groups at the turn of the century persisted in using their native languages, for example (as had previous non-English speaking immigrants from the 17th century on), and they found numerous ways of recreating or sustaining their social customs. Folkways that had been transparently adapted from native lands found places in the immigrant communities of America, and many have been sustained for a century or more as a way to remind immigrants of their original identity.

During the early years, however, the immigrant's ethnic or national identity was reinforced daily by the settlement patterns of most immigrants. The great majority of the immigrants who arrived between 1880 and 1920 lived together in ethnic and national enclaves. Whether in New York's crowded Lower East Side, less intense neighborhoods in other cities across the land, or rural midwestern Scandinavian "ghettos," the new immigrants formed identifiable clusters. They lived in boarding houses with their fellow countrymen, and they socialized in taverns or coffee houses where their own languages were spoken and their customs catered to.

The impact of the immigrants was certainly greatest in the cities, however, and the influx of so many millions in such a short time altered the urban landscape of America. Many cities—Chicago and New York are only the most prominent examples—achieved an astonishing mixture of peoples almost overnight. Moving through the dense immigrant sections of a city presented a kaleidoscope of language, dress, and customs.

Although later research has shown that few ethnic immigrant enclaves achieved anything close to a 100 percent solidarity, the effect of urban living patterns at the time was spectacular. Neighborhoods appeared to be completely Jewish or Italian or Greek or Polish and were disorienting for the visitor. An often-cited example of the confusing mixture is the industrial town of Lawrence, Massachusetts, where it was said that around 1912 there were 25 nationalities and 45 languages or dialects.

Moreover, far too many of the immigrant districts were slums of the most vicious kind, a relatively new phenomenon in American urban life, at least on the scale achieved in the decades of highest immigration. The newcomers had slim resources and had to live wherever they could afford, and there were always landlords willing to create the most profitable rental housing, without regard for squalor or concern for the occupants. Many older Americans were shocked by the revelations of books like Danish immigrant Jacob Riis's *How the Other Half Lives* in 1890 and the report of the Dillingham Commission that conditions had only gotten worse 20 years later. Slums were apparently a consistent part of the lives of recent immigrants, whether in New York, the industrial cities of the Midwest, or the mining camps of more isolated regions.

In the cities, ethnic neighborhoods often presented a sort of running anthropological graph of change over time: because housing was cheapest in such neighborhoods, they attracted the newest arrivals, who in turn pushed out those who had come before. For example, Irish neighborhoods established 40 or 50 years earlier as the home of the working Irish immigrant poor became centers of Italian or Jewish life by the turn of the century—the Irish having reached a relative prosperity were ready and able to move to more expensive and diffused places.

Typically, however, changes showed up in the children of the immigrants. The second generation of almost all the major immigrant groups at the turn of the century reacted to the effects of their double environment—heavily ethnic at home but multicultural outside—and were transformed into "hyphenates"—Italian-Americans, Slovene-Americans, Greek-Americans, etc. The second generation usually failed to learn or at least to use the mother tongue of their parents, and exposure to the "outside" world in the public schools often produced a skepticism about the absolute value of their immigrant heritage. While the second generation fought to free itself from the confines of an exclusive immigrant heritage, it nonetheless maintained an inescapable connection. Even into the third and fourth generations, the offspring of immigrants demonstrate at least some form of direct connection, even if it be only an occasional community ritual or family observance, and among several ethnic groups the third or fourth generations have sponsored cultural revivals, including renewed interest in study of original languages.

RELIGION AND THE IMMIGRANTS

The effect of immigration on religious life in America has been enormous. Immigrants imported distinctive forms of religion that have since become standard in the United States, in some instances maintaining a nationalistic flavor and in others transforming into entirely new entities. Perhaps most interesting was the cycle whereby an immigrant religion or church was changed by exposure to the new environment and then changed again or reformed by the impact of subsequent new immigration.

This pattern was almost predictable, starting with the earliest immigrants such as the Calvinist Puritans of Massachusetts Bay Colony. The Puritans arrived in America as religious reformers, bringing with them as the centerpiece of their social, intellectual, and cultural lives their fierce belief in a "pure" form of Calvinist Protestantism. The entire colonial immigrant enterprise was based on their church. In time, however, and with the changes wrought by living in America, they modified their beliefs and practices, in general falling away from the original rigid doctrines and forms. Eventually, however, renewed religious fervor, brought to America in many cases by Scotch-Irish immigrants of the 18th century, struck sparks with the older churches, and an intense revival movement altered the practice of religion yet again.

The Lutheran experience also illustrates this history. The first Lutheran immigrants were the Germans of the 18th century. For the most part, they were very strong observers of "Old World" Lutheranism, a fundamental form of Lutheran Protestantism that concentrated on salvation by faith alone. As time went by, however, many Lutheran congregations moved perceptibly away from their original "Germaness" and adapted more and more to the American culture around them. This trend was seen particularly in a tendency to adopt an interest in "good works" rather than strict attention to faith. Many took up social causes, began ecumenical relations with other Protestant churches, and—most significantly—allowed English instead of German to be spoken in worship.

In the mid-19th century, reformers and more recent immigrants attacked this acculturalization. Led by a Lutheran pastor from Saxony, Carl F.W. Walther, the reformers insisted on dragging the Lutheran church in America back into practices closer to the original European model. When a tough split developed among Lutherans, the reformers founded their own branch of Lutheranism in America, the Missouri Synod with its center in St. Louis, and in effect created a permanent split between conservative and liberal.

The situation of the Lutherans was made even more complex by the arrival of very large numbers of Scandinavian Lutherans after the Civil War. The Swedes, Norwegians, and Danes all brought with them specifically national forms of Lutheranism because these were official state churches in their homelands. To complicate the picture, however, many among the Scandinavian immigrants—particularly the Norwegians—were at odds with the extremely conservative state churches, and some had been motivated at least in part to immigrate because of religious disputes. The formation of nationality-based Evangelical Lutheran denominations in America was in part a response to this situation. These influences and experiences have sifted down to today when some American Lutherans are classified by criteria defined by immigrants of several generations ago.

The experience of the Roman Catholic church in America demonstrates even more sharply the effect of succeeding waves of immigration. The story is perhaps the best-known aspect of religion and immigration: Roman Catholicism was imported to the United States primarily by immigrant groups who were subsequently displaced or challenged in church affairs by later immigrant nationalities, all of which took place against a background of recurring persecution and suspicion from the majority Protestants.

The tale began with the establishment of the church in America by English Catholics in Maryland (originally founded by Lord Baltimore as a haven for persecuted co-religionists), who at their most influential were accepted grudgingly by the political and social elite of the 18th century. The Carroll family, for example, was both Catholic and part of the leadership of the American Revolution. The Catholic presence was small, however, and was by the 1840s a mixture of nationalities—part English, part French, part German, and part from elsewhere in Europe.

Then came the Irish. With the great migrations of the late 1840s and early 1850s, the Irish in their hundreds of thousands swamped the Catholic church in America. The Irish were not genteel Catholics, but strong believers who were accustomed to taking religion seriously and placing the parish and the clergy at the center of daily life. Within a remarkably short time, the Irish immigrants had virtually taken over the hierarchy of the church in America and had control of church affairs. For example, almost all of the influential American Roman Catholic bishops and archbishops in the later decades of the 19th century had been born in Ireland.

The capture of the church by the Irish led to conflicts with some of the older immigrant nationalities, particularly the Germans, who were distressed to see control and ministry of their local parishes and dioceses pass from fellow countrymen to whom they considered alien priests and bishops. By the 1880s and 1890s, there was a full-blown controversy within the Roman Catholic church over how strongly the church was to make national claims. Some proposed that national-based parishes should be given priority, although the Vatican tended in the end to deny this principle.

The massive influx of Catholics from Italy and southern Europe affected the church at the turn of the century, but because the Italians were relatively indifferent to the institutional side of religion—they had only a slight interest in dominating the hierarchy as compared to the Irish before them—and ethnic groups such as the Croats tended to be relatively low-key in church affairs, the overall impact seemed muted when compared to the controversies of previous decades.

The exception was the Poles, who were perhaps the most intense of the immigrant groups in their Catholicism. In fact, being Catholic was one of the essential characteristics of being Polish, and Polish immigrants were particularly active in setting up and supporting parochial schools as a way to reinforce and maintain their ethnic identity. When large numbers of Polish Catholics arrived in the United States around the turn of the century, they were confronted with an American Catholic church that seemed ill-equipped to meet their religious needs. Even more than the Germans, the Poles chafed at the control of the hierarchy by Irish or Irish American bishops and the lack of Polish-speaking priests. The immigrant Poles insisted on Polish churches in Polish neighborhoods. The conflict grew so intense that some Polish immigrants broke away from the Roman Catholic church and formed a schismatic Polish National Catholic Church, although the great majority of immigrants stayed with the traditional church.

Next to the Roman Catholics, the old-line Jews of America were the religious group most affected by the influx of eastern Europeans at the turn of the 20th century. Their experience also reflected the pattern seen in the mainstream Christian denominations. The practice of Judaism in America, of course, went back to the 17th century, but on a relatively small scale and considerably evolved from its original Iberian and German roots. Reform Judaism had been imported from Germany during the middle of the 19th century, which meant many American Jewish congregations practiced a form of their religion that emphasized the liberal intellectual and cultural heritage of the Jews and more or less encouraged accommodation to the surrounding Christian majority by de-emphasizing the more extreme differences between Christian and Jewish practices.

This reasonably comfortable direction for Judaism was swept away by the hundreds of thousands of Polish and Russian Jews from the *shtetls* who had developed intense devotion to an uncompromising and all-inclusive form of Judaism in their relative isolation under the Russian Empire. Because of their experiences, most were fiercely devoted to what seemed arcane beliefs and practices to American Jews. They were educated in little beyond the basics of the Jewish scriptures and commentaries, but they were overwhelmingly versed in these texts, which they viewed as the center of spiritual and social life. There were strong elements of mysticism and paranoia in Eastern European Judaism that were very much at odds with the easy-going, acculturated Judaism of the older American Reform congregations. By sheer weight of numbers, the new Jews became the dominate factors in American Jewish life in the early part of the century.

The Eastern European nationalities who were adherents of the Orthodox Church had a slightly different experience from groups such as the Lutherans, Roman Catholics, or Jews, simply because there was virtually no existing Orthodox presence when the hundreds of thousands of Greeks, Serbs, and others arrived between 1880 and 1920. There was nothing for them to react against. Instead, these groups typically understood their own specific national form of the Orthodox Church to be an immutable part of their ethnic and national identity. In short, a Greek could scarcely be a Greek if he or she did not adhere to the Greek Orthodox Church; a Russian Orthodox or a Serb Orthodox church was not in the least acceptable as a substitute.

As soon as practically feasible, the eastern Orthodox groups imported their own priests and set up local parishes in America. In most cases, the immigrant Orthodox churches became the focal points of intense nationalism, and what outsiders would think of as almost purely political conflicts were worked out as church schisms or disputes. These intense divisions often reflected differences that sprang from current domestic politics in the homeland.

POLITICS

Politics is about power: how to get it and how to keep it. In a democracy such as the United States, political power comes through votes, so any large bloc of the population that can be labeled by a distinctive characteristic such as nationality or ethnicity is of tremendous interest to politicians hoping to get and keep power. It is not surprising, therefore, that immigrants and immigration have been the focus of political attention since early in the history of the Republic. During those periods when immigrant votes were available in huge numbers, immigrants moved close to the center of the political stage.

The first immigrants to have a major impact on American politics were the Irish. Soon after they began to arrive in large numbers during the late 1840s, the Irish started to work the American political system to their advantage. By the end of the century, Irish politicians and Irish voters had achieved a lasting importance in the American political scene.

The basic goals of the Irish immigrants were not particularly lofty or noble. In fact, the immigrants correctly viewed local political machines as primary providers of social services. In the absence of governmental agencies, the local political parties supplied support for urban Irish immigrants, from handouts to job-finding services. In return, the political organizations asked only that the immigrants support the candidates and issues suggested by the bosses.

It was a simple and effective exchange, although it outraged a certain class of older Americans, who claimed to want voters to take a loftier view of civic responsibility but were actually distressed at the loss of local power. Whatever the reason, the Irish voter was almost always at odds with the older stock American reformers. The Irish saw very little of the abstract in politics and the very potential for politics to change society for the better. Instead, their experience taught them that votes gave them direct power to achieve personal, local goals—better jobs, freedom from police harassment, etc.— and so the Irish saw politics as one of few arenas of influence. To exchange desperately needed services for voting loyalty (and turning a blind eye to the deep corruption of the urban political system) seemed to most Irish a cheap and easy bargain.

The greatest early example of the unity of the Irish immigrants' voting power and local political control came in New York City. There an the old-line Democratic urban organization known as Tammany Hall, led by older Americans such as "Boss" William Marcy Tweed, discovered that Irish voters could be marshalled on a significant scale. Tammany Hall came to control the government offices of the city through manipulation of the Irish (and other immigrant voters) in return for providing the things the immigrants needed to cope and survive in the city. The Irish themselves soon showed a flair and aptitude for urban machine politics, and by the 1870s Irish leaders such as Richard Coker had captured local government.

Their success spread to other cities with large Irish and immigrant populations. By the end of the century, many of the nation's largest cities were controlled by Irish bosses and Irish mayors and Irish councils who proceeded to build and solidify their local power by folding in succeeding waves of immigrant voters.

Other early and mid-19th century immigrant groups had less impact on the American political system. The Germans had a few cases of notable political influence and electoral success, such as Carl Schurz's rise to national political prominence and the election of John Peter Altgeld as governor of Illinois. In the states of the upper Midwest, the Scandinavian vote came to be significant by the end of the 1800s. On the whole, however, immigrant voters were not concentrated enough outside a few major cities nor was there sufficient interest among immigrants to allow capture of widespread political power.

Although the Catholic Irish were closely aligned with the Democratic Party, many of the Protestant ethnic groups tended to vote Republican, which also diffused their potential power. Historians have devised elaborate theories concerning the attraction of one or the other political party to specific groups, but the simple explanation is probably that ethnic rivalries and self-interest guided most immigrants' political choices. When the Irish, for example, entered cities where the pro-English older immigrants were Republicans, they quite naturally gravitated toward the Democrats, who obligingly acted to strengthen what became a cooperative political relationship. When other groups arrived to find the Irish in control, they opted to support the Republicans out of simple self-interest. Thus, in places where Scandinavians faced Catholic Irish Democrats, they voted Republican.

An interesting example of this inter-immigrant political dynamic was in New England, where large numbers of French Canadian immigrants discovered the Irish in control of both local politics and the Catholic church. A fierce rivalry developed over the space of several decades, with the French Canadian immigrants slowly organizing well enough to wrest political power from the Irish in a few New England manufacturing cities. By the turn of the century, the French Canadians had become a significant political force in New Hampshire, Maine, and Rhode Island, electing a governor in the latter state in 1908.

As previously noted, the very large numbers of so-called "new" immigrants from southern and eastern Europe were on the whole relatively indifferent to American domestic politics, or at least they appeared to be much less interested than were the Irish or the Germans. There was virtually no political organization of the Italian or eastern European immigrant voters, other than groups whose interests were in the political life of the old country, not in taking over the local city or country government. In only a few isolated cases, such as Anton Cermak's takeover of Chicago, did these new immigrant groups challenge the supremacy of the entrenched Irish or other city political machines.

The approach of World War I, however, activated the eastern and southern European immigrant communities, because almost all of them came from places that were involved as belligerants in the war. Most of the immigrant groups were finally motivated to organize politically in order to lobby for specific American foreign policies that would benefit their national homelands. Significant numbers of recent immigrants came from places that were subject to rule by one of the empires that made up the enemy Central Powers. Poles, Croats, Slovenes, and many others saw the war as an opportunity for their homelands to regain sovereignty. Others, such as the Italians and the Serbs, saw the war as a chance for their homelands to expand in territory and power. These aspirations led to initial widespread support for President Woodrow Wilson's ideas for self-determination of small nations in eastern Europe after the war, but they also resulted in severe disappointment with the final postwar settlement and subsequently translated into domestic political opposition against Wilson and his party.

CHAPTER 6

·········

The Nativist Movement and Immigration Restriction

In 1886, a giant statue of a woman with the torch of freedom raised high in her hand was dedicated in New York Harbor within sight of Ellis Island. Almost immediately the figure came to symbolize for Americans the traditional role played by the United States as an asylum and a haven for the world's restless and oppressed. A few years later, the base of the statue was inscribed with "The New Colossus," a poem by Emma Lazarus (speaking in the voice of Liberty) that concluded:

> Give me your tired, your poor,
> Your huddled masses yearning to breathe free,
> The wretched refuse of your teeming shore.
> Send these, the homeless, tempest-tost to me,
> I lift my lamp beside the golden door!

Great irony rings through this message. Not only were immigrants demeaned as "huddled masses" and "wretched refuse," but less than 40 years after the dedication of the Statue of Liberty, the golden door was slammed shut and the image of America as an asylum for European masses yearning to breathe free was tossed on the scrap heap, replaced by the image of America as a fortress against the assaults of immigrant hopefuls.

By the early 1920s, immigration was no longer simply a phenomenon of American life but a problem to be solved with laws that restricted and limited immigration; it has remained so ever since. Despite a touching persistence in the belief that America has been a refuge for the world's oppressed, the truth is that since the early part of this century, America has

The Statue of Liberty in New York Harbor, dedicated in 1886, has served since the 19th century as a symbol of immigration to America. The colossal statue was a gift from France in commemoration of American-French friendship. (Photo courtesy the Statue of Liberty National Monument)

welcomed only selected immigrants at selected times and under selected circumstances. The qualifications have changed from time to time to reflect current political belief and prejudice, but since the early 1920s the constant has been significant barriers to immigration.

Until 1882, immigration to the United States had been free and open. Congress and individual states had occasionally imposed conditions on aliens and on the process of naturalization, but immigration itself was almost uniformly unrestricted. The bar against Chinese imposed in 1882, however, was the first in a long series of legal restrictions.

The Chinese Exclusion Act sprang from a combination of prejudice and economic fear. These two motivating factors have been the engines driving the movement for immigration restriction ever since, and they have proven to be powerful. Nativism and prejudice against groups perceived to be "other" are ugly but deep-seated human traits that Americans have not escaped. When these are wedded with cyclical economic downswings, the result is an overwhelming desire to keep out immigrants who are perceived as dangerous. That desire has usually been translated into restrictive immigration laws.

Around the turn of the century, the restrictionist movement received impetus from related social and intellectual developments. First, many American from older immigrant groups were overwhelmed and frightened by the arrival of millions of newcomers, especially because the immigrants were not from northern Europe and seemed in appearance and behavior to be alien and strange. In historical perspective, it seems clear that Italian or Greek peasants were no more alien than had been Irish or Norwegian peasants before them, but the terrific onslaught of huge numbers made a great psychological difference. Older American were accustomed to the Irish by the early 1900s; they were frightened by the Slavs.

The second development expressed by the proponents of restriction was a fear that the large masses of newcomers would never fit in to American life. The contention that these new peoples could not assimilate or Americanize was a reverse way of saying that the restrictionists feared that newcomers would change America in ways unknown and therefore threatening. The restrictionists, of course, assumed that the America they and their forebearers had created was the best of all possible nations and it could only be damaged by change. Therefore, they agitated for maintenance of the status quo—a status quo in which they defined what was right about society and they held the most political and economic power.

Finally, the decades at the end of the 19th century and the beginning of the 20th were full of disturbances that caused anxiety on many levels. From the end of the Civil War to World War I, the nation underwent a phenomenal period of industrial growth that sparked rapid and often bewildering social changes. The response of many Americans was to establish (or reestablish in their view) a kind of national unity that would smooth out the most drastic of the disruptive new elements in American life. It is not surprising that these reformers saw the immigrants of the period as the sources or at least the instruments of social evil. When middle-class urban reformers looked at the squalor of the immigrant neighborhoods or when political reformers, striving to rid local governments of corruption, looked at the immigrant support of political machines, they saw the things they wanted to eradicate.

THE NATIVIST REVIVAL

The nativist-inspired movement for immigration restriction between the 1880s and its final triumph in 1924 drew support from lower-class laborers, who were afraid of losing their jobs, and the social and intellectual elites of the nation, who fashioned elaborate "scientific" theories to justify exclusion. They were all united in a belief that immigrants, or at least immigrants like those currently flooding Ellis Island, were a threat to the unity of American life. The drive toward unity and conformity was, perhaps, motivated by more than just fear and suspicion of immigrants, but that was a recurrent central theme.

For many Americans, the revival of nativism was expressed as a fear of the political radicalism believed to be in the heart of nearly every immigrant. In the popular mind, the eastern European immigrant was almost certain to be an un-American anarchist or syndicalist bent on subverting American democracy or blowing up law-abiding Americans simply to destabilize society and allow radicals to take control. There was just enough evidence of immigrant radicalism—for example, the Molly Maguire Conspiracy in the Pennsylvania coal fields during the 1870s and the Haymarket Affair bombing of 1886 in which genuine radicals were involved—to give an air of credibility to the nativist fears. The truth, however, was that most immigrants either supported one of the mainline American political parties or were indifferent to domestic politics.

In 1887 in the Midwest, the American Protective Association was founded by Harry Bowers as an overtly nativist organization, aimed at revoking the imagined evil influence of immigrant radicals specifically and foreigners in general. As had been true of the Know-Nothing Party 40 years earlier, the attack centered on Roman Catholicism, which was still seen as synonymous with foreign malevolence. The true believers of the APA saw conspiracy and foreign Catholic subversives everywhere, and they genuinely feared Catholic violence wherein babies would be killed and Protestant houses burned by night-riding Catholic murderers. The strength of the APA (it may have included more than 100,000 members) was in the rural Midwest, but the organization failed to convert paranoia into votes, so it faded relatively quietly by the mid-1890s.

Less shrill in tone than the American Protective Association was the just beginning American labor movement. The first significant attempt to organize workers in industrial America was the Knights of Labor, which came to national prominence during the 1880s. At the head of the Knights was Terrance V. Powderly, a second-generation Irish-American, who eventually left the union to become U.S. Commissioner General of Immigration. Powderly and his fellow Knights were not aggressively hostile to immigrants (the organization faded before the full impact of the so-called new immigration), but they were definitely edgy about the effect of a large influx of foreign workers.

The lines were more sharply drawn by Samuel Gompers, the founder of the American Federation of Labor, who led his organization to modest successes from the late 1890s on. Gompers based his approach to labor organization on unions of skilled workers, who would judiciously use the peaceful strike to win concessions from owners. Ironically, Gompers was himself an immigrant, but he consistently supported anti-immigrant policies, because he saw the arrival of hundreds of thousands of unskilled workers as a threat to his plans for skilled unionism.

INTELLECTUAL NATIVISM

The most powerful source of nativist ideas and propaganda was the intellectual and educational elite of the northeast. Beginning in the early 1890s, academic and literary leaders of great national reputation spoke directly against immigration and the influence of immigrants in American life. Nativist academics in the universities—many of them the most prominent professors of their time—developed supposedly scientific theories to back blatantly prejudiced attacks on southern and eastern European immigrants and to support the political movement to restrict immigration.

The keynote of the genteel nativists was sounded in 1892 by Thomas Bailey Aldrich, the most famous and influential magazine editor of the day, in a poem "The Unguarded Gates" in the *Atlantic Monthly*:

> Wide open and unguarded stand our gates,
> And through them presses a wild motley throng—
> Men from the Volga and the Tartar slopes,
> Featureless figures from the Hoang-Ho,
> Malayan, Scythian, Teuton, Kelt, and Slav,
> Flying the Old World's poverty and scorn;
> These bringing with them unknown gods and rites,
> Those, tiger passions, here to stretch their claws . . . .

> (Quoted in Bernard A. Weisberger, *The American Heritage History of the American People* [New York: American Heritage, 1971], 247.)

The new nativists were not simple-minded, uneducated working-class people who feared Catholics and therefore all foreigners, but rather, as

Aldrich illustrated, they were people who feared and loathed the influence of cultures and foreign ethnic groups that might accelerate changes taking place in American society. Aldrich's ethnology and knowledge of immigration history was faulty—"figures from the Hoang-Ho" (China) had been barred since 1882—but his sentiment was clear: immigrants were to be feared and loathed, and some ethnic groups more than others.

There developed among these intellectuals the basic idea that the new disciplines of the social sciences could draw distinctions between good and bad ethnic groups. Almost all of these distinctions were based on intellectual hot air, and in historical perspective it is easy to see that these ideas were nothing more than a fancy way of dressing up prejudice. At the time, however, the theories carried immense weight and were used to support the political decisions necessary to restrict immigration.

The most vocal theorizers were a group of New England intellectuals who espoused the idea that there was a dominant "Anglo-Saxon" strain in America that had descended from early English settlers (themselves influenced to some degree by Germanic tribal peoples), and that these Anglo-Saxons were the source of almost all American civic virtues, especially a devotion to democracy and freedom. The Anglo-Saxonists claimed that love of liberty was inherent among Anglo-Saxon peoples, and—arguing by extension—other immigrants, such as the distinctively different Italians, Greeks, and Slavs who were flooding into Ellis Island, were unfit to participate in American life and were physically, culturally, and socially inferior.

The public writings of figures such as E.A. Ross, John R. Commons, and Richmond Mayo-Smith were crucial in developing the theory of Anglo-Saxonism. They were buttressed by many lesser figures who developed an entire pseudoscience of ethnography that was little more than an elaborate form of extreme prejudice. These thinkers emphasized the idea that Europe (and the rest of the world) could be divided precisely into racial types and distinct racial characteristics could be assigned to each. Moreover, these supposedly racial differences were thought to be fixed and immutable—in other words, Anglo-Saxons would always be vigorous democrats and eastern Slavs would always be degenerate subjects of empires. In retrospect, modern social scientists see that there was no basis whatsoever for dividing up Europe in such a fashion.

The modern view is that most of what the turn-of-the-century social theorists perceived as racial differences were little more than superficial cultural and national distinctions. There are undeniably racial distinctions among humans, but even the most obvious physical differences among races mean very little culturally—modern anthropology is hard pressed to clearly define what race means in any concrete sense beyond gradations of skin color and physiognomy.

The nativist New England theorizers, however, were certain they could place everyone in a particular "racial" slot and assign them fixed characteristics. To no one's surprise, the results put people like themselves at the top and people unlike themselves at the bottom. Even worse, several of these nativists went a step further and developed a more dangerous theory, known as "eugenics," which said all the good and bad traits of the supposed races were passed on by heredity. In their view, people of "good" stock should breed only among themselves and that "bad" stock should be excluded from intermarriage and kept from overbreeding. This was perhaps the ultimate expression of the nativist Americans fear of the new immigrants. There were many alarmist books, articles, and speeches on the theme that inferior stock was about to overwhelm the American scene and that intermingling would soon debase the American race.

Perhaps the most influential statement of racial-based eugenics was a widely read 1916 book by Madison Grant, called *The Passing of a Great Race*. Grant was a vocal racist who unabashedly supported the exclusion of all but what he called the "Nordic" peoples. Everyone from southern and eastern Europe and all Jews were to be kept out, Grant warned, or the nation would decline into weakness and dissipation.

(It should be noted that this eugenics theory in its most extreme form was the basis for the campaign of Hitler and Nazi Germany to exterminate the Jews of Europe. Few American nativists would have gone so far, but ideas similar to theirs, when carried to an ultimate conclusion by the Nazis, led to the Holocaust and the murder of millions.)

In 1894, a small but influential group of New Englanders formed the Immigration Restriction League of Boston as a way to formally protest open immigration and to lobby for immigration restriction. The league was in the forefront of efforts over the following decades to secure passage of national restrictions, and it enlisted the public support of some of the nation's leading intellectual and cultural leaders, including (in addition to E.A. Ross and John R. Commons) people such as Senator Henry Cabot Lodge; David Starr Jordan, president of Stanford University; and Francis A. Walker, president of the Massachusetts Institute of Technology.

The League eventually adopted the goal of using literacy tests as the major legal device to restrict immigration, which did not play directly to the racist issue. However, its official position was made clear when it asked rhetorically if Americans wanted "to be peopled by British, German, or Scandinavian stock, historically free, energetic, progressive, or by Slav, Latin and Asiatic [Jewish] races, historically downtrodden, atavistic, and stagnant." (Quoted in Roger Daniels, *Coming to America* [New York: HarperCollins, 1990], 276.)

THE DILLINGHAM COMMISSION

Shortly after the turn of the century, with immigration numbers reaching their all-time highs and nativist-restrictionist pressure building, the federal government turned to one of its favorite devices to deal with controversial issues: a commission was appointed to study the issues of immigration and restriction.

In 1906, at President Teddy Roosevelt's urging, Congress created the Dillingham Commission, named after its chairman, Senator William P. Dillingham of Vermont. The commission's appointed task was to explore the nature and consequences of immigration and provide a basis on which to formulate further legislation. While the pretense of scientific objectivity was preserved on the surface, the cards were stacked toward nativism and restrictionism from the beginning. The chief staff expert of the commission was an avowed nativist, and the commission's secretary was hired on the advice of Senator Lodge, the leader of the Immigration Restriction League.

Despite what seemed to be foregone conclusions, the Dillingham Commission energetically embraced the assignment to study the economic and social effects of immigration. With a staff of more than 300 and a budget of more than a million dollars (an immense sum for the time), the commission gathered and compiled data for more than three years. The actual statistical and demographic data put together by the commission were objective, extremely useful, and not by themselves slanted toward a foregone conclusion. Much of the interpretation of the facts was blatantly manipulated, however, including the compilation of a "Dictionary of Races" that classified immigrants into superficial racial categories that coincided with the current intellectual nativist fashion. After looking into all aspects of the immigration issue, the commission published its findings in more than 40 volumes, more than half devoted to economic matters.

The commission's conclusions, published in 1911, pointed toward restriction of immigration as the most desirable national policy. By cleverly arranging the actual data into skewed categories, the facts were made to support the preconceived conclusions of the restrictionist members of the commission and to buttress the preconceived desires of politicians who wanted to pass restriction laws. The commission came down heavily in favor of literacy qualifications as the most desirable technique to keep out unwanted immigrants.

IMMIGRATION RESTRICTION LEGISLATION BEFORE 1917

Even though the legislative history was haphazard and uncoordinated, several immigration restriction laws were passed between the Chinese Exclusion Act of 1882 and the first restrictionist literacy law in 1917. The Congress more or less chipped away at the idea of an open door to immigration by slowly adding more and more qualifications over several decades. Individual laws were usually passed in response to specific political situations and were not yet part of an overall strategic plan to end or limit immigration, but they established several important long-term principles.

The first general federal immigration law was passed in 1882, soon after Congress had taken action to bar Chinese immigration. The general law was mostly aimed at regulating the day-to-day procedures for receiving immigrants, which were still in the hands of state officials. The U.S. Supreme Court had ruled immigrant head taxes in New York and Massachusetts as unconstitutional. However, these states, which bore the most responsibility for handling the growing numbers of immigrants, wanted relief. New York finally threatened to halt operations at Castle Garden unless the federal government did something.

The response was an act that imposed a head tax of 50 cents on all incoming immigrants to finance the receiving centers. Almost as an afterthought, the law set up categories of immigrants that would be excluded automatically: no idiots, lunatics, or criminals were to be admitted, nor anyone who might become a public charge. The latter qualification became one of the linchpins of restrictionist policy in the first half of the 20th century and was the first official legal coupling of economic issues with immigration restriction. The principle established almost casually in the 1882 act is still at the heart of basic American immigration policy, which says that immigrant refugees may not enter for strictly economic reasons.

The next legislative action was passage of the Foran Act in 1885, a specific measure to prohibit the importation of contract labor. Congress was responding to pressure from the newly established American labor unions, such as the Knights of Labor, who feared that cheap immigrant labor would rob native Americans of jobs. There was almost no organized importation of unskilled contract laborers at the time, but it was an issue for American workers who were very insecure in their developing relationship with American big business. Again, this relatively early and almost casual law established a long-term principle of restriction, because fear that immigrant labor will "take away jobs from Americans" has been a recurring factor ever since.

In 1891, a new law gave the federal government complete control over regulation of immigration and set up the first federal office to deal with matters of immigration. Congress created a Bureau of Immigration, headed by a Superintendent of Immigration (a title later changed to Commissioner-General of Immigration), and prepared the way for the establishment of the federal reception center at Ellis Island a year later. The law also added several new categories of excluded aliens: paupers, persons suffering from contagious or "loathsome" diseases, convicted felons or those convicted of misdemeanors involving "moral turpitude," and polygamists. The latter was aimed at reducing the immigration of foreign Mormons, growing numbers of whom the Utah church was successful in recruiting abroad. (Note that the provision excluding people with diseases has been used in the 1990s to bar immigrants who have AIDS.)

Congress acted again in 1903 to prohibit entry of several additional categories of aliens. The most significant part of the act was the barring of anarchists or people thought to advocate the violent overthrow of the American government. Not only did this provision reflect the widespread and persistent belief that the large influx of southern and eastern European immigrants harbored dangerous political radicals, but it was a specific reaction to the assassination of President William McKinley in 1901 by Leon Czolgosz, an anarchist who was a native-born American despite his foreign-sounding name. Again, this relatively casual law established a long-term restrictionist principle, and the provision against those advocating the overthrow of the government was used extensively during the mid- and late 20th century to prohibit entry of anyone the U.S. government suspected of being a Communist or a Communist sympathizer.

The 1903 act also excluded epileptics, prostitutes, and professional beggars. One wonders how many hopeful immigrants identified themselves as either prostitutes or professional beggars when interviewed at Ellis Island. In fact, it appears that, even though the piecemeal erection of immigration barriers eventually added up to significant restriction policies (most of the restrictions were codified in a new law in 1907), there was little in the way of strict or consistent enforcement. The great numbers of immigrants entering the nation every day during these peak years and the relatively small numbers of immigration officials made it virtually impossible to apply the laws on a routine basis.

LITERACY TEST LAWS

The advocates of literacy tests as a condition for entry into the United States may have genuinely seen their idea as a method to improve the quality of immigrants. However, because most of the advocates were on record as holding unpleasant nativist views, it is tempting to believe the real motive behind the literacy test movement was to restrict immigration without having to be more specific about the reasons why.

The first literacy test for immigrants to pass Congress was sponsored by Senator Henry Cabot Lodge, the leader of the restrictionist forces, in 1896. It called for the exclusion of any potential immigrant who could not read 40 words in any language. President Grover Cleveland vetoed the bill, setting a precedent in the relations of Congress and the chief executive on this issue. Cleveland's veto message castigated the act as a gross violation of America's tradition of open immigration, a factor he said had allowed the nation to grow rich and prosperous. He also thought it better to admit hard-working illiterates than well-educated political radicals.

Literacy test bills came up repeatedly in Congress, but they were defeated in 1898, 1902, and 1906. In 1913 and 1915, Congress passed literacy bills, but they were vetoed by President Woodrow Wilson, who did not believe in such devices although he was on public record was a nativist.

The restrictionists finally triumphed in early 1917, when a bill containing literacy clauses was vetoed by Wilson but passed over his objection. The Immigration Act of 1917 was one of the first comprehensive restriction laws in the nation's history. It brought together and codified all the previous piecemeal restrictions and exclusions, and it raised the immigrant head tax, which had been creeping upward since the 1890s, to eight dollars. The law established several new categories for exclusion, including vagrants, alcoholics, and the psychopathically inferior. Perhaps most significantly, the 1917 act created a zone of exclusion in the southwestern Pacific that extended the disbarment of the Chinese and Japanese to virtually all Asians. The final provision was the exclusion of any potential immigrant who could not read a test passage in English or some other language (immigrant families were allowed in if the male head of the household passed the literacy test).

THE VICTORY OF RESTRICTIONISM

The impact of World War I on American immigration policy was crucial. The entry of the United States into a European war for the first time in 1917 set off a wave of hypernationalism that can scarcely be imagined. The nation became intensely preoccupied with eradicating anything that smacked of the foreign or the alien, and the effect on immigration was not hard to predict.

The most vicious examples of antiforeign hysteria were directed against German Americans, most of whom were native citizens. The public at large, however, made no distinction between disloyal Germans and German Americans who had simply kept alive their German heritage. The most extreme form of the anti-German hysteria resulted in the lynching of Illinois coal miner Robert Prager, hung by fellow miners who accused him of spying for the Germans. Less severe measures were carried out all over the country. German American culture, which had flourished since well before the American Revolution, was virtually wiped out in a few months of cultural terrorism.

Before the war ended in the fall of 1918, the anti-German sentiments had been extended to include nearly all foreigners, and the dissatisfaction most

Americans felt about the peace settlement after the war colored American feelings about European immigrants. A nationwide outbreak of fear of Bolshevikism in 1919—known as the Great Red Scare—cemented the national antiforeign stance. When these effects of the war were added to the long-brewing anti-immigration campaign, the stage was set for the final victory of those who demanded restrictions on immigration.

In fact, immigration had fallen to a mere fraction of its prewar pace. Travel was restricted during the conflict, and from a level of more than 1.2 million in 1914, immigration fell to only 326,000 in 1915. By 1918, the figure was barely over 110,000. Although most Americans completely missed the signals at the time, the great movement of large masses of immigrants from Europe to the United States was over, whether restrictions were placed on entry or not. The great bulk of those who wanted to come to America from Europe had already done so by the time the restrictionists won on the legislative front.

In December 1920, the U.S. Congress almost passed a emergency measure suspending immigration entirely, but decided at the last minute to shelve temporary measures and take up instead a comprehensive immigration policy sponsored by William P. Dillingham, the chairman of the study commission that had submitted its report a decade earlier.

When the new law passed in 1921, it was the first of a series of immigration restriction laws that established for the first time the basic ideas that have controlled immigration for most of this century. The Dillingham bill placed a limit on the total number of immigrants that could be admitted in any one year, and more significantly, it apportioned admissions on a system of national quotas. In other words, the law specifically singled out nationalities and gave immigration slots to each according to a formula that was meant to reflect how Congress regarded each nation of origin. This quota system stayed in effect until the mid-1960s and still lurks in the background of American policy on immigration.

The Dillingham bill did not actually come out and say that northern Europeans were more desirable and therefore should have the largest quotas, but rather used an oblique device to achieve the same effect. National quotas for new admissions were set as percentages of the total number allowed for the year and were based on the percentage of the nationality in the existing American population. This sounds complex, but it was in effect a way to freeze the ethnic mix of the country at least as far as European immigration was concerned. By carefully selecting the basis year, the Congress could restrict immigration from Europe to whatever mixture existed during that year.

Specifically, the 1921 immigration bill chose the 1910 census (the most recent available) as the initial standard. Henceforth immigration from all European countries could be no more than 3 percent in total of all the foreign-born Europeans in the nation as of 1910, and this percentage was to be divided according to the proportions of each nation of origin as of 1910. With this formula, a total of only about 350,000 new immigrants would be allowed in.

Virtually the entire program of the Immigration Restriction League was now the law.

Interestingly, the new restriction policy completely ignored the Western Hemisphere. National attention so focused on Europe as the only important source of immigration, that the restrictionists failed to mention Canada or Latin America, so the overall restriction of numbers and specific national quotas did not apply to any immigrants coming across the north or south borders. And, of course, immigration from Asia (except for a tiny quota for Japan) was already prohibited.

By 1924, there was no longer the slightest doubt that Congress intended to move even more forcefully to impose immigration restrictions. A temporary extension of the 1921 law was due to expire, so the legislators took up the issue with the goal of tightening the system even more and of openly slanting the numerical quotas to exclude southern and eastern Europeans.

The result was the Johnson-Reed Act of 1924, the definitive restrictionist legislation. The new law called for a two-step phase-in, but essentially lowered the total number of immigrants to about 150,000 per year. Moreover, the division of the quotas among European nations was to reflect the national origins of the American population as recorded in the 1890 census. This latter change was a clearly stated attempt to reflect the population as it existed before the great influx of "new" immigration from southern and eastern Europe. A further provision of the law, which was never carried out, called for future percentage quotas to be set according to a historical study of the American population from the first days of the Republic. The idea was to establish very large quotas for Great Britain, Scandinavia, and Germany and to freeze out the Italians, Greeks, Slavs, Jews, and others from the "undesirable" parts of Europe.

The Johnson-Reed Act completely cut off all immigration from Asia, ending even the tiny quota for the Japanese, but it—like the previous 1921 law—exempted the Western Hemisphere from all quotas or restrictions.

When the quotas went into effect, the largest share was assigned to natives of the British Isles who got more than half of the total admissions for a single year; Italians, on the other hand, received fewer than 6,000 slots.

CHAPTER 7

•••••••••

The Decline of Immigration

S ome historians believe that even without the imposition of restriction laws, immigration would have declined after World War I. The full provisions of the Johnson-Reed Act did not take hold until 1929, but before then it was clear that the mass movement of people from Europe was over. The devastation of the war, the imposition of travel restrictions by several of the repressive new governments of eastern Europe, and an end to the population growth that had fueled immigration all pointed to the exhaustion of the explosive "push" factors that had existed for decades. The new restrictive laws and the end of economic prosperity in America simultaneously spelled the lessening of the "pull" of the United States as well.

By the end of the 1920s, the overall percentage of immigration from Europe had dropped significantly. And re-immigration from America to Europe became a more and more important factor as the net balance for any one year grew smaller and smaller. At the same time, immigration from the Western Hemisphere, especially Mexico, began a climb that has never crested.

It also became apparent during the 1920s that there were to be many exceptions and unanticipated consequences of the quota system. For example, returning resident aliens who had traveled abroad, the wives and dependent children of U.S. citizens, and several other classes of people were allowed to enter the country over and above the quota for their nation of origin. There were also special admissions for people with desirable skills or professions. These two off-quota exceptions—families and those with skills— grew to be important categories of immigrants.

The greatest change in immigration, however, came with the Great Depression of the 1930s. In 1930, the number of immigrants slipped below

Immigrants study under the watchful eyes of native-born schoolmarms for the naturalization examination in 1937. Even though immigration had fallen to very low levels during the Depression, there was still a strong emphasis on such Americanization classes. (Photo courtesy State Historical Society of Iowa, Iowa City)

100,000 a year, and the annual total remained there until after World War II. In a development that would have seemed inconceivable only a few decades earlier, during several years of the 1930s there was actually a net loss: more people returned to their nations of origin than immigrated to the United States. Not only did the Depression make America less attractive to many potential immigrants, but the Hoover Administration intentionally used the "likely to become a public charge" section of the 1917 literacy test immigration act to effectively bar many who might otherwise have come. By stringently interpreting the clause, immigration and consular officials kept out all but wealthy Europeans during the 1930s.

REFUGEES AND WORLD WAR II

The legislators had missed one aspect of immigration that arose during the years immediately before and during World War II and that has continued to occupy the attention of policymakers ever since: refugees. After Adolph Hitler and the Nazis took power in Germany in 1933 and especially after German's annexation of Austria in 1938, tens of thousands of German Jews sought to leave the country and immigrate to the United States, creating the first refugee "problem."

Refugees had, of course, sought haven in America from political persecution before—the German political activists, for example, fled the consequences of a failed revolution in 1848—but now with restrictionist barriers in place, the situation was altered. German Jews could not simply escape Europe and enter the United States. Before leaving they had to be cleared by U.S. consular officials and fitted into the quotas and criteria for admission.

The American State Department, unfortunately, was filled with many officials who were blatantly anti-Semitic, and they prevented large numbers of Jews from obtaining permission to immigrate. Even after the beginning of the Nazi round-up of Jews for deportation to concentration camps in eastern Europe, the American government refused to alter or loosen the regulations or fixed quotas. It was no secret that Hitler was murdering Jews in large numbers (accounts appeared in the Washington, D.C., newspapers), but the U.S. government would not budge to save lives. In fact, Congress refused to vote on a special bill to allow 20,000 Jewish refugee children in.

A relatively small number (tens of thousands) of refugees from Hitler and Mussolini did manage to escape and immigrate, including many intellectual and cultural luminaries. Ironically, it was only the presence of European scientist-refugees such as Albert Einstein, Leo Szilard, and Enrico Fermi that allowed the United States to develop the atomic bomb during the course of the war. Most of the successful European refugees tended to be educated and reasonably well-off—these were defining characteristics, because poor, unskilled applicants were unable to gain entry—and once acclimatized to America, many of them made valuable contributions to their new nation.

The entry of the United States into the war after the attack on Pearl Harbor in December 1941 prompted what has become one of the saddest tales in American history. The government decided that Japanese immigrants and their second- and third-generation families constituted a threat of subversion and sabotage on the West Coast. In a move that crushed the Constitution and civil rights, the government rounded up all the Japanese Americans it could find, including both aliens and American citizens, deprived them of their property, in effect placed them illegally under arrest, and moved them all to internment camps. While it might have been legitimate to show concern for the dangers of harboring enemy aliens, the action directed against the Japanese American community was clearly motivated by racist sentiments: the millions of German Americans and Italian Americans were barely disturbed.

Not all Asian immigrants suffered during the war, however. The Chinese, who had been completely excluded from immigration since 1882, became American allies in the fight against imperial Japan. Apparently the idea of excluding a major ally from immigration because of alleged racial inferiority was too embarrassing, so a tiny crack in the door was opened for the Chinese during the war. They were granted a minuscule quota—only 105 places for all immigrants of Chinese ethnicity no matter what the country of origin—and the 1882 exclusion act was repealed. Perhaps most significantly, the bar against Chinese naturalization was finally dropped, clearing the way for immigrant Chinese to become citizens.

During the war years themselves, of course, immigration from Europe or Asia came almost to a standstill. No one could move around at will, and there was no commercial transport to bring immigrants across oceans that were little more than watery battlefields for most of the conflict.

Despite a build-up of demand for immigration from Europe that developed during the war, there was not much movement in the months immediately following the end of hostilities, in part because of a continuing acute shortage of civilian transportation. One major exception was the immigration of about 150,000 wives and 25,000 children of American servicemen who were given special dispensation to immigrate in 1946 under an emergency war brides act. The same act facilitated the largest immigration of Chinese since the 19th century, and about 5,000 Chinese women entered as war brides. (Probably another 5,000 Chinese women immigrated legally between 1945 and 1952 under new provisions that generally allowed off-quota admissions of wives of American citizens.)

THE MEXICANS: THE FIRST WAVE

The most important aspect of immigration to America in the second half of the 20th century has been the massive influx of people from Mexico, our neighbor to the south. The exact number of Mexicans who have immigrated is impossible to fix because of many complicated factors, not the least of which is that a large percentage of Mexican immigrants have entered the country illegally. However, even the most conservative guesses about Mexican immigration since 1900 put the number at between eight and 10 million; liberal estimates run as high as 20 million. Whatever the exact figure, it is safe to say that Mexican immigration has had a greater impact on American history than has any other in this century by a wide margin.

An objective view of Mexican immigration over the past 50 years reveals the same stages as did immigration from southern and eastern Europe at the turn of the century. However, because the Mexican influx is still in progress and the public's view is influenced heavily by the issue of illegal immigration, the parallels are not often recognized or acknowledged. The early immigration consisted of large numbers of dispossessed agricultural workers—primarily young males in the first wave—who left home to seek a better economic fortune in America. When they arrived, they took some of the lowest-paying jobs in the American economy. The first wave included large numbers of sojourners who returned to their homeland and families after working for a period in America. In the case of Mexican immigrants, however, the return was more like a back-and-forth movement because of the proximity and relative ease of crossing the border. As time went on, more and more women and families joined the immigration stream, and increasing numbers of Mexican immigrants became American citizens, extending citizenship to a second and third generation of native born Mexican Americans.

There were relatively few Mexican immigrants before the 1940s, however, and the total Mexican American community in the United States was surprisingly small. The origins of Mexican American culture were, of course, found in the people of Mexican heritage who became Americans when California and large portions of the Southwest passed into American hands at the middle of the 19th century. There is no accurate data for annual immigration to 1924, but the best guess puts the total Mexican American community at less than half a million in 1900. When compared to the estimated two-and-a-half million Americans of Mexican birth in 1945 and the 12 million Mexican Americans in the 1980 census, this figure shows the dramatic increase.

The restrictionists who wrote the new laws in the early 1920s to keep out southern and eastern Europeans completely ignored immigration from Mexico (and other Latin American nations) by excluding the Western Hemisphere from the national quota system. Therefore Mexicans could immigrate at will, as long as they met the other requirements. This has been essentially true ever since, although the legalities have been manipulated constantly in response to economic swings in both Mexico and the United States.

Because there has almost always been a major disparity between the standard of living in Mexico and in the United States, the greatest single factor by far in motivating immigration has been economic. When economic times became especially bad for the average worker or peasant in Mexico or when times were especially good in the parts of the American economy that attracted unskilled workers, both legal and illegal immigration blossomed. When there has been a combination of both economic push and pull, then immigration has exploded.

The first important movement of immigrants from south of the border began shortly after 1900. A shortage of agricultural workers in the Southwest and especially California (where new lands in the fertile southern valleys were being irrigated) attracted Mexican immigrants. The official records show slightly less than 50,000 between 1900 and 1910, with over 200,000 in the following decade, and 459,000 between 1920 and 1930.

For these figures to be accurate for all Mexican immigrants, they should be inflated by considerable numbers of illegal aliens after 1924. Even though there was no quota or upper limit on immigration from Mexico, it became more expensive and difficult after the passage of the restriction laws because potential immigrants had to pass the literacy tests and pay a head tax. It was simpler to just cross the border and go to work in the fields. The great majority of Mexican immigrants before 1930 moved no further than California, Texas, or Arizona, and they became the central source of field labor in the rapidly growing fruit and vegetable production business.

From these beginnings, there has been an inseparable tie between the desire of poor Mexican immigrants to improve life for themselves and their families by seeking jobs in the United States and the perceived needs of American business, especially the seasonal agricultural industry, for cheap labor. Official American attitudes toward both legal and illegal Mexican immigration have been guided by political and economic pressures, vacillating between welcome and rejection depending on the state of the economy and the immediate labor needs of California and Southwestern agriculture. The relationship has been even more complex because it has also been tinged with racist attitudes, especially on the local level in the Southwest, directed against Mexicans, most of whom represent an ethnic mix of Spanish and native Indian ancestors. There has usually been a good deal of exploitation and manipulation by American businessmen and government officials. This has only recently begun to change to any significant degree because of the economic and political organization of the huge numbers of Mexican American (and other Hispanic) citizens.

When the Great Depression hit the United States, there was a drastic decline in demand for immigrant labor in the farm fields, and immigration statistics fell during the 1930s to very low levels. In addition, state governments in the Southwest were allowed to round up and deport illegal Mexican aliens—more than 400,000 between 1930 and 1934—who were thought to be taking jobs from needy Americans. The reality is that until the extreme provocation of the Depression, most Anglos had avoided the difficult, exploited, and poorly paid labor in the farm fields. The deportation net caught not only illegal aliens, but also many Mexican American citizens who had immigrated legally, in some cases decades before.

The onset of World War II changed conditions drastically, however. Not only did the agricultural sector regain prosperity but the demands of wartime brought on an acute labor shortage. At the same time, economic conditions in Mexico hit bottom, so when the United States proposed a program of importing Mexican workers to serve the growers of the Southwest, the Mexican government agreed, despite reservations about how Mexican citizens might be treated. The result was the *bracero* program, which was to be a temporary solution to the war shortage but proved so advantageous to American growers that they pressured the government to continue it beyond 1945. In fact, the program lasted until 1964 and brought large numbers of

Mexican workers into the United States, between 100,000 and 200,000 a year during the war and as many as 400,000 a year at the peak in the late 1950s. Workers were screened and recruited by the Mexican government and then transported across the border where they signed individual contracts with growers.

The *bracero* program also inadvertently spurred illegal immigration, because the prevailing need for workers meant many American officials cast blind eyes toward undocumented laborers and it proved simpler in many cases for Mexicans to find work if they avoided the formal paperwork required by the *bracero* procedures. The large number of illegal Mexican immigrants—called *los mojados* or "wetbacks" in reference to swimming the border at the Rio Grande River—were ripe for exploitation and ill-treatment by employers, because their status was precarious and they had virtually no legal or practical recourse if cheated or abused.

Taken together, the legal and illegal immigrations of the 1940s created a large and ever-growing Mexican American community in the United States. It was at first concentrated in California and the Southwest, but eventually spread to other parts of the nation as Mexicans and Mexican Americans began to follow a long trail of seasonal work, pushing as far north as Michigan and Minnesota. There were also growing pockets of Mexican American settlement in some of the larger American industrial cities by the early 1950s.

NEW LAWS AND NEW POLICIES

The two decades following the end of World War II saw a series of changes in the nation's immigration laws and policies, which by the mid-1960s resulted in a revised basic structure that is still in place, although it has been tinkered with and amended often over the last 30 years. Throughout these important postwar decades, American law makers and officials continued to view immigration from Europe as the major element in the equation. In fact, European immigration had long since passed its greatest importance and was be only a minor factor. For much of the period, the Cold War global struggle between the United States and the Soviet Union controlled American reaction to immigration.

The first legal and policy issue to arise after the war was how to deal with the hundreds of thousands of European refugees created by the long struggle. The question of how to treat refugees has not left center stage of the immigration policy arena since, but the late 1940s were the first years in which America had to face up to whether large numbers of refugees would be welcome. In nearly every instance then and since, the question has hinged almost entirely on politics: if the refugees were deemed politically worthy (for many decades this was measured almost entirely by the standard of pro-Communist versus anti-Communist), they were let in; if seen as a political threat, they were excluded.

In 1948, the U.S. Congress passed the Displaced Persons Act, which allowed a limited number of Europeans displaced by the war and the subsequent takeover of Eastern Europe by Communist regimes to immigrate to America. There were many in the United States who feared that a flood of undesirables would enter if unlimited refugee immigration was allowed, so the refugee law was less than an open-armed welcome.

The Congress also wanted to maintain the idea that national quotas were still the controlling factor in regulating immigration, so an elaborate system was devised to allow European displaced persons to come in through longterm borrowing against future national quotas. This polite fiction was necessary because a large number of refugees came from places whose quotas had been set intentionally low during previous decades to keep them out. About 400,000 European refugees were admitted under the Displaced Persons Act between 1948 and 1952.

By the time the four-year temporary Displaced Persons Act expired, it was evident that political refugees were a category of potential immigrants that was unlikely to go away and would probably increase. In 1953, Congress enacted a Refugee Relief Act, mostly in response to a failed anti-Communist revolt in East Germany. Slightly more than 200,000 temporary visas were created to allow refugees to enter and live in the United States, although they were on a form of extended parole until they qualified as permanent resident aliens or as citizens.

During the rest of the 1950s, a time of the most intense American concern about the spread of international Communism and domestic subversion, the lawmakers responded to world events by creating immigration exceptions to accommodate those considered worthwhile refugees. In 1957, for example, a special category for Hungarians was created over and above the national quota to let in about 40,000 refugees of the suppressed 1956 Hungarian Revolution. Other exceptions were made, too, even allowing refugees from Communist China, people who would have been the targets of anti-Asian policies under almost any other circumstances.

Overall immigration certainly increased during the 1950s—more than two-and-a-half million were admitted during the decade—but in retrospect the level appears relatively low. It is evident now that in reality there was no massive, pent-up desire for immigration to America from Europe, but most American policymakers were still under the thrall of the impact of the great immigration at the turn of the century (a full 50 years previous) or concerned obsessively with the perceived threat of Communism.

The McCarran-Walter Immigration and Nationality Act of 1952 was intended as a reform of the system, but in fact it did little more than reflect the long-term principles of restriction inherited from an era before World War I, wedded to the prevailing paranoia about Communism. The act was pushed through Congress by Senator Patrick McCarran of Nevada, an old-line reactionary at the end of his political career, and passed over President Harry S Truman's veto, which attacked the entire notion of limiting immigration by national origins.

The new law affirmed the quota system, however, even though the entire basis for national origins quotas was now outdated, and it slapped on top provisions to test the political orthodoxy of potential immigrants. The idea was to preserve restrictions and at the same time prevent aliens with "un-American" ideas from infecting the nation. One of the most repugnant provisions of the law allowed the U.S. Attorney General to deport without due process any alien declared to be engaged in activities against the public interest.

While the 1952 act was something of a step backward rather than a progressive reform of the nation's immigration policy, it also stimulated a new official study by a committee appointed by Truman. The result of the commission's work was one of the most clear-eyed public statements ever on immigration. The commission's close scrutiny of historical data led it to conclude that far from being a threat and a problem, immigration had been a great stimulus to the growth and development of the United States, especially in the economic sphere. The commission recommended changing national policy to encourage immigration, especially of people with needed skills and training, and to significantly raise the limit on the numbers of immigrants to be admitted.

THE IMMIGRATION AND NATIONALITY ACT OF 1965

More than four decades after the enactment of restriction laws, the nation changed course again and reformed basic immigration policy. During a period of relative national optimism and self-confidence, the Congress passed a major reform bill in 1965 as part of the larger attempt sponsored by President Lyndon Baines Johnson to transform America into a "Great Society." Johnson and a cooperative Congress put in place a series of laws affecting basic parts of national life, and the new immigration act was among them. However, neither at the time nor since has it received as much attention as did Johnson's more dramatic civil rights and voting rights laws, or the War on Poverty.

The Immigration and Nationality Act of 1965, signed by Johnson on Ellis Island with the Statue of Liberty in the background, eliminated the national

origin quotas and substituted upper limits on total immigration with a system
of graded family and occupational preferences determining who would be
allowed to fill the overall quotas. This major change finally did away with
favoring certain nations of origin over others and dropped the attempt to
freeze the ethnic profile of the nation as it had existed before 1890. The 1965
law has remained the basic template controlling U.S. immigration policy
ever since, although it has been tinkered with and amended several times.

The new act divided the world into two hemispheres and established
slightly different policies for each. The Western Hemisphere was defined
basically as North, South, and Central America, and the Eastern Hemisphere was all the rest of the world. This was a progressive move for it ended
the virtual exclusion of Asians that had existed since the late 19th century
and essentially put them on an equal footing with potential immigrants from
the rest of the world. However, it also imposed the first limits on legal
immigration from Latin America.

The 1965 law set an upper limit of 170,000 legal immigrants per year from
the Eastern Hemisphere with individual countries limited to no more than
20,000 each admitted on the basis of the preference system. The Western
Hemisphere was limited to 120,000 total, but originally had no specific
national limits and was on a first-come-first-serve basis rather than preferences.
(Applicants for immigration visas still had to meet most of the old individual
requirements of health, political correctness, and financial solvency.)

One effect of the reform was to create temporarily a dual policy: one for
the Western Hemisphere and another for the Eastern. In 1976, however, the
law was amended to put all immigration on the same footing, with the
overall totals for the entire world set at 290,000 (no increase), the nations of
the Americas subject to the 20,000-per-country limit, and immigrants from
the Western Hemisphere admitted according to the preference system.

The list of preferences—really an extension and codification of existing
practices—was relatively complex, but it aimed at achieving immigration of
basically two classes of people: family members of U.S. citizens and people
who might fill important needs in the then-booming American economy.
Each preference was also allotted a percentage of the allowable annual total,
which was intended to further regulate the specific configuration of admissions.

The first preference category, given 20 percent of the total, went to
unmarried adult children of U.S. citizens. The second ranking, also set at 20
percent, was for spouses and adult unmarried children of resident aliens. The
fourth preference was for married children of citizens up to 10 percent of the
total, and the fifth preference category allotted 24 percent of the total to
brothers and sisters (over 21 years of age) of citizens. Because all spouses,
unmarried minor children, and parents were already exempt from both the

preference system and the overall immigration quota totals, the new law meant that virtually all members of an immigrant's family were eligible for immigration.

The third ranking preference, amounting to 10 percent, was reserved for professionals, scientists, and artists of "exceptional ability," a provision that aimed at prolonging or accelerating the so-called brain-drain to the United States. The sixth preference was for skilled or unskilled workers, up to 10 percent of the total, who could fill spots in needed occupations. Both of these preferences assumed that the American economy would continue to expand indefinitely and were in stark contrast to the cyclically recurring anti-immigrant arguments that foreigners should not be allowed to take jobs from native-born Americans.

The final preference category allowed immigration up to 6 percent of the total for refugees from Communism and the Middle East. The sweeping changes in the immigration laws put in place by the 1965 Act altered the basic configuration of the development of immigration over the next three decades. They created the legal conditions that resulted in a massive new wave of immigration from unexpected sources.

CHAPTER 8
. . . .

The Drama of Modern Immigration

I n retrospect, there is little doubt that the effects of changing the immigration policy and law in 1965 were almost entirely unanticipated. The history of immigration since then has been the story of how large numbers of people from new places have taken advantage of the laws to enter the United States at a rate that has been increasing steadily over the last 20 years and now stands at a level comparable to the great immigration flow at the turn of the century. This is nothing less than a third great wave of immigration whose end is not in sight and the consequences of which are not yet fully understood.

The lawmakers in the mid-1960s genuinely thought they were primarily dealing with a pent-up source of immigration from southern and eastern Europe that had been stymied since the 1920s by the restrictive and biased national origins quotas. There was in fact a brief burst of immigration from Europe after 1965 as family members joined those already here, but within a few years the statistics began to show a massive tilt toward the developing countries of the "Third World." By the end of the 1970s, the flow from Europe was reduced to a trickle and the flow from all parts of Asia and Latin America was a flood.

Not even the limits set for total immigration had much effect, because the nonquota family categories and off-quota exceptions for refugees came to be very important. In short, the new family preference laws gave official sanction to the old practice of chain migration, and one immigrant could legally bring in several family members, many of whom entered over and above the supposed annual limits of 290,000 in total world wide and 20,000 per nation. Furthermore, international events such as the Communist revolution in Cuba and the war in Southeast Asia produced large numbers of eligible refugees. The actual annual average of legal immigrants during the 1970s was almost 439,000, with more than 600,000 entering in 1978 alone. The numbers for 1980 illustrate the situation: 289,479 immigrants entered under the legal limits, but an additional 165,325 came in who were exempt from the quotas and 341,552 more entered as refugees.

Many of the same factors that had stimulated European immigration during the 19th century affected Asia and Latin America during the 1970s and 1980s. Many areas, particularly in Asia, experienced population booms in conjunction with growing industrialization, with the result that there was considerable excess population no longer able to find enough land to support traditional ways of life. When this strong set of push factors was joined to a vision of the material prosperity of America as seen in the movies and on television, the impetus to emigrate grew strong.

Moreover, yet another revolution in transportation occurred, with the slow, dangerous sea voyage replaced by the astonishingly rapid modern airliner. The trip from any homeland in the world to America is now measured in hours rather than weeks or months. Only the most desperate refugees or illegal aliens now try to arrive by ship or boat; most overseas immigrants step off an airplane.

THE CONTINUING REFUGEE PUZZLE

The immigration law of 1965 included for the first time a specific formula for admitting refugees, but the act accommodated only 17,400 refugees per year and only from Communist countries or the Middle East. World events since have produced far more refugees and in political circumstances far more complex than the simple-minded Cold War formula could deal with.

The collapse of the American-backed government in South Vietnam and the defeat of American forces in 1975 produced a very large number of war refugees, primarily Vietnamese whose lives would have been in danger after the American pullout. President Jimmy Carter used the traditional presidential power to create additional admission slots for refugees by putting them on parole, which allowed around 400,000 refugees from the war to enter the United States between 1975 and 1979. This system of dealing with refugees, however, was entirely inadequate—a puzzle not yet solved.

In 1980, the Carter administration pushed a new bill through Congress aimed at clearing up the refugee situation. In fact, it did little more than formalize the president's power of parole by creating a possible annual total of 50,000 refugee immigrants. The law also recognized those seeking asylum as a new category of political refugee. During the year following passage of the Refugee Act, the nation admitted 156,466 refugees and asylum-seekers,

A refugee family arrives in the United States from Southeast Asia in the late 1970s. In this case the people are Tai Dam, a small ethnic group originally from Vietnam who were forced to flee to camps in Thailand at the end of the Vietnam War. (Photo courtesy State Historical Society of Iowa, Iowa City)

so it was made clear immediately that historical events would surpass the lawmakers' attempts to legislate.

The infamous Mariel boatlift of Cuban refugees in 1980 also illustrated the difficulty of the refugee problem. All American administrations since the early 1960s have been eager to take in refugees from Castro's Communist Cuba. More than 400,000 fled to the United States, principally settling in Miami, during the years following Castro's rise to power in 1959. In 1980, after a complex series of maneuvers, Castro agreed to release thousands more all at once. The result was a mass exodus of 125,000 refugees in only a few weeks time. These arrivals caused chaos in the immigration procedures and mocked the completely inadequate American refugee laws. By the late 1980s, close to a million Cubans and Cuban Americans had established strong roots in the United States, particularly in Florida where they have come to dominate the economic and political life of Miami and Dade County. There is still a strong interest among the Cuban community in the affairs of Castro's Cuba, however, and the collapse of Communism elsewhere has sparked discussion among Cubans in America about what will happen when and if Castro falls. The older generation still voices a desire to return to the homeland from exile, but many American-born descendants seem much less eager to disrupt their lives in the United States.

The disruptive potential of the Cuban situation was highlighted during a crisis in 1994. When Castro announced he would not obstruct Cubans who wanted to leave, thousands took to the sea in makeshift rafts, heading for Florida. The Clinton Administration responded by finally slamming shut the door to Cuban refugees, and the U.S. Coast Guard intercepted rafters at sea (as many as 3,000 a day during the peak of the crisis) and interned them at the American naval base at Guantanamo Bay. A negotiated agreement for Castro to stop the rafters and for the United States to increase the number of legal Cuban immigrants ended the immediate crisis after a few weeks, but a long-term solution was not in sight.

Under the Reagan administration, which was staunchly anti-Communist, the existing refugee laws allowed the government to encourage immigration from Communist nations, including significant numbers of Soviet Jews. However, people from nations controlled by right-wing anti-Communist governments such as El Salvadorans were not granted political asylum or refugee status.

Apart from this explicitly political stance, the American government also developed the policy that all refugees must be fleeing political oppression and not merely seeking to improve their economic lot. In practice this distinction has been impossible to apply with any rational consistency and it has led to embarrassing consequences. The most conspicuous case involves the tens of thousands of black Haitians who have attempted to flee their homeland for America. Haiti is both one of the poorest nations in the Western Hemisphere, and a country in the throes of political repression and misgovernment since the late 1950s. Throughout the 1960s and 1970s, many Haitians immigrated legally to the United States, but thousands more tried to do so illegally. American policy has been consistent in ruling Haitian refugees ineligible for immigration, despite the clearly repressive nature of the Haitian governments under "Papa Doc" and "Baby Doc" Duvalier and a subsequent military regime that ousted an elected president. The rejection of Haitian refugees on the basis that they are motivated by economics and not fear of their violent and dictatorial government was very difficult to maintain in the face of facts about Haiti. Many critics accused the American government of racism in rejecting the predominantly black Haitians while accepting the mostly white Cubans virtually without restriction. Almost simultaneously with the 1994 Cuban refugee rafter crisis, the Clinton administration decided to intervene in Haiti, and several thousand American troops occupied the nation after a last-minute negotiated agreement to avoid armed invasion. Although ostensibly a move to "restore democracy" to

Editorial cartoonist Bryan Duffy comments on a 1993 decision by the Supreme Court to allow the U.S. government to continue to turn away Haitian boat refugees. (Illustration courtesy of Bryan Duffy. Reprinted by permission of *The Des Moines Register*)

Haiti, the intervention was also clearly designed to staunch the flow of refugees.

A second difficult area has developed as the result of a practice adopted by immigrants arriving by air in New York City. They immediately declare themselves in peril of persecution at home and make application for political asylum. They are released to await a hearing on the merits of their cases, but because the backlog of cases is immense and hearings cannot be scheduled for years, thousands upon thousands of these immigrants disappear into the general population and are never heard of again.

The question of how to deal with refugees will certainly not disappear from the American political agenda anytime soon, unless the warring and contending nations of the world decide to cease fighting each other and to quit oppressing their own citizens.

THE HISPANIC MIGRATION

Mexican immigrants and their offspring make up far and away the largest percentage of Spanish-speaking people in the United States and have accounted for about a sixth of all immigration to the United States since 1960, making them the largest single immigrant group by country of origin. Even after the immigration act of 1965 placed restrictions on immigration from the Western Hemisphere, the great flow of Mexican immigrants did not

A Mexican American mother and child living in migrant workers' housing during the 1970s. (Photo courtesy State Historical Society of Iowa, Iowa City)

stop or even slow appreciably. There were 450,000 during the decade of the 1960s, 640,000 during the 1970s, and 1.6 million during the 1980s, with no decrease in sight during the 1990s. Since these figures count only legal immigrants, the real total would be staggering if it could be known.

The Mexican American communities in the United States have been known traditionally for their cultural cohesiveness and the seeming resistance of Mexican Americans to acculturate to American society. For example, Mexican immigrants seem to prefer to be bilingual rather than adopting English as their exclusive language. The tendency to live in relatively exclusive neighborhoods (barrios in Spanish) also reenforces the strong sense of cultural solidarity. The relatively low rate of naturalization among Mexican Americans indicates less than an overwhelming desire to trade in their native identity.

The majority of Mexican Americans now live in cities and are likely to work in industrial or service sector jobs, which is a change from previous decades when the term "migrant worker" was thought by many Americans as synonymous with Mexican immigrant. There are still hundreds of thousands of Mexican and Mexican American farm workers, of course, but their economic status has improved considerably since the immediate post–World War II years, due in part to the efforts of such activists as César Chávez in the late 1960s and early 1970s.

Although they make up by far the largest percentage of first- and second-generation Hispanics in the general American population, Mexicans and Mexican Americans are by no means the only national or ethnic group from Latin America. By the late 1980s, there were almost 19 million Americans who were either born in a Spanish-speaking country of Central or South America or were children of immigrant parents. About 12 million were of Mexican origin, but the remaining seven million came from other places, including 2.3 million Spanish-speaking Puerto Ricans.

Puerto Rico is an American Commonwealth, and all Puerto Ricans are by birth American citizens, so those who move to the mainland are not, technically speaking, immigrants. The huge growth in the number of native Puerto Ricans living in the mainland began after World War II when air transport became relatively cheap and easy. There are no official statistics about such internal movements, but the evidence is strong that hundreds of thousands of Puerto Ricans traveled back and forth from the island to the mainland—principally New York City—seeking the best jobs.

This upsurge in the number of non-Mexican Hispanic Americans was a fairly recent phenomenon, since as late as the 1960 census, fewer than 400,000 first- and second-generation residents were counted. Since then, though the actual numbers of Mexican immigrants continue to increase in an absolute sense, the percentage of Mexicans among Hispanic immigrants has declined; in other words, increasingly large numbers of Mexicans have immigrated to the United States in the last three decades, but there has been an even greater increase in the number from places such as Cuba, the Dominican Republic, and the Central American nations.

If demographic projections prove to be correct, the influx of more immigrants from Latin America and a robust birth rate among those already here will produce an ever larger percentage of Hispanics in American society by around the turn of the 21st century, and they will eventually surpass black Americans as the largest single minority. Much will depend, of course, on international economic and political developments that affect immigration.

THE ASIANS

Before the changes in immigration law and policy wrought by the 1965 act, it was nearly impossible for Asians to immigrate to the United States. Only a handful of national quota slots were open for Chinese (or any person of Chinese ancestry no matter what the country of origin) and Filipinos as the result of a token loosening of the Exclusion Act during World War II, and immigration from the rest of Asia was virtually banned.

In the census of 1960, Asian Americans represented only a tiny fraction of the U.S. population, and the majority were two, three, or even four generations removed from their original immigrant forebears. Twenty years later, however, there were almost 3.5 million Americans of Asian ancestry, including significant numbers of not only Chinese and Japanese Americans, but also first- and second-generation immigrants from the Philippines, Korea, India, Vietnam, and other Southeast Asian nations.

By the 1980s, Asians represented almost 50 percent of all legal immigrants to the United States, whereas 30 years earlier they had counted for only 6 percent.

The 1965 immigration reform bill had finally opened the door to Asians, and they poured through in large numbers, including many well-educated and trained professionals who immigrated under the economic skills provisions of the new law. There were also many thousands who came as relatives of previous immigrants under the family preference sections of the law. Many Asians perfected the new system of chain migration made possible after 1965: one person immigrated, then used the family preference to bring in close relatives who in turn invoked the family preference for even more.

One often-cited example of this chain system (sometimes called "pyramid" immigration) was a Filipina nurse who entered the United States in the early 1970s under the skilled worker provisions—very large numbers of nurses have immigrated from the Philippines and are disproportionately represented in the nursing profession in some parts of the United States—

and as a permanent resident brought in her parents. Then, she gained entry
for her nine brothers and sisters under the family preference provisions. Her
siblings in turn sponsored their spouses and children, until by 1982 there
were 45 members of the original nurse immigrant's family in the United
States. (First reported in *Time* magazine and cited in Maldwyn A. Jones,
American Immigration, 2nd ed. [Chicago: University of Chicago, 1992], 271.)

Important numbers of Asian immigrants also arrived as refugees or
semirefugees after the mid-1970s, including about a quarter million Vietnamese and others mistakenly listed on the official records as Laotians or
Thais, because they entered directly from refugee camps set up in those
countries after the American withdrawal from Vietnam in 1975. Buried in
the statistics are several small but ethnically distinct groups such as the
Hmong, a tribe of warriors from the hills of Vietnam who had been American allies during the war. More than 5,000 Hmong were transplanted to the
United States, almost all to cities, although thousands more remain in Asian
refugee camps. Such groups have often found it difficult to adjust to the
vastly different conditions of life in America after endless generations as
farmers or rural villages, and the cultural difference between old and new
environments has been very sharp. It is estimated that by 1990, there were
approximately one and a quarter million refugees from the Vietnamese War
living in the United States.

THE CHINESE

Immigration of Chinese to the United States since 1965 represents two
distinct streams. On the one side are the highly skilled and educated ethnic
Chinese who have come here from places such as Hong Kong, Indonesia,
and Taiwan and who have joined the ranks of the relatively affluent and
successful. On the other side are unskilled, undocumented workers who have
entered the country illegally from mainland China and who have created an
underground labor force in cities such as New York and Los Angeles.

The numbers of legal Chinese immigrants have been significant since the
mid-1960s, with an estimated increase in the Chinese population of close to
600,000 between the censuses of 1960 and 1980, making the Chinese the
largest single ethnic group among Asian Americans. The large influx has
been so recent, in fact, that foreign-born Chinese still form the majority of
the Chinese American population.

The mainline Chinese community in the United States is distinguished
by its recently acquired reputation for high-educational and high-commer-
cial achievement—an image in stark contrast to the racism toward of the
Chinese during earlier eras—and statistics back up the popular viewpoint.
Chinese rates for completion of college are more than twice than that for

white Americans and four or five times than that for blacks or Hispanics. And median income figures are also appreciably higher among legal immigrant Chinese than that of the average American.

Though there are still large, densely populated Chinatowns in San Francisco, Los Angeles, and New York, many second- and third-generation Chinese Americans (and well-to-do first generation immigrants) are moving away from the ethnically exclusive neighborhoods and intermarrying extensively with the general American population. Both of these trends are major changes from the Chinese American patterns of previous decades.

The underside of Chinese immigration, however, presents a starkly different picture. There is no way to calculate the numbers of illegal Chinese immigrants who have entered the country in recent years, but there is clear evidence that tens of thousands, perhaps hundreds of thousands, have been brought in by a criminal network that preys on victims intent on leaving rural China at any cost.

The immigrants—many of them from the impoverished Fujian Province—are so desperate to escape the grinding poverty of their homes that they agree to pay smugglers fees as high as $30,000 each. If they reach America successfully, they usually are thrust into low-paying jobs in a thriving underground economy and work for years to pay off their debts to the smugglers. Those who resist are intimidated by physical violence. The system has been described repeatedly by journalists but so far escapes the efforts of police or immigration officials to eradicate it.

THE FILIPINOS

By the early 1990s, the number of Filipinos in the United States was closing in on one-and-a-half million, which represented a very large jump from the 180,000 or so counted in the census of 1960. The history of Filipino immigration is complicated, but this recent dramatic upsurge represents basically the same forces at work as among other Asian national or ethnic groups.

The Philippine Islands, of course, became possessions of the United States in the late 19th century after the American victory in the Spanish-American war. Filipinos were then technically allowed to immigrate freely, but in fact they were barred from eligibility for citizenship as were all other Asians. The largest concentration of Filipinos for many decades was in Hawaii, where more than 100,000—mostly males—were imported during the 1920s to work as farm laborers. At the same time, racist state laws in California discriminated against and excluded Filipinos. In 1934, a federal law set the annual quota for legal immigration from the Philippines at only 50. At the end of World War II, Filipinos were made eligible for citizenship in the United States, but the annual quota was raised to only 100.

The act of 1965 finally removed all the discriminatory barriers and opened immigration for relatively large numbers of Filipinos. The influx has been unusual because a very high percentage of women and trained professionals has made up the majority since the mid-1960s. However, the impetus for the huge numbers during recent decades is familiar: the push of a poor domestic economy and unstable political system combined with the pull of American prosperity and the need for qualified workers.

THE KOREANS

The story of the Koreans is similar in basic outline to other Asian immigrant groups—decades of exclusion and discrimination ended with the new law of 1965, and immigration has exploded since then. The Koreans, who were under the imperial rule of the Japanese from 1905 until 1945 and the end of World War II, were specifically barred from citizenship although several thousand came to Hawaii and California as agricultural workers around the turn of the century.

With the occupation and partition of Korea in 1945 and the subsequent involvement of the United States in the Korean War, a significant number of Korean women were admitted as war brides or spouses of American citizens, and there have been a large number of Korean children adopted by American families. However, massive immigration did not begin until after the legal and policy reforms of the mid-1960s.

By 1990, there were more than 800,000 first- and second-generation Koreans in the United States with the largest concentrations in Los Angeles and New York. A very high percentage of Korean immigrants are well-educated professionals—perhaps as many as one-quarter—and the rest have demonstrated a high capacity for commercial success. The Korean-owned produce grocery, for example, has almost become an urban cliche during the 1990s. Unfortunately, this relative prosperity made merchants in Los Angeles' Koreatown the victims of black rioters during civil disturbances in 1992.

Although Korea is a nation primarily of Buddhists, a very high number of Korean immigrants to the United States are Protestant Christians.

THE ASIAN INDIANS

The most significant numbers of immigrants from India have also arrived since 1965. Before the changes in U.S. policy, India had been part of the barred Asia area excluded from admission. Only a handful of Indians had migrated before 1965, although they tended to be high-profile professionals and businessmen—many of them members of the Sikh minority.

Since 1965, immigration has produced an Indian population in the United States that stood at about 680,000 by 1990. Several other Asian groups demonstrate a high percentage of educated and well-employed immigrants, but the rates of income and high employment are greatest among the Asian Indians. The median family income among Indians, for example, was nearly 13 percent higher than other Asian immigrant groups in 1980.

THE REFORMS OF 1986 AND 1990

Two decades after the passage of the landmark 1965 immigration act, Congress enacted a major reform bill, primarily aimed at dealing with the growing problem of illegal immigrants and undocumented workers.

Yet another federal immigration study commission, formed by Congress in 1981, declared that illegal immigrants were in effect stealing jobs from Americans. Because this finding came during a period of economic recession in the United States, it received a warm welcome from those who were willing to point fingers at immigrants when jobs grew scarce.

An observer who is armed with the facts of history tends to see this argument as an emotional response to bad economic times, but policymakers, union leaders, and politicians are often inclined to use immigration as a convenient scapegoat. Roger Daniels, an expert on the history of Asian immigration and the author of a recent comprehensive survey of immigration, has put it succinctly in *Coming to America* (390): "Germans, Irish, Chinese, Japanese, French Canadians, Italians, Jews, and almost every conceivable immigrant group have been, at one time or another, accused of lowering the American standard of living, and the question of the impact of immigration on the standard of living is a debate without end. What is not debatable is that the argument has much more force and appeal in an era of economic stringency and lowered expectations."

The 1986 reform of immigration law was directed specifically at two issues: the hiring of illegal aliens by unscrupulous American employers and the large number of aliens (mostly agricultural workers) who had made illegal residence and work a way of life. The act put tough sanctions and requirements on employers and moved to regularize most current illegals.

Under the new law, anyone who knowingly hired illegal aliens was subject to a series of escalating penalties, beginning with stiff fines for each worker hired and ending with the possibility of a six-month jail sentence. All employers were also required to ask for documents before hiring workers in order to judge potential workers' status. While many question the efficacy of the increased penalties in reducing the hiring of illegals, the latter provisions have been built into the employment procedures of nearly every American business, and all job applicants are now routinely asked to show driver's licenses, birth certificates, passports, or resident alien cards.

The most dramatic part of the 1986 act was the creation of a one-time amnesty program that was intended to allow thousands of workers to regularize their legal status. Illegal aliens who had lived in the country since 1982 or earlier were allowed to become legal residents if they could document their years in America with pay stubs or rent records. They had a year to file applications, and if accepted, they became temporary legal residents and were eligible for permanent residency after an additional year and a half. After five years as permanent resident aliens, they could apply for citizenship. The law was particularly lenient in allowing agricultural workers to apply, so it was seen by many to be aimed specifically at Hispanic farm workers.

The regulations called for a great deal of complex paperwork and the ability to deal with the immigration and naturalization bureaucracy, so the situation spawned the growth of a service industry of attorneys and immigration counselors who assisted thousands of illegal aliens who wanted to take advantage of the amnesty program.

More than three million illegal aliens qualified under the amnesty—about 1.4 million of these coming under the agricultural worker provisions. Almost seven out of every 10 successful applicants were from Mexico, and the majority of these were young males living in California. Overall, 90 percent of those who applied for amnesty came from the Western Hemisphere.

In the years immediately following the passage of the 1986 reform law, there was considerable debate about whether it was achieving its intended effects. There was some evidence initially that employers were abiding by the laws about hiring illegal aliens, but it has eventually become clear that there are still massive numbers of illegal aliens entering the country each year to seek jobs. And the effect of the prevailing family preference sections of the basic immigration system seemed to have complicated the workings of the amnesty, because many who regularized their status were then eligible to bring in family members.

In 1990, Congress attempted another reform of the immigration system, this time aimed at manipulating immigration so that it specifically aided the national economy. A new act focused on workers and skills that could benefit the nation and limited the number of immigrants who could be admitted under the family provisions.

The 1990 act capped total immigration annually at 700,000 (reduced to 670,000 within five years) and set quotas by family or economic category. There could be no more than 480,000 family-related immigrants, which put a limit on chain or pyramid migration, and 140,000 slots were reserved for immigrants who could qualify under a complicated set of criteria for professional training or job skills. Ten thousand places were set aside for immigrants who agreed to invest at least one million dollars in the United States economy and 55,000 for "diversity" immigrants, who were to be natives of countries previously discriminated against under the 1965 immigration regulations—the Irish for example. The 1990 act also finally did away with the anti-Communist political tests built into immigration law during the Cold War.

THE FUTURE

Like almost all aspects of modern life in America, the issues surrounding immigration are complicated and often puzzling. Americans of all backgrounds continue to show a strong and persistent pride of ethnicity and origin, while at the same time there is a discernable public celebration of a single, overarching American identity. This seems unlikely to change at any foreseeable time in the future: the pot never quite melts immigrants, but it does bubble and produce a rich national stew.

The most difficult problems related to immigration will probably continue to be illegal immigration and refugees. As long as economics and domestic politics remain important influences, immigrants and immigration policy will continue to make news. The movements in several states in 1994 to sue the federal government to recover of the costs of providing services to illegal aliens are indicative of the situation, and in California this apparent economic and political question has been tied by the governor explicitly to a revived nativism in his proposal that American-born children of illegal aliens be denied citizenship.

Another illustration of the difficult problems connected with immigration is the inability of the federal government to deal with those immigrants who use the refugee provisions to gain illegal entry. The flood of entrants who immediately claim political asylum and take advantage of an immense backlog of cases—the number was growing by 10,000 a month and totaled 364,000 in mid-1994—to slip into the work force of the country has mocked the system. The government response has been to institute a $130 fee for each entrant who wants to claim refugee status and to impose a 150 day waiting period for work permits. Whether these tactics will succeed remains to be seen.

When one looks back, however, over the 400 years of immigration history, it is abundantly clear that immigration has been the lifeblood of the American experience and that no matter what problems arise—usually the same ones over and over again in slightly different forms—the nation will find ways to channel the energy of immigrants into positive pathways for the future.

BIOGRAPHIES

• • • • • • • • •

Adams, John (1735–1826). The second president of the United States and one of the most important political figures of the American Revolution, Adams was a native of Braintree, Massachusetts (now known as Quincy) who practiced law after graduation from Harvard. He was at the center of the anti-British agitation before the Revolution and served in the both the First and the Second Continental Congresses as the principal spokesman for the New England colonies. During most of the war, he was one of the American representatives to the court of France, and he was the nation's first ambassador to England after the peace. In 1789, Adams was elected as vice president to George Washington as part of the first federal administration under the new constitution. He served ably as the head of the Senate, setting many long-term precedents as the new nation took shape. With Washington's withdrawal after two terms, Adams was elected president over Thomas Jefferson in 1796, although by a slim margin in the electoral college. The greatest challenge of his term was the undeclared naval war with France and the growing agitation between two developing political points of view. Adams was severely hampered during his presidency by the rivalry of Alexander Hamilton within the Federalist party, which limited his room to maneuver. The Federalist Congress passed the Alien and Sedition Acts in 1798, which were directed specifically against immigrant radicals and potential subversives and against the growing opposition party of Jefferson. Adams signed the bill, but he was lukewarm in carrying out its provisions. He did sign a few alien warrants that would have deported specific individuals, but the papers were never served. Adams refused to sign blank warrants for others to use, and he declined to act against several prominent foreign spokesmen. Defeated in the election of 1800, Adams withdrew from public life to his farm in Massachusetts. He died the same day as Jefferson, on the 50th anniversary of the signing of the Declaration of Independence.

Aldrich, Thomas Bailey (1836–1907). Although his name is scarcely remembered today, at the end of the 19th century Aldrich was one of the nation's best-known and most influential literary figures, especially in his role as editor of *Atlantic Monthly*. His 1892 poem "The Unguarded Gates" was an important anti-immigrant statement. He came from Anglo American New England families and was born in New Hampshire, although his childhood was spent in New York and New Orleans. As a teenager, he returned to Portsmouth, New Hampshire, after his father's death. Aldrich did not attend college but went to work at age 16 in a relative's business in New York. In his spare time, however, he wrote poetry and won a minor reputation that led to his appointment as a literary critic and junior editor of several periodicals. He served briefly as a war correspondent during the Civil War and returned in the early 1860s to New York and another editorship. In 1865, Aldrich moved to Boston and turned increasingly to writing novels and short stories. He was named editor of the prestigious *Atlantic Monthly* in 1881 and remained at the magazine's head until 1890. He continued to write actively until his death.

Altgeld, John Peter (1847–1902). Altgeld was one of the most successful immigrant politicians and leaders, though a figure of some controversy and judged by historians since to have been ahead of his time. Born in Germany, he was brought to the United States by his parents when he was young. He lived in Ohio until 1869, then moved to Missouri and eventually became a lawyer. In 1875, Altgeld moved to Chicago and made a fortune in real estate in the booming city. He was elected governor of Illinois in 1892 after serving as a Cook County judge. He was a liberal politician, oriented strongly toward social welfare issues such as penal reform and reform of the labor laws affecting children and women. His most controversial decision as governor was to pardon the remaining imprisoned anarchists convicted in the Haymarket Riot of 1886. He correctly believed that they had been unfairly prosecuted at least in part because of their political beliefs and foreign backgrounds. In all spheres of public life, Altgeld defended the rights of immigrants and others on the underside of American society, but—perhaps because of his own immigrant background—he was perceived by many voters as radical and was defeated for a second term as governor. He returned to Chicago as a legal partner of Clarence Darrow, the most famous lawyer of the time.

Bowers, Henry F. (1837–1911). After he helped begin the American Protective Association at a small meeting held in his Clinton, Iowa, law office in 1887, Bowers became the leader of the anti-Catholic, anti-immigrant forces that coalesced for a while around his organization. He was born in Maryland, the son of a German immigrant father, who died while Bowers was still a child, and raised by his mother, a native of New England. Bowers grew up in the state that was among the strongest in support of the Know-Nothing Party; he was nearly an adult when Millard Fillmore won Maryland for the Know-Nothings in 1854. Three years later, Bowers and his mother moved to rural eastern Iowa, where they failed as farmers, and then to Clinton, a bustling manufacturing town with two-fifths of its population foreign-born, including many Irish Catholics. Bowers eventually became a self-educated lawyer and community leader. After beginning the APA, apparently in response to the defeat of a candidate he supported in a local mayoral election, Bowers served as its president and chief spokesman until 1891, when he relinquished the position as the movement gained wider national membership and prominence. Nonetheless, he remained an important leader of the association and kept it alive, at least nominally, until his own death.

Calvert, George (Lord Baltimore) (circa 1580–1632). Calvert was an important and influential courtier and government officeholder under the early Stuart monarchy. He came from a wealthy Yorkshire family and first gained prominence as private secretary to Sir Robert Cecil, the chief minister of James I. Taking office in 1606, Calvert thereafter was elected to Parliament and served as a diplomat. In 1619, he was appointed one of the two principal secretaries of state. In 1625, however, he announced that he had converted to Roman Catholicism and therefore left office, although he kept a seat on the Privy Council and was made Baron of Baltimore in the Irish nobility. Calvert had long been interested in the American colonies and held a proprietorship of part of Newfoundland. He visited the northern colony in 1627 and returned to Newfoundland the following year, although he began to petition the crown for an exchange of grants that would give him a colony further to the south. He landed at Jamestown in 1628 but was hounded out of the colony because he was Catholic. He returned to England and was granted proprietorship of a large colony in the Chesapeake region— the area of modern-day Maryland—by Charles I. Calvert died before taking possession of what he intended to be a haven for Catholics; the charter was taken over by his son.

Carter, Jimmy (1924–). An energetic and highly intelligent man, Carter's term between 1977 and 1981 as the only Democratic president during a long run of Republicans was a difficult if not disastrous administration. He was a native of Georgia, trained as a Navy nuclear engineer, who came to symbolize a new moderation while governor of Georgia in the early 1970s. He was a strong supporter of civil rights and government reform when he captured the

Democratic presidential nomination in 1976 and then very narrowly defeated Gerald Ford, mostly due to voter reaction to the Nixon administration and the Watergate scandal. Although his administration had some high moments, Carter was plagued by disasters—mostly on the international front—that were largely beyond his control. An energy crisis set off by a Mideastern oil embargo plunged the economy into trouble and the Soviet invasion of Afghanistan created extreme difficulties and tensions. Worst of all was the fall of the shah of Iran and the subsequent seizure of American hostages—a situation Carter could not solve during his term in office. The low point was probably a failed attempt to rescue the Iranian hostages. Carter dealt energetically with the question of international human rights and tied his concern for the immigration of political refugees to this issue. The 1980 Refugee Act was one of his administration's largest accomplishments. He was smashed in the 1980 election by Ronald Reagan, but over the following years took an active role in social and human rights causes and made a considerable impact. In 1994, Carter led the diplomatic mission that negotiated the American occupation of Haiti, a move designed in part to ease a refugee crisis.

Cermak, Anton (1893–1933). Cermak was born in Prague, part of the Austro-Hungarian Empire at the time, and was brought to the United States by his Czech parents when he was an infant. After an early career as a businessman, he became the most successful eastern European immigrant politician of his day and established the long-lived Democratic political machine of Chicago, based largely on appeal to the diverse immigrant and ethnic population of the city. He was elected to the state legislature in 1902 and thereafter held many city and Cook County offices, until 1928 when he became chairman of the county Democratic Party. His chief opponent in city politics was the corrupt Republican boss Big Bill Thompson, who disdained the immigrant-ethnic vote. Cermak skillfully organized a precinct-level coalition and defeated Thompson for mayor in 1931. He proceeded to build a classic urban working-class political machine that used patronage, jobs, and government favors to establish the Democratic Party as the major social and economic power in the immigrant neighborhoods. Cermak strongly supported Roosevelt for president in 1932 and was invited to appear with Roosevelt in Miami the following year. When an attempt was made to assassinate the president, Cermak was shot and killed by mistake.

Chávez, César (1927–1993). Chávez was a native-born American, but his career was tied almost entirely to the organization of farm laborer and migrant workers, principally Mexican immigrants or those of Mexican American heritage. He was born on a small farm near Yuma, Arizona, but the Great

Depression forced his family on the road as migrant workers, an experience that colored Chávez's life thereafter. He himself worked as a migrant in Arizona and California before becoming a labor organizer in the early 1950s for the Community Service Organization. In 1962, Chávez formed the National Farm Workers Association with headquarters near Delano, California. After successfully organizing farm workers in the local area, Chávez expanded to the national scene in 1966 with the creation of the United Farm Workers Organizing Committee, the beginning of a long struggle with the grape growers of California. Chávez built an effective organization of workers and used a well-publicized national boycott of grapes to eventually win an agreement with the majority of growers. He subsequently won contracts for workers in the lettuce and citrus industries. Chávez was a tireless and charismatic leader, who improved and publicized the lives of hundreds of thousands of immigrants and their families.

Cleveland, Grover (1837–1908). Cleveland was born and died in New Jersey, but almost all of his political life was tied to New York state. He was a Buffalo lawyer during his early career and used local offices to launch himself into the larger arena. As Democratic governor of New York from 1882 to 1884, Cleveland gained a wide reputation as a liberal reformer and social moderate. He defeated James G. Blaine in 1884 for the presidency after a raucous campaign, the first Democrat to win the office since before the Civil War. He was a reasonably popular president who energetically enforced his ideas of good government by holding down costs (he vetoed several bills to pay veterans' pensions) and working against the protective tariff. He lost the presidency in 1888 to Benjamin Harrison, even though he had a slight plurality of the popular vote—the peculiarities of the electoral college gave the Republican the victory. Cleveland, however, ran again in 1892 and won, becoming the only president of the United States to serve nonconsecutive terms. His second stint in office was controversial, including his veto of a anti-immigration literacy law in 1896, and he was judged ineffectual in dealing with rapidly changing social and economic conditions. He failed to win his party's nomination for a third term and retired from politics.

Commons, John R. (1862–1945). Commons was one of the generation of professors of the new social sciences around the turn of the century who combined a faith in scholarship with impulses toward both social reform and nativism. He was a native of Indiana, educated at Oberlin and Johns Hopkins. He studied economics and taught briefly at three different schools, losing his job at each. During a subsequent stint as an independent researcher, Commons compiled a report on immigration for the U.S. Industrial Commission. In 1904, he joined the faculty of the University of Wisconsin, where he became well known for his studies of the labor movement. At Wisconsin, Commons became part of the alliance of academics and government reformers labeled the "Wisconsin Idea," but he also grew increasingly anti-immigrant. In 1907, he published *Races and Immigrants in America*, in which he assigned inferior "racial" traits to Eastern Europeans, Italians, Jews, and blacks. Commons supported immigration restriction and was particularly vocal about the need to force "Americanization" on immigrants in order to quell what he saw as political radicalism. Although he enjoyed a period as a well-known public authority, often testifying before Congressional committees, his personal life took a turn for the worse about the time of his wife's death in 1928, and his remaining years were filled with unhappiness.

Croker, Richard (1841–1922). Croker was born in Ireland and brought to America at age three. He became a product of the New York streets, gravitating to Tammany Hall and the orbit of the political bosses when only a teenager. By 1870, Croker was an alderman of the city and one of the Tammany faction trying to wrest political power from Boss William Tweed. With Tweed's fall, Croker's star began to rise and he moved through a series of municipal offices that resulted in his accumulation of a huge fortune through graft and bribes. In 1885, Croker became head of the Tammany political machine, which relied on immigrant votes to retain power in the city. He brought the art of dispensing government patronage to a high state during his years of control. He was ousted as Tammany boss in 1894 and moved to England. Although he returned to New York briefly a few years later, he essentially lived the balance of his life as a rich horse breeder on estates in England and Ireland purchased with the money stolen during his sojourn in the United States.

Dillingham, William P. (1843–1923). Dillingham's name is tied inextricably with the movement to erect legal barriers to immigration during the first two decades of the 20th century. As a U.S. senator from Vermont, he headed the study commission that bore his name and sponsored the bill that ultimately established national quotas. He was born and educated in Vermont, though he briefly read law with his sister's husband in Milwaukee when a young man. His was a political family (his father was governor of Vermont), and the young Dillingham received public office early, serving as state's attorney and several terms in the state legislature. In 1888, he was elected governor of Vermont. Twelve years later, Dillingham was appointed to fill an unexpired seat in the U.S. Senate, and he was re-elected by the state legislature and then by the public when the method of selecting senators changed to popular vote. Dillingham was the Senate's principal authority on immigration almost from the beginning of his service. He became chairman of the Senate Committee on Immigration during his first term and was still serving on the committee when he died in office. In 1907, he was named to chair the committee commissioned to prepare a comprehensive study of the effects of immigration. He officially presented the results of the Dillingham Committee study four years later, endorsing the idea of restriction. He introduced a bill in 1913 that incorporated the principle of assigning restricted quotas on immigration, based on nation of origin. The initial bill never became law, but the same idea, known thereafter as the "Dillingham Bill," was carried over to several subsequent bills and eventually passed in 1921. The national quota system remained in effect until 1965.

Fillmore, Millard (1800–1874). Brought to the presidency by the death of Zachary Taylor in 1850, Fillmore served only part of a term and subsequently allowed himself to be nominated by the nativist Know-Nothing Party in 1856. He was a native of New York state and a lawyer. He served in the state legislature and as a U.S. representative, emerging as a leader of the Whigs in the House during the early 1840s, when the Whig Party enjoyed its greatest strength. Fillmore was out of the national limelight and serving as controller of the State of New York when nominated by the Whigs in 1848 to balance the ticket with southerner Taylor, the hero of the Mexican war. After Taylor's death, Fillmore was in an important position to help pass the Compromise of 1850 that many hoped would settle the question of slavery without war. His support and signing of the Compromise, however, created enough controversy to prevent his nomination at the 1852 Whig convention, and the rejection ended his career as a Whig (a party that lost most of its standing almost overnight). Fillmore returned to Buffalo and practiced law, but allowed himself to be nominated by the nativist, anti-Catholic Know-Nothings in 1856 and by the remnants of the Whigs. He ran a miserable third in the national election, winning only the state of Maryland and a total of eight electoral votes. He withdrew to Buffalo and almost complete obscurity.

Franklin, Benjamin (1706–1790). One of the most familiar figures of American history, Franklin was born in Boston and learned the printing trade as an apprentice to his brother. He ran away to Philadelphia in 1723 and within a few years was owner of a prosperous printing shop and newspaper. While building his fortune in business, Franklin also began to dabble with scientific experiments (the most famous of which had to do with electricity and lightning) and by midcentury was well known in Europe for his scientific accomplishments. He essentially retired from business in the 1740s and devoted most of the rest of his life to politics. In 1751, he was elected to the Pennsylvania Assembly and soon after began service in a series of government posts that lasted until the outbreak of the American Revolution. During the 1750s and 1760s, Franklin was leader of the political forces in Pennsylvania that opposed the proprietary power of the Penn family, and he saw the large numbers of Pennsylvania German immigrants as allies of his enemies, a fact that was to some degree responsible for his anti-German utterances. During the Revolution, Franklin served first as a prominent member of the Continental Congress and then as the nation's chief minister in France. Following the peace with England, which he negotiated and signed, Franklin returned to Pennsylvania and resumed public office. His advanced years did not prevent him from playing a key role in devising the new Constitution at the Philadelphia convention.

Gompers, Samuel (1850–1924). Born in London, Gompers immigrated to the United States at age 13. He became a cigarmaker and joined the Cigarmakers' Union the year after his arrival. By 1877, he was the president of the union and on his way to becoming the most influential and well known of America's early labor leaders. Gompers did not believe in the sort of unionism that aimed at reforming the industrial or capitalist system, rather he was the principal proponent of trade unionism that strove solely for better pay by peaceful means. He opposed strikes and violence, opting instead for what became known as "pure and simple" unionism. He helped organize the Federation of Organized Trades and Labor Unions in 1881, which eventually became the American Federation of Labor. Gompers served as president of the federation for most of the rest of his life. He believed that immigrant labor was one of the major threats to the well-being of American workers, so he strongly supported restrictionist measures. Ironically, by the end of his life the immigrant cigarmaker became a nativist and anti-immigrant spokesman.

Grant, Madison (1865–1937). A lawyer and naturalist, Grant was one of the more vocal genteel racists of the early part of this century. He was a native of New York whose family wealth allowed him to no more than dabble in a law practice after graduation from Yale and Columbia while fulfilling his interests in travel and study of animal life. He was a founder of the New York Zoological Society and what became the Bronx Zoo. He was also active in the nature preservation movement, helping to sponsor an organization, for example, to save California redwoods. Despite these worthwhile endeavors, Grant was a vocal bigot who believed in the eugenic theories of racial superiority. He thought there was a Nordic race that was the source of most virtue and that people from southern or eastern Europe were not only inferior but should be prevented from intermarriage or interbreeding with Nordic mates, for this would debase the superior stock. He published several books espousing these racist theories, the most famous, *The Passing of a Great*

Race, in 1916. He was vice president of the Anti-Immigration League and worked for passage of immigration restriction laws in the early 1920s.

Hamilton, Alexander (1757–1804). Hamilton was one of the most important and complex figures in the early history of the United States. He was the only foreign-born member of the so-called founding fathers, though his general political stance in later life was antiforeign and anti-immigrant. He was born in the British West Indies, the son of a divorced French Huguenot mother and a Scots father, making him illegitimate under the law of the day. He was orphaned at age 11, and in 1772, was sent to college at Princeton in New Jersey. He was a strong revolutionary despite his tender years and organized his own volunteer military company to fight the British. He served during the first part of the war as an aide to George Washington and then later in the field under Lafayette. He was one of the primary leaders of the Federalist faction during the struggle to ratify the Constitution and wrote several of the *Federalist Papers*. He was named by Washington as the first secretary of the treasury and served until 1795. Thereafter, Hamilton controlled the conservative faction of the Federalist party and supported the Alien Acts and suppression of foreign influence. His major concern, however, was to engineer the defeat of Adams in 1800, which he did only to see Jefferson eventually take the prize—Hamilton himself was barred from the highest office because of his foreign birth. He was killed in a duel by Aaron Burr, a political rival, in 1804.

Jefferson, Thomas (1743–1826). Among the two or three greatest men in American history, Jefferson was a Virginia planter by birth and a lawyer and politician by profession, although his accomplishments are many. He wrote the Declaration of Independence and served as governor of Virginia during the Revolution. He was appointed as the first post-Revolution ambassador to France, and soon after his return to America became the nation's first secretary of state. He found himself at odds politically with the Federalists and resigned from the cabinet in 1793. He missed election as president by only three votes in 1796, and under the Constitution he became John Adams' vice president, although by this time Jefferson was the key figure in the developing opposition political party. He received strong support from Scotch-Irish immigrants, and he was the leader of the pro-French faction during the turbulent late 1790s. When the Federalists passed obstructionist naturalization laws and the infamous Alien and Sedition Acts in 1798, Jefferson secretly wrote the Kentucky Resolutions, which claimed individual states need not enforce such laws. Jefferson defeated John Adams in the election of 1800, but tied in the electoral college with his intended vice president, Aaron Burr. Under the provisions of the Constitution at the time, the election was thrown into the Congress when Burr refused to withdraw. Jefferson was awarded the presidency, however, and took office in 1801. The new Congress, controlled by Jefferson's Republicans, allowed the Alien acts to expire and redrew the naturalization laws to require only a five-year wait, though Jefferson urged an even shorter period. After serving two terms as President, Jefferson returned to Virginia. He died on the 50th anniversary of the signing of the Declaration, only hours before Adams.

Johnson, Lyndon Baines (1908–1973). One of the most dramatic presidential figures of the latter part of the 20th century, Johnson accomplished large works during his terms in office. However, involvement in the Vietnamese War and Johnson's failed policy in that conflict will always color history's view of his leadership. He was a Texan through and through, having won fortune and then political fame as resident of the hill country. As a young man he came to Washington as a representative and signed on as an ardent New Dealer. Despite his personal faults, he maintained a passionate lifelong devotion to the causes of social reform and improvement and a faith in classic New Deal liberalism. By the mid-1950s he was a powerful majority leader of the Senate. He was nominated to the Democratic ticket as vice presidential candidate in 1960 to help balance John Kennedy's New England Catholicism. When Kennedy was assassinated three years later, Johnson became president and in 1964 won his own term in one of the largest landslides to that date. He proceeded to push through a willing Democratic Congress a series of major laws aimed at reforming and improving society: welfare reform, civil rights reform, voting reform, environmental protection, and more. Among his achievements was the 1965 immigration law that finally abolished the overtly nativist national quota system. By 1968, however, the increasingly controversial Vietnam involvement had sapped his popularity and strength, and Johnson declined to run again.

Jordan, David Starr (1851–1931). Jordan was born in New York state and attended college at Cornell University. He taught at many schools early in his career, principally in the Midwest, and by the late 1870s he had received both a medical degree and a Ph.D. His reputation in the field of natural science and in particular the study of fish grew significant after 1882, when he published what became the standard survey of the fish of North America. In 1885, he assumed the post of college president at Indiana University. Six years later, he moved to the presidency of Stanford, where he remained for the rest of his life. He was an active public speaker and was widely published in popular magazines, and thus he became one of the best widely known and respected educators of his day. He supported nativism and the restriction of immigration because, like many other public intellectuals of his time day, he believed that the Anglo-Saxon "race" was somehow superior to other peoples.

Kearney, Denis (1847–1907). Kearney was the leader of the working-class anti-Chinese agitation in California during the late 1870s. He was an Irish sailor who had settled in San Francisco around 1872 after working on a coastal steamer for several years. There Kearney operated a hauling business, but his real love was public speaking of the roughest kind. There was very little systematic thinking behind his speaking but he loved to address a crowd of workers. In 1877, Kearney began to hold meetings of workingmen in a sandlot next door to City Hall, where he harangued the crowds on the evils of the Chinese and the threat they represented to the native-born workers of California. Soon the sandlot meetings were followed by anti-Chinese rioting and violence, though Kearny himself seems not to have incited such behavior directly. He was also an officer of the Workingman's Trade and Labor Union, essentially a political organization, but he broke with the party in 1880. Two years later, a federal Exclusion Act barred Chinese immigrant workers, but Kearney had already withdrawn from the public scene. He devoted the rest of his life to business and amassed a considerable fortune.

Lazarus, Emma (1849–1887). The daughter of an old-stock New York City Jewish family, Lazarus was a poet from childhood and enjoyed a considerable reputation even as a teenager. She published regularly in the leading magazines of the day and dabbled in writing plays. In the early 1880s, she became an ardent defender of the Jews of Eastern Europe who were suffering a renewed burst of violence at the hands of the Russians. She not only wrote extensively about the issue—notably in *Songs of a Semite*, published in 1882—but also personally organized relief efforts for Jewish refugees. Lazarus became one of the leading American Zionists, seeking a Middle-Eastern homeland for the Jews, and she spent much of the time during her last years of life in England and Europe working with Zionists there. Her most famous lines of poetry come from "The New Colossus" and are inscribed on the base of the Statue of Liberty. She died young from cancer.

Lodge, Henry Cabot (1850–1924). Lodge not only was a man of great ability and accomplishment but also a narrow-minded aristocrat. He was a native Bostonian and a graduate of Harvard, where he earned not only his undergraduate degree but also a law degree and a Ph.D. in history. Most of his life was devoted to a combination of scholarly or semischolarly writing and a prominent political career. He combined an assistant editorship of the *North American Review* (the most important opinion magazine at the time) with service in the Massachusetts state legislature during the 1870s, then went on to the U.S. House of Representatives. In 1892, he became a U.S. senator and remained one of the most important Senate members, especially where foreign affairs was concerned, for the rest of his life. He was heir to much of the liberal Republican reform tradition and espoused many important reforms, but he was also an aggressive imperialist, tying American expansion to the economic well-being of the nation. He thought the United States would prosper only if it could achieve dominance over large sections of the world. Not surprisingly, Lodge was also a nativist who played a leading role in the spread of the idea of a superior Anglo-Saxon "race" and the movement for immigration restriction. He introduced several bills into the Senate to establish literacy tests as a means of choking off the influx of what Lodge thought were inferior immigrants from eastern and southern Europe. One such bill passed Congress in 1896, during Lodge's first term in the Senate, but was vetoed by Grover Cleveland. Lodge is best remembered for his implacable opposition to President Woodrow Wilson's policies, and he was the pivotal political figure in defeating American ratification of the Treaty of Versailles and the League of Nations.

McCarran, Patrick (1876–1954). McCarran was an archconservative western senator who during the later years of his career vigorously attacked supposed radicals in the government and the nation and who was the guiding force behind the McCarran-Walters Immigration Act of 1952. He was a second-generation Irish Catholic born in Nevada, who married into a wealthy Episcopalian family and took up the study of law while sheep farming. He began his public career with a seat in the Nevada state legislature. As he gained prominence in the state, McCarran moved on to a seat on the state supreme court. He was elected to the U.S. Senate in 1932 as a Democrat, but for the next 20 years, McCarran was essentially at odds with the liberal leadership of his party, first Franklin Roosevelt and then Harry Truman. By the late 1940s, McCarran was one of the most powerful members of the Senate, and he chose to use his power to promote anti-Communist paranoia, much of which carried over into the immigration policies he supported. As chairman of the Senate Internal Security committee, McCarran worked along side Senator Joe McCarthy to attack supposed Communists and subversives in government, creating one of the most shameful episodes in American political history. In line with his political paranoia, McCarran opposed the admission of postwar refugees during the late 1940s, because he feared subversives would enter the country and take over the nation. His immigration legislation of 1952 retained the old national quotas and added political tests aimed at enforcing a political purity on immigrants. McCarran engineered the bill's passage and an override of President Truman's veto.

Mayo-Smith, Richmond (1854–1901). Mayo-Smith was born in Ohio, the descendent of a Massachusetts Puritan family. He was educated at Amherst and spent most of his professional life as a professor of economics and statistics at Columbia University. Like many of his fellow prominent pioneer social scientists during the late 19th century, Mayo-Smith used the principles of his developing intellectual discipline to support a nativist (or even racist) viewpoint toward immigrants. He was one of the first professors to offer courses in statistics and actually did much to develop the practice of data gathering and analysis in the United States. He published *Emigration and Immigration* in 1890, in which he tried to analyze the effect of population movements on social structures and ethical standards. His conclusion, which in retrospect seems to have nothing to do with statistical evidence and only to do with Mayo-Smith's prejudices, was that the large numbers of immigrants coming into the United States at the time were a threat to the American way of life because of their diversity and that they should therefore be excluded or restricted. His book and his academic reputation gave a legitimacy to groups such as the Immigration Restriction League. Mayo-Smith's life ended tragically with insanity and suicide.

Minuit, Peter (1580–1638). Minuit was closely involved in both New Netherlands and New Sweden. He was born into a Protestant Dutch family living in a German state on the Rhine and moved to Holland when the Spanish captured his native city in 1624. He there involved himself with the Dutch West India Company, which had established a colony in North America at the site of modern day New York. Minuit visited New Netherlands in 1626 and returned a year later when he became governor of the colony. One of his most famous acts, which has passed into American mythology, was to purchase Manhattan Island from a local Indian tribe for goods worth about $24. He established the colony's chief town on the island, calling it New Amsterdam, but he was recalled to Holland and dismissed from the Dutch West India Company's service because of political differences with the directors. Minuit resurfaced in 1637 as one of the sponsors of a Swedish colony to be established along the Delaware River in the region of modern-day Wilmington. He arrived on the site in March 1638 and supervised the building of a fort. In June, Minuit left on a trading expedition to the Caribbean and was drowned in a hurricane.

Oñate, Juan de (circa 1549–1624). Oñate was born in the New World, the son of a Spanish official who had grown wealthy from mining. Oñate himself helped develop Spanish mines early in his career. The Spanish government always sought to pursue new possibilities for plunder and colonization of Indian tribes, so by the early 1590s, it was eager to have the region to the north of Mexico explored and settled. Oñate won a contract in 1595 to colonize "New Mexico," and in return for providing settlers and financing the expedition, he was named governor of the new province. Three years later, he set off with a force of 400, crossing the Rio Grande and heading north to the site of modern-day Santa Fe where he established the headquarters of the new colony. There was actually very little to exploit easily in the region and several expeditions to the north and west yielded no new sources of precious metals or other treasures. The colony hung on precariously but was severely threatened by an uprising of the local Pueblo Indians. Dispirited and nearly bankrupt, Oñate asked to be relieved of his duties in 1607 and returned to Mexico two years later. Like many other colonial administrators, he was accused of ill-treatment by disaffected colonists.

Pastorius, Francis Daniel (1651–1720). Pastorius was born into a prosperous German Lutheran family. He was very well educated, received a law degree, and briefly practiced in Windsheim. In 1679, however, he moved to Frankfurt-am-Main and turned from the law to a passionate preoccupation with religion, specifically Quakerism. He became acquainted with friends of William Penn and learned through them of Penn's intent to settle Pennsylvania. In 1683, Pastorius was appointed the land agent for a group of Frankfurter Quakers who wanted to immigrate to America. He arrived in Philadelphia in August and within three months had negotiated the purchase of 15,000 acres nearby from Penn. Pastorius laid out the settlement of Germantown and became its first mayor when the city was chartered. He was an active land agent, sat in the provincial assembly, and taught school.

Penn, William (1644–1718). Penn was the son of a prominent English admiral who had great influence at the Restoration court due to a friendship with the Duke of York (later James II). From his teenage years, the younger Penn was attracted to the Quaker religious philosophy and, though an aristocrat, he put his beliefs at the center of his career. By the age of 22, Penn had fully converted to Quakerism and from then on used his position and influence to campaign for fair political and social treatment for religious dissenters, especially his fellow Quakers. He looked to the New World as a haven for Quakers, originally dealing with the proprietors of New Jersey, but eventually obtaining a charter to found a colony to be called Pennsylvania. Penn and his family were to be the sole proprietors of the colony, which he intended as a religious experiment in toleration but also as a permanent source of wealth. He actively recruited immigrants from Europe and hoped to settle his colony to a large degree with non-English immigrants. He succeeded in attracting large numbers of immigrants and settlers to Pennsylvania, where they found an abundance of fertile farmland and relative peace with the Indians, with whom Penn dealt fairly on the whole. When the reign of James II ended in the Glorious Revolution, Penn fled England to live in Pennsylvania for three years, after which he returned to England.

Powderly, Terrance V. (1849–1924). Powderly was the son of Irish immigrants, but put distance between himself and immigrants throughout most of his career as a labor leader and immigration official. He was born in Pennsylvania and worked as railroad machinist in Scranton, where be became interested in the efforts to organize unions. In 1874, Powderly joined the Knights of Labor, a secret organization with religious overtones as well as aspects of trade unionism. He rose rapidly in the hierarchy of the Knights, and at the same time he took an active interest in politics. He was elected mayor of Scranton in 1878 on the Greenback-Labor ticket, and he continued as mayor for several years while also becoming one of the nation's best-known labor leaders. As his influence in the Knights' organization increased, Powderly managed to get the group to abandon much of its secrecy and semireligious ritual and to concentrate more on labor issues. He became head of the Knights in 1879. Although he personally had a long-term socialist vision for society, Powderly was under pressure from many of his union members to support local strikes as a major tactic. When a series of strikes won concessions from business owners, the popularity of the Knights jumped dramatically, and by the mid-1880s Powderly headed an organization of 700,000 members. The industrial owners retaliated, however, and subsequent strikes failed—Powderly never agreed to strikes as a weapon of labor—and the movement collapsed. Powderly turned from the Knights in the early 1890s, and in 1897 he became the first federal commissioner of immigration.

Raleigh, Walter, Sir (1552–1618). Raleigh was one of the great romantic figures of a very romantic period of British history. He was also responsible for much of the early exploration of what became British North America. He was a soldier and a poet who gained the personal favor of Elizabeth I and was granted lavish honors and privileges. He was intensely interested in settling the New World, and with his brother-in-law Sir Humphrey Gilbert, he either personally conducted or sponsored several explorations to establish settlements in America. None of them were successful, however, though a two-ship expedition dispatched by Raleigh in 1582 claimed for the crown a region he named Virginia. After the Queen's death, Raleigh fell from favor. He was convicted falsely of treason in 1603 but was allowed freedom until a failed expedition for South American gold caused James I to imprison him again. Raleigh was beheaded in 1618 on the old conviction.

Riis, Jacob (1849–1914). One of the nation's most famous journalists and urban reformers at the turn of the century, Riis was a native of Denmark who immigrated to the United States at age 11. His first years in his new home were difficult, and he never forgot the poverty and struggle associated with new immigrants. Within a few years, however, Riis became a reporter, eventually specializing in the New York City police beat. He spent his work days on the Lower East Side, where hundreds of thousands of immigrants had crowded and terrible slums had developed. Riis began to write regularly about the crime, lack of sanitation, poor housing, and other ills of the slums. By the late 1880s, he was well known for his dramatic reporting of the human costs of city life—especially the effects on women, children, and families. In 1890, Riis published *How the Other Half Lives*, which delineated for a wide national audience the problems he had been describing to his newspaper readers. The book made Riis famous and helped mobilize efforts to improve slum life. He continued to investigate and write for several years thereafter, publishing more books and becoming a popular public speaker.

Roosevelt, Theodore (1858–1919). Born in New York City to an old Dutch family, Roosevelt became one of the best-known and most colorful Presidents. He was educated at Harvard and throughout his life pursued intellectual life as an historian and a writer. He was attracted also to politics. Roosevelt won a seat in the New York legislature in 1882, lost a run for the mayor's office of New York City thereafter, and became first the federal civil service commissioner and then the head of the New York City police board. The outbreak of the Spanish-American War found him as an assistant secretary of the Navy, but he resigned, formed an Army unit from westerners, and won lasting heroic fame at the head of the Rough Riders at San Juan Hill. He returned home to become governor of New York, then vice president, and finally president after the assassination of McKinley in 1901. His two terms in office were marked by his vigorous pursuit of an aggressive foreign policy and a reform, antimonopoly program at home. He was no particular partisan of immigration and was on record as fearing the effect of the masses of newcomers, but he was careful in how he treated the issue. Roosevelt won the Nobel Peace Prize for helping to negotiate the end of the Russo-Japanese War, so he was in a good position to deal with the difficulties caused by growing discrimination against Japanese immigrants in California. In 1907, he concluded the so-called Gentleman's Agreement with Japan that effectively ended Japanese immigration without provoking an international conflict. Roosevelt was also responsible in part for promoting the Dillingham Commission to study the effect of immigration. He left office in 1909 and made another run as a reform, third-party candidate in 1912, losing to Woodrow Wilson.

Ross, Edward A. (1866–1951). Born in Illinois and educated at a small college in Iowa, the University of Berlin, and Johns Hopkins, Ross was the founder of the study of sociology in America, a social reformer, and one of the generation of nativist social scientists who advocated immigration restriction around the turn of the century. After teaching at Stanford and the University of Nebraska, he settled into a professorship at the University of Wisconsin, where he remained for more than 30 years until his retirement. He was a prolific writer and public speaker and was well known among a surprisingly large segment of the general population. His early work centered on the study of American social institutions and what was required to maintain them. These ideas tied in closely to his nativist views on immigration, because he espoused the idea that Anglo-Saxons were superior to recent immigrants and that the society of the United States was in danger of debasement from the flood of newcomers. He also became a strong supporter of eugenics (see Chapter Six). Somewhat surprisingly, Ross outlived his early nativism. By the 1930s, he had changed his mind and began to write and speak more about civil liberties than the dangers of inferior races.

Sacco, Nicola (1891–1927). Sacco was an Italian immigrant who came to the United States at age 17. His name is linked forever in history with his friend Bartolomeo Vanzetti, also an Italian immigrant. Together they became the focus of one of the most famous criminal prosecutions in the annals of America. Sacco was a family man, employed in a shoe-making factory in Milford, Massachusetts, and Vanzetti was a footloose bachelor with no steady employment, but they shared a belief in anarchism, the violent abolition of all government, a political idea attractive to a fringe minority among some immigrants at the time. Both had briefly fled the United States to evade the draft during World War I. In May 1920, they were arrested and charged with the robbery of a shoe factory the previous month in which two employees had been killed. Their trial turned into a showcase for the issues of political radicalism and class struggle. They were eventually convicted and sentenced to death, though the evidence against them was not entirely clear cut. The real drama came over the next six years of appeals during which they came to be seen by liberal intellectuals as political victims, whose immigrant status hastened their condemnation by conservative, nativist officials in Massachusetts. Several committees and courts examined the records, but no one overturned the verdicts, and Sacco and Vanzetti were electrocuted in 1927, becoming symbolic martyrs to a generation of left-wing Americans.

Schurz, Carl (1829–1906). During the second half of the 19th century, Schurz was seen by many Americans to be the classic immigrant success story. He was born near Cologne and attended the University of Bonn during the great period of revolution in Germany. He was caught up in the struggle of 1848 and 1849, playing a role in what turned out to be an unsuccessful attempt to liberalize the German states. Escaping from German in a series of adventures, Schurz made his way to America, where he became one of many such German "Forty-Eighters." By 1856, he was living in Wisconsin and became one of the important figures in the formation of the new Republican Party, already assuming a significant place in American affairs. When the Republicans won in 1860, Schurz was rewarded with an appointment as minister to Spain. With the outbreak of the Civil War, he returned to the United States and took a commission as a general in the Union Army, serving with only mediocre skill. After the War, he became a journalist for a few years, but was elected as a U.S. senator from Missouri in 1869. He became disaffected with the corruption under President Grant, so in 1870, Schurz helped found the reformist Liberal Republican movement. He served as secretary of the interior under President Rutherford B. Hayes from 1877 to 1881 and thereafter returned to journalism with a succession of newspapers and magazines and continued activity in reform movements.

Smith, John (1579–1631). Smith was a great adventurer who played the key role in the survival of the first successful English colony at Jamestown. He traveled and fought around Europe as a soldier of fortune while still in his early twenties. He became a member of the Virginia Company after his return to England and sailed for Virginia in 1607. The first months and years of the Jamestown settlement were brutally difficult and only the grit and authority of Smith allowed the disorganized colonists to survive. He almost single handedly forced the colonists who were unaccustomed to actual labor to work for their own salvation, and he kept a remnant alive by trading with the local Indian tribes for food. The colonists were not grateful, however, and seized him and sentenced him to death. He was reprieved and again took up authority in the colony, but he tired of the bickering and left for England in 1609. He sailed a few years later again to the American coast, exploring the region off New England. In his later years, Smith wrote extensively about the New World and helped inspire many Englishmen to immigrate.

Stuyvesant, Peter (circa 1610–1672). A strong-willed Calvinist, Stuyvesant was the final and most able of New Netherlands' governors. He was born in Friesland, the son of a Dutch Reformed minister. As a young man he joined the service of the Dutch West India Company, rising in the ranks of the company's colonial South American officers. By 1643, Stuyvesant was governor of the Dutch colony at Curaçao. While leading an attack on the Portuguese at St. Martin, he suffered a leg wound that required amputation. Two years later, he was appointed director general of New Netherlands, the principal Dutch settlement in North America with headquarters in New

Amsterdam (modern-day New York). He proved to be a stern governor who imposed what seemed at times a harsh rule on the cosmopolitan inhabitants of the town. Stuyvesant insisted on a Calvinist order and probity in conduct, and he made the inhabitants of New Netherlands follow taxes regulations and trading restrictions. He quashed all attempts to establish a separate municipal government for New Amsterdam. In 1655, he swooped down on the Swedish settlements on the Delaware River and absorbed them into the Dutch colonial empire. Unfortunately for Stuyvesant, the English king Charles II wanted New Netherlands for his brother, so an English squadron sailed into New Amsterdam's harbor in 1664 and with the help of disaffected colonists seized the entire Dutch settlement and deposed Stuyvesant. After a trip to Holland, Stuyvesant returned to what was by then New York and retired on a farm.

Truman, Harry S (1884–1972). A man little regarded by many of his contemporaries, Truman's stature as a President has grown steadily in recent years, and he is now generally judged as one of the more able chief executives of this century and a man who made a host of difficult decisions. He was born in Missouri, a state he was closely identified with during his entire life, and after service as an artillery officer in the field during World War I returned to Kansas City and became a minor official in the Pendergast political machine. In 1934, Truman was elected to the U.S. Senate, where he served as New Deal Democratic loyalist. He came to widest public attention during World War II as chairman of a Congressional watch-dog committee, and when Roosevelt decided to drop Henry Wallace from the ticket in 1944, the hitherto nondescript Truman was substituted as vice president. Within months Roosevelt was dead and Truman was President. Thrust into one of the most difficult situations imaginable, Truman made the crucial decision to use the atomic bomb to end the war with Japan, and he proceeded to guide America into the postwar era, pushing such monumental programs as the Marshall Plan, the United Nations, and NATO. Consistently underestimated by his opponents who ruled in Congress, Truman won his own term as president in 1948. He was constantly under pressure from right-wing conservatives who were entering the most paranoid phase of the early years of the Cold War, and the North Korean invasion of South Korea in 1950 created insurmountable problems for Truman. He consistently opposed restrictive immigration legislation, and he vetoed the McCarran Walter Act of 1952, but it was passed over his veto. Truman also supported a study commission on immigration that resulted in one of the most positive official views ever. He declined to run for another term and retired after the 1952 election.

Tweed, William Marcy (1823–1878). Tweed came to epitomize 19th-century urban political corruption in the public mind, due in no small part to the striking political cartoons of Thomas Nast. Tweed, who was known always in his adult life as "Boss," was born in New York City and worked as a saddlemaker and a clerk in his young days. He joined the Tammany Hall political organization and moved into leadership by his late twenties. He served in the U.S. House of Representatives and as a New York City alderman, but his major power came as the unofficial head of the city's dominant political machine, which relied increasingly on immigrant votes to maintain its control. Tweed and his cronies were corrupt on a massive scale, making millions of dollars in bribes and kickbacks from their manipulation of public works and government projects. The city tolerated his graft as long as public service did not suffer too seriously, but by 1870 the public had enough and a series of newspaper attacks on Tweed and his "ring" lead to his downfall and conviction. He served part of a 12-year sentence but was released and then jailed again. In 1876, he escaped to Cuba but was returned by the Spanish authorities to face new charges. Tweed died in a New York City jail.

Vanzetti, Bartolomeo (1888–1927). See **Sacco, Nicola**.

Walker, Francis A. (1840–1897). Walker was another of the prominent intellectuals from New England who espoused nativist ideas and supported immigration restriction. He was born in Boston, educated at Amherst, and served as a Union general during the Civil War. In 1869, Walker was named to head the bureau of statistics in the U.S. Treasury department and supervised the national census of 1870. He followed this with a two-year term as the first commissioner of Indian Affairs. In 1872, he joined the faculty of Yale University and there began to teach statistics and gain a national reputation as an expert in population and demographics. He returned to government to supervise the 1880 census and then became president of the Massachusetts Institute of Technology. He wrote many books and articles and was looked to as one of the leading authorities on statistics. Unfortunately, his chief conclusion about the demographics of immigration was a complete fallacy. He proclaimed that by some mysterious process immigration did not add to the total population because the birth rate among the native-born would fall in proportion to the influx of immigrants. This "displacement" theory had no basis in fact whatsoever and resulted entirely from Walker's nativist prejudices.

Walther, Carl F.W. (1811–1887). The leader of a conservative reform movement among Lutherans in America and founder of the Missouri Synod, Walther was a native of Saxony who had studied theology at the University of Leipzig and had become deeply ingrained with a fundamental form of German Lutheranism. He became a follower of the religious dissident Martin

Stephan and followed Stephan to the United States in 1839, settling with a colony of like-minded believers near St. Louis. The group soon discarded Stephan, and Walther was his successor. He and his fellow immigrant Lutherans founded the school that became Concordia Seminary, and then used the school as the base to launch a conservative reform movement against what Walther considered to be backsliding and inappropriate liberalism among Lutherans in America. He founded the Missouri Synod in 1847 and served as its head for the rest of his life. A powerful debater and writer, Walther dominated the conservative wing of the Lutheran church until his death, raising repeated controversies throughout his career.

Wilson, Woodrow. (1856–1924). Elected to office as the president after a career as an academic and an aristocratic reformer, Wilson confronted the gravest crisis in American life since the Civil War when the United States was pulled into the general European conflict of World War I. His attitudes toward immigrants were mixed; he had spoken and written nativist sentiments before he became president, but consistently vetoed restrictionist legislation and saw a relationship between his efforts to establish self-determining nations in eastern Europe and the large number of eastern European immigrants in the United States. He was born in Virginia and educated at Princeton and the University of Virginia. He practiced law for a few years, then went to Johns Hopkins and earned a Ph.D. before taking up a career as a professor of political science. He began teaching at Princeton in 1890 and became its president in 1902. His tenure was cut short in 1910 when he was forced out of office over the issue of educational reform. In the same year, however, he was elected governor of New Jersey, and he pushed for a range of social reforms during his two years in office. Receiving the Democratic nomination for president in 1912, Wilson won a three-way race against former President Teddy Roosevelt and the incumbent William Howard Taft. Wilson's two presidential terms began with an emphasis on domestic reform but soon turned to pressing issues of foreign policy, first in Mexico and then in Europe where war broke out in 1914. In 1915, Wilson vetoed a restrictive literacy test act aimed at slowing the flow of immigrants, and he did the same in 1917, though the Congress overrode him. America was eventually drawn into the European conflict on the side of the Allies, and Wilson hoped to use his influence to reshape Europe. In this he failed and then met political defeat at home when isolationists refused to go along with his peace treaty and his plan for a League of Nations. He suffered a paralyzing stroke in 1919 and for the rest of his term was only a shadow executive. Many historians believe his wife and top advisors actually functioned as president while Wilson vegetated. If so, it was they who used the pocket veto to stifle the Dillingham Bill in 1921. The national quota restrictions were passed again shortly after Wilson left office.

Winthrop, John (1588–1649). Winthrop was a member of the landed English gentry who became the indispensable man of the Puritan immigrants. He was born in Suffolk and inherited his family estates there at age 21. He was a convinced Puritan and like many of his fellow believers thought the social and political disruptions in England during the early 17th century showed evidence of a deep evil. When it was suggested that he accept the governorship of the proposed Massachusetts Bay Colony and thus embark on setting up a model Puritan state in the New World wilderness, Winthrop could not refuse. He gathered the first draft of Puritan immigrants and sailed for Massachusetts in 1630. For nearly 20 years, Winthrop headed the government of the colony, shaping it as a "city on a hill" and a realization of a Puritan theocracy. He enforced the strict Puritan codes of belief and social order, acted as the civil authority in matters of religious dissent, and ably administered the day-to-day affairs of Massachusetts. He welcomed hundreds and then thousands of new immigrants to Massachusetts Bay, but only so long as they were firm Puritan believers—he wanted to keep out all others.

Zangwill, Israel (1864–1926). Zangwill was an English Jewish writer and Zionist activist who invented one of the most lasting cliches of immigration when he published his 1909 play "The Melting Pot." He was born in London and became a teacher and writer concerned mostly with the plight of impoverished Jewish immigrants to England. He gained wide public notice for his journalism and books, especially *The Children of the Ghetto*, published in 1892. He was one of the principal founders of the international Zionist movement and worked throughout his life to establish a Jewish home state in Palestine. He neither lived nor worked in the United States, but he apparently was the first to use the melting-pot term that became the favorite metaphor for generations of writers and politicians.

CHRONOLOGY

· · · · · · · · ·

1492   Christopher Columbus sails from Spain to a landfall somewhere in the Caribbean, marking the first encounter of Europeans with the New World.

1584   Sir Walter Raleigh sends ships to explore part of the east coast of America, establishing a British claim to "Virginia," as he calls the region.

1587   A British trading company establishes an ill-fated colony of immigrants on Roanoke Island off the coast of Carolina. All disappear without a trace.

1598   Juan de Oñate heads a group of Spanish colonists that moves into the area of modern-day New Mexico. These are the first European immigrants to establish a permanent settlement in what will become the United States.

1607   British immigrants land at the mouth of the James River in Virginia and establish the village of Jamestown, the first successful British colony.

1619   The first contingent of black African slaves arrives at Jamestown and is sold, marking the beginning of black slavery in America.

1620   The *Mayflower*, blown off its course, lands at Plymouth in Massachusetts with the Pilgrims on board. They establish a settlement, which survives the first winter only with the help of local natives, and begin the colonization of New England.

1623	Dutch settlers begin the colony of New Netherlands as an outpost of the Dutch West India Company.
1629	A large contingent of English Puritans arrives in Massachusetts with a charter and the mission to set up a Puritan Commonwealth. Nearly 20,000 English immigrants arrive within the next decade, part of what is known as the Great Migration.
1634	Maryland founded as a proprietary colony by George Calvert, Lord Baltimore.
1654	The first Jewish immigrants to America arrive in New Amsterdam as refugees from a Dutch colony in South America. They are Sephardic Jews who have been forced out of Spain by the Inquisition.
1660	The end of significant English migration to the Puritan Massachusetts Bay colony. Immigration is officially discouraged hereafter.
1664	England seizes New Netherlands by force, turning the former Dutch colony over to the Duke of York, the king's brother and the future King James II.
1669	Carolina founded.
1681	The colony of Pennsylvania is founded by William Penn, a British Quaker. He intends to populate it with immigrants.
1683	The first German immigrants arrive on the *Concord* and settle in Pennsylvania.
1685	Louis XIV revokes the Edict of Nantes, thereby banishing all French Protestants, known as Huguenots. Many Huguenots eventually immigrate to America.
1710	Immigration from the German Palatinate to America begins with a group recruited by British colonial officials.
1717	Changes in land leases set off the beginnings of large-scale immigration of the Protestant Scotch-Irish from northern Ireland to the American colonies.
1718	The British Parliament prohibits the immigration of skilled workers from the British Isles.

1730   German immigrants and Scotch-Irish from Pennsylvania begin to settle in the back country of the Carolinas, taking up small farm holdings on the frontier.

1732   The *Philadelphische Zeitung* is founded as the first German-language newspaper in America.

1745   The Jacobite rebellion in Scotland attempts to restore the Stuarts to the British throne. A crushing defeat stimulates Scots Highlanders to immigrate to the American colonies.

1775   The outbreak of revolutionary violence and the beginning of the long War for Independence stops immigration from Great Britain. The subsequent naval blockade of American ports by the Royal Navy curtails immigration from most of Europe for several years to come.

1789   The beginning of the French Revolution, followed by a small immigration of French political refugees to the United States.

1789   The new Constitution of the United States (which replaces the Articles of Confederation) authorizes Congress to adopt naturalization laws that will grant citizenship to immigrant aliens, but contains no specific provisions. The Constitution also grants foreign-born citizens the right to hold all government offices except the Presidency.

1790   Congress passes the first national naturalization laws, granting citizenship to all "free white persons" after only two years residency.

1793   European warfare breaks out and will continue intermittently for nearly a quarter century. Free travel and immigration from Europe is at a virtual standstill for most of this period.

1795   A second naturalization law increases the waiting period for citizenship to five years.

1797   The Federalists propose a tax of 20 dollars on certificates of naturalization as a way to bar recent immigrants from becoming citizens, but the measure is defeated.

1798   Congress again changes the naturalization law and increases the waiting period to 14 years.

1798   The Federalists pass the Alien and Sedition Acts, which include two laws aimed at controlling aliens within the United States. The Alien Enemies Act never takes effect, but several aliens are required to register with the government under the Alien Friends Act, which also grants the President the power to deport aliens.

1801   After a shift in political power following the election of 1800, the new Congress passes a naturalization law that eliminates the registration requirement and sets the waiting period for citizenship at five years.

1803   The British Passenger Acts, in an attempt to make trans-Atlantic travel safer for immigrants, limits the number of passengers on ships.

1807   Congress officially outlaws the black slave trade, but illegal slave smuggling continues for decades.

1818   A British sailing company begins regular passenger service between Liverpool and New York.

1820   The United States begins to collect immigration statistics, recording individuals by the immediate country of origin.

1825   The first contingent of Norwegian immigrants lands from the *Restauration.*

1825   The British laws against immigration are repealed, allowing free travel to the United States from the British Isles.

1834–36 Violence breaks out against Roman Catholics in general and Catholic immigrants in particular in several eastern states.

1844   Nativists riot against Catholics in Philadelphia.

1845   Anti-Catholic, anti-immigrant Know-Nothing Party is founded to seize political power in order to limit the rights of Catholics and immigrants.

1845–49 A blight strikes the potato crops of the British Isles and Europe, pushing hundreds of thousands to the United States as immigrants. The Irish are particularly hard hit and begin a tremendous burst of immigration to America.

1846–47 Widespread crop failures in northern Europe stimulate increased immigration, particularly from Germany.

1847 New York establishes a Board of Emigration to regulate the influx and processing of immigrants.

1848 Failed political revolutions throughout the German states send many intellectuals and professionals into exile. Thousands of these "Forty Eighters" immigrate to the United States.

1849 The U.S. Supreme Court rules in the *Passenger Cases* that regulation of immigration is a federal matter under the Commerce clause of the Constitution. State-imposed head taxes in New York and Massachusetts are ruled unconstitutional, but the policing powers of the states are left in place.

1854 The Know-Nothings capture all the state government offices in Massachusetts and gain considerable power in Pennsylvania and Delaware. Massachusetts passes anti-immigrant laws.

1855 New York opens a reception center for immigrants at Castle Garden, which remains the major depot for immigrants for almost 40 years.

1856 Former President Millard Fillmore runs for the presidency on the Know-Nothing ticket, but carries only Maryland. The political threat of the nativist Know-Nothings collapses.

1861 The American Civil War begins. During the ensuing four years of brutal conflict, hundreds of thousands of immigrants fight for the Union cause, creating a new measure of acceptance for immigrants in the North.

1870 A federal Naturalization Act limits naturalization to whites and people of African descent, barring Asians from citizenship.

1871–75 Molly Maguire "conspiracy" among immigrant miners in the Pennsylvania coal fields results in riots.

1875 A U.S. Supreme Court decision invalidates state head taxes on immigrants and affirms that only the federal government has jurisdiction over immigration; however, officials decide to pay the states—primarily New York—to continue to process immigrants at the points of entry.

1876   Nativists riot and attack Chinese immigrants in San Francisco. The violence spreads and continues for several years.

1880   The so-called new immigration begins, bringing more than 23 million immigrants to America over the next 40 years, mostly from southern and eastern Europe.

1882   Congress passes the Chinese Exclusion Act, prohibiting immigration by male Chinese workers and extending Chinese ineligibility for naturalization, creating the first legal limit to immigration from a foreign nation.

1882   Congress passes the first general immigration law, regulating reception of immigrants, imposing a 50-cent head tax, and excluding idiots, lunatics, criminals, and anyone likely to become a public charge.

1885   Foran Act prohibits importation of immigrant contract labor.

1886   The Statue of Liberty, which eventually becomes a symbol of America's status as an immigrant asylum, is dedicated in New York Harbor.

1886   In what comes to be known as the Haymarket Affair, anarchists bomb police ranks during a Chicago labor demonstration, killing seven. As a result, political fear of immigrants grows.

1887   The American Protective Association is founded in the Midwest as an anti-Catholic, anti-immigrant, nativist organization.

1890   Jacob Riis's exposé of urban immigrant life, *How the Other Half Lives*, is published.

1891   Congress takes over of regulation of immigration and sets up the Bureau of Immigration. Paupers, persons with contagious diseases, felons, and polygamists are excluded.

1892   Ellis Island is opened by the federal government as the main reception point for immigrants from Europe. Millions pass through its gates for processing and admission.

1894   Immigration Restriction League of Boston is founded by New Englanders who fear the influence of southern and eastern European immigrants. Their intent is to lobby for immigration restriction.

1896   President Grover Cleveland vetoes a literacy test bill passed by Congress as a restrictive measure.

1903   Congress enacts new categories of exclusion, including anarchists, epileptics, prostitutes, and professional beggars.

1905   Immigration to the U.S. surpasses one million in a single year.

1906   Congress creates the Dillingham Commission to study the effects of immigration on the country.

1907   Existing restrictions and immigration exclusions codified by Congress in new law.

1907   The "Gentleman's Agreement" between the United States and Japan effectively ends Japanese immigration.

1907   The highest single year of immigration in American history: 1,285,349 immigrants arrive.

1909   Playwright Israel Zangwill coins term "melting pot" to describe immigrant America.

1911   The Dillingham Commission publishes its 40-volume report, urging immigration restriction through literacy tests.

1913   President Woodrow Wilson vetoes literacy test bill.

1914   Beginning of World War I in Europe essentially halts immigration.

1915   Wilson again vetoes a literacy test bill.

1916   Madison Grant's racist book, *Passing of the Great Race in America*, is published.

1917   Congress passes an Immigration Act over President Woodrow Wilson's veto, enacting the first literacy test for immigrants, excluding all Asians, and raising the head tax to eight dollars.

1917   America enters the European war on the side of the Allies. Participation in war sets off wave of domestic anti-German terrorism.

1919   A national wave of political fear, known as the Big Red Scare, grips America.

1921   Congress passes the first comprehensive immigration restriction law, setting a limit on total immigration and imposing a quota system based on nations of origin. The intent is to choke off immigration from southern and eastern Europe. The Western Hemisphere is not included in the restrictions.

1924   National Origins Law (Johnson-Reed Act) is passed by Congress as a permanent extension of immigration restrictions and national quotas. The law is even more ethnically biased than the 1921 law and aims at slowing eastern and southern European immigration to a minimum and excluding all Asian immigration.

1927   Italian radicals Sacco and Vanzetti executed in Massachusetts.

1929   The stock market crashes, signalling the beginning of the Great Depression and a drastic decline in immigration.

1930   A four-year period of negative immigration begins: more immigrants leave the U.S. than arrive.

1933   Hitler takes power in Germany and soon after begins his campaign against Jews.

1937–38   The growing threat of European war creates political refugees, especially Jews eager to escape the Nazis. Few are permitted to immigrate to America.

1939   World War II begins in Europe, ending almost all immigration for the time being.

1941   America joins global war after an attack on Pearl Harbor by the Japanese. Official immigration subsequently falls to the lowest annual rates since the 1820s.

1942   Japanese Americans on the West Coast interned as enemy aliens and sent to detention camps.

1942   The *bracero* program to bring Mexican workers to the United States begins.

1946   The War Brides Act provides for immigration of servicemen's spouses over and above national quotas.

1948   Congress passes the Displaced Persons Act as a four-year temporary measure to accommodate European refugees by mortgaging national quotas far into the future. About 400,000 immigrants are admitted under the act.

1952   Immigration and Naturalization Act of 1952 is passed as a reform of the immigration system, but instead it preserves the old restrictionist principles and national quotas. In addition, the new law requires tests of anti-Communist political orthodoxy.

1952   A presidential commission studies immigration and concludes it benefits the country economically. The commission recommends a new policy to encourage immigration, especially of people with needed skills.

1953   The Refugee Relief Act is another attempt to deal with the question of refugees, specifically in response to a failed revolution in Communist East Germany. The act creates 200,000 temporary visas.

1954   Ellis Island closes as a reception center as more and more immigrants arrive by air. The facility falls into severe disrepair during the following two decades.

1956   Hungarian Revolution creates political refugees, and the following year a special category of immigration exception is made to allow 40,000 to enter the Untied States.

1959   Fidel Castro stages a successful Communist revolution in Cuba, which eventually creates hundreds of thousands of political refugees.

1965   The Immigration and Nationality Act of 1965 ushers in a new era of immigration policy. It ends the national origins quota system and sets up a graded system of preferences that allows family members and those qualified in needed occupations to immigrate to the United States under an annual cap. The ban on Asian immigration is scrapped, and immigration from the Western Hemisphere is limited to 120,000 total per year.

1970   A third great wave of immigration to the United States begins as the new law comes into full effect. Millions will emigrate from Asia and Latin America over the next two decades.

1975   Communist victory in Vietnam and the American pull-out create large numbers of refugees from several Southeast Asian nations.

1976   President Carter decrees additional slots above the annual limits for refugees of the war.

1980   A new Refugee Act tries to deal with the refugee problem by raising the annual quota to 50,000, but more than three times that number are admitted during the following year.

1980   Castro allows a massive release of refugees to America, with more than 100,000 coming in a matter of weeks, most in a boatlift from the port of Mariel to Florida.

1986   The Congress passes the Immigration Reform and Control Act of 1986 in hope of mitigating the problem of illegal aliens. The act creates severe penalties for hiring illegal workers and extends an amnesty to illegal aliens already living in the country. More than three million eventually take advantage of the amnesty.

1990   The second immigration reform act passed by Congress in four years raises the annual limit on total immigration but cuts the number of family-related admissions in favor of occupational or economic development.

GLOSSARY

● ● ● ● ● ● ● ●

Acculturation: The merging of cultures as a result of prolonged contact.

Alien Acts of 1798: A package of laws that enabled the government to suppress political dissent in the name of national security and to move against noncitizen aliens at will. It included the Alien Friends Act, which required aliens to register with the government and allowed the president, John Adams, to deport any alien he deemed dangerous. These laws were allowed to expire in 1801.

"Americanization": An attempt to strip away alien culture and assimilate immigrants into the mainstream of traditional American society.

Amish: A strict sect of Anabaptist followers who settled in America chiefly in the 18th century.

Anabaptists: Members of a radical Protestant movement which was most prominent in the 16th century. Anabaptists advocated baptism and church membership of adult believers only and the separation of church and state.

Anti-Semitism: Hostility toward or discrimination against Jews as a religious, ethnic, or racial group.

Austro-Hungarian Empire (1867 to 1918): A monarchy in central Europe that included Bohemia, Moravia, Bukovina, Transylvania, Galicia, Austria, Hungary, Slovenia, Croatia, and northeast Italy.

Balkans: The countries occupying the Balkan Peninsula—Slovenia, Croatia, Bosnia and Herzegovina, Macedonia, Yugoslavia, Romania, Bulgaria, Albania, Greece, and Turkey.

Bohemia: A region of the modern-day Czech Republic that was once part of the Austro-Hungarian Empire.

The *bracero* program: A program established in 1945 during the labor shortage of WWII, whereby Mexican workers were screened and recruited by the Mexican government then transported across the border into the United States, where they signed individual contracts with growers. The *bracero* program was continued after the war and ended in 1964.

Chain migration: A pattern of immigration in which an immigrant working in the U. S. sends money back to the country of origin to pay for passage of other members of the family.

Chesapeake Colonies: Area now encompassing Maryland and parts of Virginia.

Chinese Exclusion Act of 1882: Legislation that suspended immigration of Chinese laborers to America. The act also denied naturalization to Chinese living in America and refused to allow Chinese to return to America if they left to visit China.

Coolie: An unskilled immigrant laborer, usually from the Far East, hired under contract for low or subsistence wages. It became a derogatory term.

Crimea: A peninsula in southeast Europe extending into the Black Sea.

Croatia: A county of southeastern Europe that was once part of the Austro-Hungarian Empire.

The Dillingham Commission: A commission appointed by Teddy Roosevelt in 1906 to explore the nature and consequences of immigration and provide a basis on which to formulate further legislation.

Displaced Persons Act (1948 to 1952): Temporary legislation that allowed a limited number of Europeans displaced by the war and the subsequent takeover of Eastern Europe by Communist regimes to immigrate to America.

East Anglia: Region of eastern England including modern-day Norfolk and Suffolk.

Emigrant: A person who leaves a country to take up residence elsewhere.

Federal Naturalization Act (1870): Legislation that limited naturalization to whites and people of "African descent." This law essentially allowed all immigrants except Asians to become citizens.

Forty-Eighters: Political activists and intellectuals who fled Germany after the failed revolution of 1848.

Galicia: A region of eastern central Europe that is now divided between Poland and the Ukraine and was once part of the Austro-Hungarian Empire.

Greenhorns: A slang expression originating in the early days of immigration and still used today that means newly arrived immigrants who are unacquainted with local manners and customs.

Hessians: Germans from the state of Hesse, which is located in central Germany; also, mercenaries whose services were purchased by England to fight against Americans during the Revolutionary War.

Illegal aliens: Immigrants who enter the United States against the law.

Immigrant: A person who comes to a country to take up permanent residence.

Immigration and Nationality Act of 1965: Legislation that eliminated the national origin quotas and substituted upper limits on total immigration with a system of graded family and occupational preferences determining who would be allowed to fill the overall quotas. This act has remained the basic template of U.S. immigration policy ever since.

Indenture: A contract that many 17th century English immigrants agreed to in exchange for passage to Virginia or Maryland and the promise of land at the end of service. The indenture required them to give up most of their rights and work for landowners in America, usually for four to seven years.

Internment camps: Camps where Japanese Americans, considered potential enemies during WWII, were confined.

Jacobites: Highland Scots of the 18th century who were loyal to the deposed house of Stuart and had fought unsuccessfully to put Bonny Prince Charlie on the throne.

The Johnson-Reed Act of 1924: Legislation that lowered the total number of immigrants to about 150,000 per year and set up quotas for the origin countries around the world. This act restricted emigration from southern and eastern Europe and completely cut off all emigration from Asia.

Magyars: The dominant people of Hungary.

Massachusetts Bay Colony: The colony set up by the Puritans in the 1600s, with Boston as its capital.

The McCarran-Walter Immigration and Nationality Act of 1952: Legislation intended to reform the immigration system, the McCarran-Walter act did little more than affirm the quota system.

Melting pot: The idea that a new kind of person will emerge from a mixing and blending of all the distinctive people who immigrated to the United

States. This has not been the case, but immigrant groups have maintained their unique identities for generation after generation.

Mennonite: A member of an Anabaptist Protestant sect derived from the Anabaptists and characterized by congregational autonomy and rejection of military service. Originally founded by Menno Simons.

***Los mojados* or "wetbacks":** Illegal emigrants from Mexico. This derogatory slang term is derived from the emigrants swimming the Rio Grande River to reach America.

Moravia: A region of the modern-day Czech Republic that was once part of the Austro-Hungarian Empire.

Nativism: A belief favoring native inhabitants as opposed to immigrants. This set of ideas can lead to a virulent, often violent, paranoid, and irrational hatred and fear of immigrants.

Naturalization: The process whereby foreigners may become citizens of their new country.

New Amsterdam: The capital of the 17th century Dutch colony New Netherlands; it was located at what is today New York City.

New Netherlands: A 17th century Dutch colony that is modern-day New York State.

Palantinate Germans: Germans from the Rhineland region.

Pogroms: Attacks on 19th century Russian Jewish settlements by neighboring groups that destroyed homes and businesses and claimed the lives of thousands of defenseless Jews.

Push-pull theory: A theory of immigration that says that elements must be in place at both the immigrants' place of origin and their destination for immigration to occur. Elements in the old land must push immigrants to uproot themselves and leave home; other elements in the new land must look so attractive that immigrants are pulled to a new place.

Pyramid immigration: Process of immigration in which one person immigrates, then uses the family preference provision of the Immigration and Nationality Act to bring in close relatives, who in turn invoke the family preference provision to bring in even more relatives.

Quota System: A system of immigration regulation in which the U.S. government specified how many immigrants per year from each country would be allowed to enter the United States. Numbers were determined according to a formula that was meant to reflect how Congress felt about each nation of origin. Adopted in 1921, this system stayed in effect until the mid-1960s and still lurks in the background of American policy on immigration.

Redemptioners: Immigrants who offered their services to shipping companies in exchange for passage to America.

Refugee: A person who flees a country to escape danger or persecution.

The Refugee Act: Legislation that recognized those seeking asylum as a new category of political refugee and created a possible annual total of 50,000 refugee immigrants.

Refugee Relief Act: Legislation adopted in 1953 to address the need proven with the Displaced Persons Act. About 200,000 temporary visas were created to allow refugees of eastern Europe to enter and live in the U.S.

Rhineland: Area of Germany immediately west of the Rhine River.

Shtetls: Small rural villages where many eastern European Jews were forced to live.

Slovenia: A country of southern Europe that was once part of the Austro-Hungarian Empire.

Sojourner: An immigrant who intends to return to their native country.

Transylvania: A region of modern-day Romania that was once part of the Austro-Hungarian Empire.

Ulster: Northern Ireland.

FURTHER READING

· · · · · · · · ·

his bibliography is intended to provide a starting point for reading or
research about immigration and ethnic groups in America. It is not
definitive because the published information on these topics is vast
and there are literally thousands of books and articles in print; it is, however,
comprehensive in the sense that it covers a wide range of topics.

The bibliography is divided into categories, and books are listed alpha-
betically by author's last name within the classifications. There are 15
categories plus a long list of ethnic or national groups. Many books are cited
in more than one topic category. For example, Carl Wittke's 1957 book on
the German language press in America is listed under both "Germans" and
"Literature and Journalism."

These books have been selected with bias toward more recent works, but
many important older books are included, especially if recently reprinted.
Most are written for the general adult audience, though a few young adult
titles are included. These books are noted with an asterisk (*).

GENERAL

Albovias, Benjamin C. *Immigration to the United States*. Chicago: B.C. Albovias.
1988.

Anzovin, Steven. *The Problem of Immigration*. New York: H.W. Wilson. 1985.

Archdeacon, Thomas J. *Becoming American: An Ethnic History*. New York:
Free Press. 1983.

*Ashabranner, Brent. *The New Americans: Changing Patterns in U.S. Immi-
gration*. New York: Dodd Mead. 1983.

Baldwin, Beth C. *Capturing the Change*. Santa Ana, CA: Immigrant and
Refugee Planning Center. 1982.

Bentz, Thomas. *New Immigrants: Portraits in Passage*. New York: Pilgrim Press.
1981.

Blegen, Theodore C., ed. *Land of Their Choice: The Immigrants Write Home.* Minneapolis: University of Minnesota. 1955.

*Blumenthal, Shirley. *Coming to America: Immigrants from Eastern Europe.* New York: Delacorte. 1981.

*Bode, Janet, ed. *New Kids in Town: Oral Histories of Immigrant Teens.* New York: Scholastic. 1991.

Bodnar, John E. *Immigration and Industrialization: Ethnicity in an American Mill Town, 1870–1940.* Pittsburgh: University of Pittsburgh. 1977.

————. *The Transplanted: A History of Immigrants in Urban America.* Bloomington, IN: Indiana University Press. 1985.

Bouvier, Leon W., and Robert Gardner. *Immigration to the United States: The Unfinished Story.* Washington, DC: Population Reference Bureau. 1986.

Bowers, David F., ed. *Foreign Influences in American Life.* Princeton, NJ: Princeton University Press. [1944] 1966.

Brownstone, David M. *Island of Hope, Island of Tears.* New York: Rawson Wade. 1979.

Bryce-Laporte, Roy S., ed. *A Sourcebook on the New Immigration: Implications for the United States and the International Community.* New Brunswick, NJ: Transaction Books. 1980.

Burton, William. *Melting-Pot Soldiers: The Union's Ethnic Regiments.* Ames, IA: Iowa State University Press. 1988.

Cafferty, Pastora San Juan, Barry Chiswick, Andrew M. Greeley, and Tensa A. Sullivan. *The Dilemma of American Immigration: Beyond the Golden Door.* New Brunswick, NJ: Transaction Books. 1983.

Chermayeff, Ivan, et al. *Ellis Island: An Illustrated History of the Immigrant Experience.* New York: Macmillan. 1991.

Coleman, Terry. *Going to America.* Garden City, NJ: Anchor Press. 1973.

Commager, Henry C., ed. *Immigration and American History: Essays in Honor of Theodore C. Blegen.* Minneapolis: University of Minnesota. 1961.

Coppa, Frank J., and Thomas J. Carran. *The Immigrant Experience in America.* Boston: Twayne. 1976.

Crewdson, John. *The Tarnished Door.* New York: Times Books. 1983.

Cummings, Scott. *Immigrant Minorities and the Urban Working Class.* Irvington, CA: Associated Faculty Press. 1980.

Daniels, Roger. *Coming to America: A History of Immigration and Ethnicity in American Life.* New York: HarperCollins. 1990.

Davie, Maurice R. *World Immigration with Special Reference to the United States.* New York: Macmillan. 1936.

*Day, Carol Olsen, and Edmund Day. *The New Immigrants.* New York: Franklin Watts. 1985.

Debouzy, Marianne, ed. *In the Shadow of the Statue of Liberty: Immigrants, Workers, and Citizens in the American Republic, 1860–1920.* Champaign, IL: University of Illinois. 1992.

Dimas, Nicasio, Donald Chou, and Phyllis Fong. *The Tarnished Golden Door: Civil Rights Issues on Immigration*. Washington, DC: United States Commission on Civil Rights. 1980.

Dinnerstein, Leonard, and David Reimers. *Ethnic America: A History of Immigration*. New York: Harper & Row. 1987.

Dublin, Thomas, ed. *Immigrant Voices: New Lives in America, 1773–1986*. Champaign, IL: University of Illinois Press. 1993.

Ehrlich, Richard L., ed. *Immigrants in Industrial America*. Charlottesville, VA: University Press of Virginia. 1977.

Fermi, Lauro. *Illustrious Immigrants: The Intellectual Migration from Europe, 1930–1941*. Chicago: University of Chicago Press. 1968.

Fishman, Joshua A. *Language Loyalty in the United States: The Maintenance and Perpetuation of Non-English Mother Tongues by American Ethnic and Religious Groups*. New York: Arno Press. [1966] 1978.

*Freedman, Russell. *Immigrant Kids*. New York: Scholastic. 1980.

Glazer, Nathan, ed. *Clamor at the Gates: The New American Immigration*. San Francisco: Institute for Contemporary Studies. 1985.

Golab, Caroline. *Immigrant Destinations*. Philadelphia: Temple University Press. 1977.

Greene, Victor R. *American Immigration Leaders, 1800–1910: Marginality and Identity*. Baltimore: Johns Hopkins University Press. 1987.

Haberstein, Robert W. *Ethnic Families in America*. New York: Elseveir. 1976.

Handlin, Oscar. *Boston's Immigrants*. Boston: Oxford University Press. 1959.

———, ed. *Children of the Uprooted*. New York: Braziller. 1966.

———, ed. *Immigration as a Factor in American History*. Englewood Cliffs, NJ: Prentice-Hall. 1959.

———. *Race and Nationality in American Life*. Garden City, NY: Doubleday. 1957.

———. *Statue of Liberty*. New York: Newsweek Book Divisions. 1971.

———. *The Uprooted: The Epic Story of the Great Migrations That Made the American People*. Boston: Little, Brown. 1951.

Hansen, Marcus. *The Atlantic Migration, 1607–1860*. Cambridge, MA: Harvard University Press. 1940.

———. *The Immigrant in American History*. New York: Harper & Row. 1940.

Higham, John, ed. *Ethnic Leadership in America*. Baltimore: Johns Hopkins University Press. 1977.

———. *Send These to Me: Immigrants in Urban America*. Baltimore: Johns Hopkins University Press. 1984.

———. *Strangers in the Land: Patterns of American Nativism, 1860–1925*. New Brunswick, NJ: Rutgers University Press. 1955.

Hoffman, Eva. *Lost in Translation: A Life in a New Language*. New York: E.P. Dutton. 1989.

Holloway, Thomas H. *Immigrants on the Land.* Chapel Hill, NC: University of North Carolina Press. 1980.

Holtzman, Wayne H., and Thomas H. Bornemann, eds. *Mental Health of Immigrants and Refugees.* Austin, TX: Hogg Foundation 1990.

Hook, J.N. *Family Names: How Our Surnames Came to America.* New York: Macmillan. 1982.

Hull, Elizabeth. *Without Justice for All: The Constitutional Rights of Aliens.* Westport, CT: Greenwood Press. 1985.

Jasso, Guillermina, and Mark R. Rosenzweig. *The New Chosen People: Immigrants in the United States.* New York: Russell Sage Foundation. 1990.

Jones, Maldwyn Allen. *American Immigration.* 2d edition. Chicago: University of Chicago. 1992.

———. *Destination America.* London: Fontana. 1976.

———. *The Old World Ties of American Ethnic Groups.* London: A.K. Lewis. 1976.

Kennedy, John F. *A Nation of Immigrants.* New York: Harper & Row. 1964.

Kessner, Thomas, and Betty B. Caroli. *Today's Immigrants, Their Stories: A New Look at the Newest Americans.* New York: Oxford University Press. 1982.

Kivisto, Peter, and Dag Blanck, eds. *American Immigrants and Their Generations: Studies and Commentaries on the Hansen Thesis after 50 Years.* Urbana, IL: University of Illinois Press. 1990.

Kraus, Michael. *Immigration, The American Mosaic: From Pilgrims to Modern Refugees.* Melbourne FL: Krieger. 1979.

Kraut, Alan M. *The Huddled Masses: The Immigrant in American Society, 1880–1921.* Arlington Heights, IL: Harlan Davidson. 1982.

———. *Silent Travelers: Germs, Genes, and the "Immigrant Menace."* New York: Basic Books. 1994.

Lacey, Dan. *The Essential Immigrant.* New York: Hippocrene Books. 1990.

Lamphere, Louise, ed. *Structuring Diversity: Ethnographic Perspectives on the New Immigration.* Chicago: University of Chicago Press. 1992.

Launer, Harold M., and Joseph E. Palenski, eds. *Crime and the New Immigrants.* Springfield, IL: C.C. Thomas. 1989.

Lerda, Valeria Gennaro, ed. *From Melting Pot to Multiculturalism.* Rome: Bulzoni. 1990.

Lieberson, Stanley. *A Piece of the Pie.* Berkeley, CA: University of California Press. 1980.

Lissak, Rivka S. *Pluralism and Progressives: Hull House and the New Immigrants.* Chicago: University of Chicago Press. 1989.

Maisel, Albert Q. *They All Chose America.* New York: Nelson. 1957.

May, Julian. *The Many-Colored Land.* New York: Ballantine. 1985.

McCabe, Cynthia J. *The Golden Door: Artist-Immigrants of America, 1876–1976.* Washington, DC: Smithsonian Institute. 1976.

Morris, Milton D. *Immigration: The Beleagured Bureaucracy.* Washington, DC: Westview. 1985.

Morrison, Joan, and Charlotte F. Zabusky. *American Mosaic: The Immigrant Experience in the Words of Those Who Lived It.* Pittsburgh: University of Pittsburgh Press. 1993.

Namias, June. *First Generation: In the Words of Twentieth-Century Immigrants.* 2d edition. Champaign, IL: University of Illinois Press. 1992.

Noble, Allen G. *To Build a New Land: Ethnic Landscapes in North America.* Baltimore, MD: Johns Hopkins Press. 1992.

Olson, James. *The Ethnic Dimension in American History.* New York: St. Martin's. 1977.

Pitkin, Thomas. *Keepers of the Gate: A History of Ellis Island.* New York: New York University Press. 1975.

Portes, Alejandro. *Immigrant America: A Portrait.* Berkeley: CA: University of California Press. 1990.

Potter, George W. *To the Golden Door.* Westport, CT: Greenwood Press. [1960] 1974.

Pozzetta, George. *Contemporary Immigrants.* New York: Garland. 1991.

———. *Ethnic Communities.* New York: Garland. 1991.

———. *Folklore, Culture, and the Immigrant Mind.* New York: Garland. 1991.

———. *Immigrant Family Patterns.* New York: Garland. 1991.

———. *Immigrant Institutions.* New York: Garland. 1991.

———. *Immigrants on the Land.* New York: Garland. 1991.

———. *Law, Crime, and Justice.* New York: Garland. 1991.

———. *Themes in Immigrant History.* New York: Garland. 1991.

———. *The Work Experience.* New York: Garland. 1991.

Reimers, David M. *The Immigrant Experience.* New York: Chelsea House. 1989.

———. *Still the Golden Door: The Third World Comes to America.* New York: Columbia University Press. 1985.

Reeves, Pamela. *Ellis Island: Gateway to the American Dream.* New York: Crescent. 1991.

Richmond, Anthony H. *Immigration and Ethnic Conflict.* New York: St. Martin's. 1988.

*Rips, Gladys N. *Coming to America: Immigrants from Southern Europe.* New York: Delacorte. 1981.

Rischin, Moses. *Immigration and the American Tradition.* New York: Macmillan. 1976.

*Robbins, Albert. *Coming to America: Immigrants from Northern Europe.* New York: Delacorte. 1981.

Santoli, Al. *New Americans: An Oral History; Immigrants and Refugees in the U.S. Today.* New York: Viking. 1988.

Seller, Maxine. *To Seek America: A History of Ethnic Life in the United States.* Englewood Cliffs, NJ: Prentice-Hall. 1977.

Solomon, Barbara. *Ancestors and Immigrants.* Boston: Northeastern University Press. [1956, 1975] 1989.

Sorin, Gerald. *A Time for Building: The Third Migration, 1880–1920.* Baltimore: Johns Hopkins University Press. 1990.

Stern, Gail F., et al., eds. *Freedom's Doors: Immigrant Ports of Entry to the United States.* Phildelphia: Balch Institute. 1986.

Steiner, Dale R. *Of Thee We Sing: Immigrants and American History.* Orlando, FL: H.B. Collegiate Publications. 1987.

Stephenson, George M. *A History of American Immigration, 1820–1924.* New York: Russell & Russell. [1924] 1964.

Takai, Ronald. *A Different Mirror: A History of Multicultural America.* Boston: Little, Brown. 1993.

Taylor, Philip. *The Distant Magnet: European Emigration to the U.S.A.* London: Eyre & Spottiswoode. 1971.

Tift, Wilton S. *Ellis Island.* Chicago: Contemporary Books. 1990.

United States Immigration and Naturalization Service. *Immigrant Nation: United States Regulation of Immigration, 1798–1991.* Washington, DC: Government Printing Office. 1991.

Weisberger, Bernard A. *The American Heritage History of the American People.* New York: American Heritage. 1970.

Weiss, Bernard J., ed. *American Education and the European Immigrant, 1840–1940.* Urbana, IL: University of Illinois Press. 1982.

ASSIMILATION

Bayer, Alan E. *The Assimilation of American Family Patterns by European Immigrants and Their Children.* New York: N.W. Ayer. 1981.

Carlson, Robert A. *The Americanization Syndrome: A Quest for Conformity.* New York: St. Martin's. 1987.

Elkholy, Abdo A. *The Arab Moslems in the United States: Religion and Assimilation.* New Haven, CT: College and University Press. 1960.

Erickson, Charlotte. *Invisible Immigrants: The Adaptation of English and Scottish Immigrants in the 19th Century.* Ithaca, NY: Cornell University Press. [1972] 1990.

Glazer, Nathan, and Daniel P. Moynihan. *Beyond the Melting Pot: The Negroes, Puerto Ricans, Jews, Italians, and Irish of New York City.* Cambridge, MA: Harvard University Press. 1970.

Gordon, Milton. *Assimilation in American Life: The Role of Race, Religion, and National Origins.* New York: Oxford University Press. 1964.

Hoffman, Eva. *Lost in Translation: A Life in a New Language*. New York: E.P. Dutton. 1989.

Jiobu, Robert. *Ethnicity and Assimilation: Blacks, Chinese, Filipinos, Koreans, Japanese, Mexicans, Vietnamese, and Whites*. Albany, NY: State University of New York Press. 1988.

Kayal, Philip, and Joseph Kayal. *Syrian Lebanese in America: A Study in Religion and Assimilation*. Boston: Twayne. 1975.

Kim, Hyung-Chan. *The Korean Diaspora: Historical and Sociological Studies of Korean Immigration and Assimilation in North America*. Santa Barbara, CA: ABC-Clio. 1977.

Pozzetta, George. *Americanization, Social Control and Philanthropy*. New York: Garland. 1991.

———. *Assimilation, Acculturation, and Social Mobility*. New York: Garland. 1991.

Rogg, Eleanor Meyer. *Assimilation of Cuban Exiles: The Role of Community and Class*. New York: Aberdeen. 1974.

Sandberg, Neil. *Ethnic Identity and Assimilation*. New York: Polish American Historical Association. 1974.

CITIES

Bayer, Ronald. *Neighbors in Conflict: The Irish, Germans, Jews and Italians of New York City, 1929–1941*. Baltimore: Johns Hopkins University Press. 1978.

Beibom, Ulf. *Swedes in Chicago*. Vajo, Sweden: Scandinavian University Books. 1971.

Birchall, R.A. *The San Franciso Irish, 1848–1880*. Berkeley, CA: University of California Press. 1980.

Bodnar, John, Roger Simon, and Michael P. Weber. *Lives of Their Own: Blacks, Italians, and Poles in Pittsburgh, 1900–1960*. Champaign, IL: University of Illinois Press. 1982.

———. *The Transplanted: A History of Immigrants in Urban America*. Bloomington, IN: University of Indiana Press. 1982.

Bogen, Elizabeth. *Immigration in New York*. Westport, CT: Greenwood. 1987.

Brumberg, Stephen F. *Going to America, Going to School: The Jewish Immigrant Public School Encounter in Turn-of-the-Century New York*. New York: Praeger. 1986.

Couzens, Kathleen N. *Immigrant Milwaukee, 1836–1860: Accommodation and Community in a Frontier City*. Cambridge, MA: Harvard University Press. 1976.

Ernst, Robert. *Immigrant Life in New York City, 1825–1863*. New York: King's Crown Press. 1965.

Esslinger, Dean R. *Immigrants and the City*. Port Washington, NY: Kennikat. 1975.

Ewen, Elizabeth. *Immigrant Women in the Land of Dollars: Life and Culture on the Lower East Side, 1890–1925*. New York: Monthly Review Press. 1985.

Fine, David M. *The City, the Immigrant, and American Fiction, 1880–1920*. Metuchen, NJ: Scarecrow. 1977.

Foner, Nancy, ed. *New Immigrants in New York*. New York: Columbia University Press. 1987.

Garcia, Mario T. *Desert Immigrants: The Mexicans of El Paso, 1880–1920*. New Haven, CT: Yale University Press. 1981.

Glazer, Nathan, and Daniel P. Moynihan. *Beyond the Melting Pot: The Negroes, Puerto Ricans, Jews, Italians, and Irish of New York City*. Cambridge, MA: Harvard University Press. 1970.

Goren, Arthur H. *New York Jews and the Quest for Community*. New York: Columbia University Press. 1970.

Gumina, Deanna Paoli. *The Italians of San Francisco, 1850–1930*. New York: Center for Migration Studies. 1978.

Handlin, Oscar. *Boston's Immigrants*. Boston: Oxford University Press. [1941] 1959.

Hertzberg, Stephen. *Strangers within the Gate City: The Jews of Atlanta, 1845–1915*. Philadelphia: Temple University Press. 1979.

Hirsch, Eric L. *Urban Revolt: Ethnic Politics in the Nineteenth Century Chicago Labor Movement*. Berkeley, CA: University of California Press. 1989.

Kessner, Thomas. *The Golden Door: Italian and Jewish Mobility in New York City, 1880–1915*. New York: Oxford University Press. 1977.

Kinkead, Gwen. *Chinatown: Portrait of a Closed City*. New York: Harper Perennial. 1993.

Laguerre, Michael S. *American Odyssey: Haitians in New York City*. Ithaca, NY: Cornell University Press. 1984.

Lieberson, Stanley. *Ethnic Patterns in American Cities*. New York: Free Press. 1963.

Markowitz, Fran. *A Community in Spite of Itself: Soviet Jewish Emigres in New York*. Washington, DC: Smithsonian Institute. 1993.

Miller, Randall M., and Thomas D. Marzik, eds. *Immigrants and Religion in Urban America*. Philadelphia: Temple University Press. 1977.

Moore, Deborah D. *At Home in America: Second Generation New York Jews*. New York: Columbia University Press. 1981.

Morawska, Ewa. *For Bread with Butter: The Life-Worlds of East Central Europeans in Johnstown, Pennsylvania, 1890–1940*. Cambridge, United Kingdom: University of Cambridge Press. 1985.

Mormino, Gary R., and George E. Pozzetta. *The Immigrant World of Ybor City: Italians and Their Latin Neighbors in Tampa, 1885–1985*. Champaign, IL: University of Illinois Press. 1987.

————. *Immigrants on the Hill: Italian-Americans in St. Louis, 1882–1982*. Champaign, IL: University of Illinois Press. 1986.

Nadel, Stanley. *Little Germany: Ethnicity, Religion and Class in New York City*. Urbana, IL: University of Illinois Press. 1990.

Nelli, Humbert S. *Italians in Chicago, 1880–1930: A Study in Ethnic Mobility*. New York: Oxford University Press. 1970.

Niehaus, Earl. *The Irish in New Orleans, 1800–1860*. New York: Arno. [1965] 1976.

Olson, Audrey L. *St. Louis Germans, 1850–1920*. New York: Arno. 1980.

Rischin, Moses. *The Promised City: New York's Jews, 1870–1914*. Cambridge, MA: Harper & Row. 1962.

Rosenberg, Stuart E. *The Jewish Community in Rochester, 1843–1925*. New York: American Jewish Historical Society. 1954.

Seaburg, Alan. *At the Fair: The Boston Immigrant Experience*. Medford, MA: A. Miniver. 1990.

Shokeid, Moshe. *Children of Circumstance: Israeli Emigrants in New York*. Ithaca, NY: Cornell University Press. 1988.

Suttles, Gerald D. *The Social Order of the Slum: Ethnicity and Territory in the Inner City*. Chicago: University of Chicago Press. 1968.

Tomasi, Silvano M. *Piety and Power: The Role of Italian Parishes in the New York Metropolitian Area, 1830–1930*. Staten Island, NY: Center for Migration Studies. 1975.

Vorspan, Max, and Lloyd P. Gartner. *History of the Jews of Los Angeles*. San Marino, CA: Jewish Publication Society of America. 1970.

Ward, David. *Cities and Immigrants: A Geography of Change in Nineteenth Century America*. New York: Oxford University Press. 1971.

Yans-McLaughlin, Virginia. *Family and Community: Italian Immigrants in Buffalo, 1880–1930*. Ithaca, NY: Cornell University Press. 1977.

ECONOMICS AND LABOR

Berthoff, Rowland T. *British Immigrants in Industrial America, 1790–1950*. Cambridge: Harvard University Press. [1953] 1967.

Bonacich, Edna, and John Modell. *The Economic Basis of Ethnic Solidarity: Small Business in the Japanese-American Community*. Berkeley, CA: University of California Press. 1980.

Dickinson, Joan Y. *The Role of Immigrant Women in the U.S. Labor Force, 1890–1980*. New York: Arno Press. 1980.

Erickson, Charlotte. *American Industry and the European Immigrant, 1860–1885*. Cambridge: Harvard University Press. 1957.

Fenton, Edwin. *Immigrants and Unions—A Case Study: Italians and American Labor*. New York: Arno Press. 1975.

Galarza, Ernest. *Merchants of Labor: The Mexican Bracero Story*. Charlotte, NC: McNally & Loftin. 1964.

Greene, Victor R. *The Slavic Community on Strike: Immigrant Labor in the Pennsylvania Anthracite Mines*. Notre Dame, IN: Notre Dame University Press. 1968.

Hartmut, Keil, and John J. Jentz, eds. *German Workers in Industrial Chicago, 1850–1910: A Comparative Perspective*. DeKalb, IL: Northern Illinois University Press. 1983.

Hirata, Lucie C., and Edna Bonacich, eds. *Labor Immigration under Capitalism: Asian Immigrant Workers in the United States before World War II*. Berkeley, CA: University of California Press. 1984.

Hirsch, Eric. *Urban Revolt: Ethnic Politics in the Nineteenth Century Chicago Labor Movement*. Berkeley, CA: University of California Press. 1989.

Korman, Gerd. *Industrialization, Immigrants, and Americanization*. Madison, WI: University of Wisconsin Press. 1967.

Light, Ivan, and Parminder Bachnu, eds. *Immigration and Entrepreneurship: Culture, Capital, and Ethnic Networks*. New Brunswick, NJ: Transaction. 1993.

Mink, Gwendolyn. *Old Labor and New Immigrants in American Political Developments*. Ithaca, NY: Cornell University Press. 1990.

Modell, John. *The Ecomonics and Politics of Racial Accomodation: The Japanese of Los Angeles, 1900–1977*. Urbana, IL: University of Illinois Press. 1977.

Parmet, Robert D. *Labor and Immigration in Industrial America*. Melbourne, FL: Krieger. 1987.

Rosenblum, Gerald. *Immigrant Workers: Their Impact on American Labor Radicalism*. New York: Basic Books. 1973.

Yearley, Clifton K. *Britons in American Labor*. Baltimore: Johns Hopkins Press. 1957.

ETHNICITY AND RACE

Altschuler, Glenn C. *Race, Ethnicity, and Class in American Social Thought, 1865–1919*. Arlington Heights, IL: Harlan Davidson. 1982.

Bernal, Martha E., and George P. Knight, eds. *Ethnic Identity: Formation and Transmission among Hispanics and Other Minorities*. Albany, NY: State University of New York Press. 1993.

Bonacich, Edna, and John Modell. *The Economic Basis of Ethnic Solidarity: Small Business in the Japanese-American Community.* Berkeley, CA: University of California Press. 1980.

Colburn, David R., and George E. Pozzeta, eds. *America and the New Ethnicity.* Port Washington, NY: Kennikat. 1979.

Cordasco, Francesco, and D.N. Alloway. *American Ethnic Groups: The European Heritage.* Metuchen, NJ: Scarecrow. 1981.

Cunningham, Barbara, ed. *The New Jersey Ethnic Experience.* Union City, NJ: W.H. Wise. 1977.

D'Innocenza, Michael, and Josef P. Sirefman, eds. *Immigration and Ethnicity: American Society: "Melting Pot" or "Salad Bowl."* Westport, CT: Greenwood. 1992.

Edmondston, Barry, and Jeffrey S. Passel, eds. *Immigration and Ethnicity: Integration of America's Newest Immigrants.* Washington, DC: Urban Institute. 1993.

Greeley, Andrew M. *Ethnicity in the United States.* New York: John Wiley and Son. 1974.

Handlin, Oscar. *Race and Nationality in American Life.* Garden City, NY: Doubleday. 1957.

Jiobu, Robert. *Ethnicity and Assimilation: Blacks, Chinese, Filipinos, Koreans, Japanese, Mexicans, Vietnamese, and Whites.* Albany, NY: State University of New York Press. 1988.

Knobel, Dale. *Paddy and the Republic: Ethnicity and Nationality in Antebellum America.* Middletown, CT: Wesleyan University Press. 1986.

Lieberson, Stanley, and Mary C. Waters. *From Many Strands: Ethnic and Racial Groups in Contemporary America.* Ithaca, NY: Free Press. 1980.

Luebke, Frederick C., ed. *Ethnicity on the Great Plains.* Lincoln, NE: University of Nebraska Press. 1980.

Nadel, Stanley. *Little Germany: Ethnicity, Religion and Class in New York City.* Urbana, IL: University of Illinois Press. 1990.

Pozzetta, George. *Ethnicity and Gender: Immigrant Women.* New York: Garland. 1991.

———. *Ethnicity, Ethnic Identity.* New York: Garland. 1991.

Sandberg, Neil. *Ethnic Identity and Assimilation.* New York: Polish American Historical Association. 1974.

Shenton, James P. *Ethnicity and Immigration.* Washington, DC: American Historical Association. 1991.

Suttles, Gerald D. *The Social Order of the Slum: Ethnicity and Territory in the Inner City.* Chicago: University of Chicago Press. 1968.

Walters, Mary C. *Ethnic Options: Choosing Indentities in America.* Berkeley, CA: University of California Press. 1990.

"HOW TO"

Canter, Lawrence, and Martha S. Siegel. *The Insider's Guide to Sucessful U.S. Immigration: Discover How to Make the New Immigration Act Work for You.* New York: HarperCollins. 1992.

Danilov, Dan. *Immigrating to the U.S.A.: Who Is Allowed? What Is Required? How to Do It.* North Vancouver, Canada: Self-Counsel Press. Not dated.

Deutsch, Howard D. *Immigration the Easy Way: Including a Guide to Canadian Immigration.* Hauppaugue, NY: Barrons. 1993.

Henry, Christopher E. *How to Win the U.S. Immigration Game: The Essential Guide to Successful American Immigration.* Chester Springs, PA: Dufour. 1989.

Kimmel, Barbara B. *Immigration Made Simple: An Easy-to-Read Guide to the U.S. Immigration Process.* Westport, CT: New Decade. 1992.

Merritt, Nancy-Jo. *Understanding Immigration Law: How to Enter, Work, and Live in the United States.* Scottsdale, AZ: Makai. 1992.

Siegel, Martha. *U.S. Immigration Made Easy: An Action Guide.* Tuscon, AZ: Sheridan Chandler. 1989.

U.S. Immigration and Naturalization Service. *Basic Guide to Naturalization and Citizenship.* Rev. ed. Washington, DC: Government Printing Office. 1990.

IMMIGRATION LAW, NATURALIZATION, AND POLICY

Aleinikoff, Thomas A., and David Martin. *Immigration: Process and Policy.* St. Paul, MN: West Publishing. 1985.

Baker, Susan G. *The Cautious Welcome: The Legalization Programs and the Immigration Reform and Control Act.* Washington, DC: Urban Institute. 1990.

Bennett, Marion T. *American Immigration Policies.* Washington, DC: Public Affairs Press. 1963.

Briggs, Vernon Jr., and Stephen Moore. *Still an Open Door? U.S. Immigration Policy and the American Economy.* Washington, DC: American University Press. 1994.

Chan, Sucheng, ed. *Entry Denied: Exclusion and the Chinese Community in America, 1882–1943.* Philadelphia: Temple University Press. 1991.

Chiswick, Barry, ed. *The Gateway: U.S. Immigration Issues and Policies.* Washington, DC: American Enterprise Institute. 1982.

Divine, Robert A. *American Immigration Policy.* New Haven, CT: Yale University Press. 1957.

Frye, Hope M., ed. *Selected Writing: Immigration Law in Transition.* Washington, DC: American Immigration Law Association. 1990.

Hing, Bill O. *Making and Remaking Asian America through Immigration Policy, 1850–1990*. Palo Alto, CA: Stanford University Press. 1993.

Hofstetter, Richard, ed. *U.S. Immigration Policy*. Durham, NC: Duke University Press. 1984.

Hutchinson, Edward P. *Legislative History of U.S. Immigration Policy, 1798–1965*. Philadelphia: University of Pennsylvania. 1981.

Kettner, James H. *The Development of American Citizenship, 1608–1870*. Chapel Hill, NC: Institute of Early American History and Culture. 1978.

Kritz, Mary M., ed. *U.S. Immigration and Refugee Policy: Global and Domestic Issues*. Lexington, MA: D.C. Heath. 1982.

LeMay, Michael. *From Open Door to Dutch Door: An Analysis of U.S. Immigration Policy since 1820*. New York: Praeger. 1987.

McKee, Delber. *Chinese Exclusion Versus the Open Door Policy*. Detroit: Wayne State University Press. 1977.

Montwieler, Nancy H. *The Immigration Reform Law of 1986: Analysis, Text, and Legislative History*. Washington, DC: Government Printing Office. 1987.

Papademetriou, Demetrios, and Mark J. Miller. *The Unavoidable Issue: United States Immigration Policy in the 1980s*. Philadelphia: Institute for the Study of Human Issues. 1983.

LITERATURE AND JOURNALISM

Andersen, Arlow W. *The Immigrant Takes His Stand: The Norwegian American Press and Public Affairs, 1847–1872*. Northfield, MN: Norwegian-American Historical Association. 1953.

Capps, Finis H. *From Isolationism to Involvement: The Swedish Immigrant Press in America, 1914–1945*. Chicago: Swedish Pioneer Historical Society. 1966.

Ferraro, Thomas J. *Ethnic Passages: Literary Immigrants in Twentieth-Century America*. Chicago: University of Chicago Press. 1993.

Fine, David M. *The City, the Immigrant, and American Fiction, 1880–1920*. Metuchen, NJ: Scarecrow. 1977.

Green, Rose Basile. *The Italian-American Novel*. Teaneck, NJ: Farleigh-Dickinson University Press. 1974.

Kim, Elaine H. *Asian American Literature: An Introduction to the Writings and Their Social Context*. Philadelphia: Temple University Press. 1982.

Metzker, Isaac, ed. *A Bintel Brief: Sixty Years of Letters from the Lower East Side to the Jewish Daily Forward*. New York: Schocken. [1971] 1990.

Peck, David R. *American Ethnic Literature: Native American, African American, Chicano/Latino, and Asian American Writers and Their Backgrounds: An Annotated Bibliography*. Englewood Cliffs, MD: Salem Press. 1994.

Roucek, Joseph, Alice Hero, and Jean Downley. *The Immigrant in Fiction and Biography*. New York: Bureau of International Education. 1945.

Skardal, Dorothy B. *The Divided Heart: Scandinavian Immigrant Experience through Literary Sources*. Lincoln, NE: University of Nebraska Press. 1974.

Wittke, Carl. *The German Language Press in America*. Lexington, KY: University Press of Kentucky. 1957.

Wong, Cynthia Sau-ling. *Reading Asian American Literature: From Necessity to Extravagance*. Princeton, NJ: Princeton University Press. 1993.

MIGRATION PATTERNS

Anderson, Virginia. *New England's Generations: The Great Migration and the Formation of Society and Culture in the Seventeenth Century*. New York: Cambridge University Press. 1991.

Bailyn, Bernard. *The Peopling of British North America*. New York: Knopf. 1986.

———. *Voyagers to the West: A Passage in the Peopling of America on the Eve of the Revolution*. New York: Knopf. 1986.

Baines, Dudley. *Migration in a Mature Economy: Emigration and Internal Migration in England and Wales, 1861–1900*. Cambridge, United Kingdom: Cambridge University Press. 1985.

Katz, William L. *The Great Migrations, 1880–1912*. Austin, TX: Raintree Steck-Vaughn. 1993.

Nugent, Walter T.K. *Crossings: The Great Transatlantic Migrations, 1870–1914*. Bloomington, IN: Indiana University Press. 1992.

Pooley, Colin G., and Ian D. Whyte. *Migrants, Emigrants, and Immigrants: A Social History of Migration*. New York: Routledge. 1991.

NATIVISM AND RACISM

Billington, Ray Allen. *The Protestant Crusade, 1800–1860: A Study of the Origins of American Nativism*. New York: Macmillan. 1938.

Higham, John. *Strangers in the Land: Patterns in American Nativism, 1860–1925*. New Brunswick, NJ: Rutgers University Press. 1955.

Saniel, J.M., ed. *The Filipino Exclusion Movement, 1927–1935*. Quezon City, Phillipines: University of Philippines Press. 1967.

Smith James Morton. *Freedom's Fetters*. Ithaca, NY: Cornell University Press. 1956.

POLITICS

Allswang, John M. *A House for All Peoples: Ethnic Politics in Chicago, 1890–1936*. Lexington, KY: University Press of Kentucky. 1971.

Daniels, Roger. *The Politics of Prejudice*. New York: Atheneum. [1962] 1973.

Fuchs, Lawrence H., ed. *American Ethnic Politics*. New York: Harper & Row. 1968

Harles, John C. *Politics in the Lifeboat: Immigrants and the American Democratic Order*. Boulder, CO: Westview. 1993.

Hirsch, Eric L. *Urban Revolt: Ethnic Politics in the Nineteenth Century Chicago Labor Movement*. Berkeley, CA: University of California Press. 1989.

Kantowicz, Edward R. *Polish-American Politics in Chicago, 1888–1940*. Chicago: University of Chicago Press. 1975.

Levine, Edward M. *The Irish and Irish Politicians*. South Bend, IN: Purdue University Press. 1966.

Mink, Gwendolyn. *Old Labor and New Immigrants in American Political Developments*. Ithaca, NY: Cornell University Press. 1990.

Modell, John. *The Ecomonics and Politics of Racial Accomodation: The Japanese of Los Angeles, 1900–1977*. Urbana, IL: University of Illinois Press. 1977.

Pozzetta, George. *Immigrant Radicals*. New York: Garland. 1991.

Roucek, Joseph S., and Bernard Eisenberg, eds. *America's Ethnic Politics*. Westport, CT: Greenwood. 1982.

Wefald, Jon. *A Voice of Protest: Norwegians in American Politics, 1890–1917*. Northfield, MN: Norwegian-American Historical Association. 1971.

REFERENCE

Allen, James P., and Eugene J. Turner. *We the People: An Atlas of America's Ethnic Diversity*. New York: Macmillan. 1988.

Cordasco, Francesco, ed. *Dictionary of American Immigration History*. Metuchen, NJ: Scarecrow. 1990.

Davidson, Darrow R. *Immigration and Emigration: Index of Modern Authors and Subjects with a Guide for Rapid Research*. Washington, DC: ABBE Publications. 1991.

Gall, Susan B., and Timothy L. Gall, eds. *Statistical Record of Asian Americans*. Detroit: Gale Research. 1993.

Historical Statistics of the United States: Colonial Times to 1970. Two vols. Washington, DC: Department of Commerce, Bureau of the Census. 1975.

Horton, Carrell, and Jessie Carney Smith, eds. *Statistical Record of Black America*. Detroit: Gale Research. 1993.

Kim, Hyung-Chan, ed. *Dictionary of Asian American History*. Westport, CT: Greenwood. 1986.

Reddy, Marlita, ed. *Statistical Records of Hispanic Americans*. Detroit: Gale Research. 1994.

Statistical Abstract of the United States. Washington, DC: United States Department of Commerce, Bureau of the Census. Annual.

Thernstrom, Stephen, ed. *Harvard Encyclopedia of American Ethnic Groups.* Cambridge, MA: Harvard University Press. 1980.

REFUGEES AND ILLEGAL ALIENS

Conover, Ted. *Coyotes: A Journey through the Secret World of America's Illegal Aliens.* New York: Vintage. 1987.

Garcia, Juan Ramon. *Operation Wetback: The Mass Deportation of Mexican Undocumented Workers in 1954.* Westport, CT: Greenwood. 1980.

Fagen, Patricia Weiss, and Serjio Aguayo. *Fleeing the Maelstrom: Central American Refugees.* Boulder, CO: Westview. 1987.

Feingold, Henry L. *The Politics of Rescue.* New Brunswick, NJ: Transaction. 1970.

Friedman, Saul. *No Haven for the Oppressed: United States Policy toward Jewish Refugees 1938–1945.* Detroit: Wayne State University Press. 1973.

Haines, David W., ed. *Refugees as Immigrants: Cambodians, Laotians, and Vietnamese in America.* Lanham, MD: Rowman. 1989.

Hall, Donald K. *The Border: Life on the Line.* New York: Abbeville. 1988.

Haskell, Grace. *The Illegals.* New York: Stein and Day. 1978.

*Hauser, Pierre N. *Illegal Aliens.* New York: Chelsea House. 1990.

Hawthorne, Lesleyanne, ed. *Refugee: The Vietnamese Experience.* New York: Oxford University Press. 1982.

Johnson, Kenneth A. *Illegal Aliens in the Western Hemisphere.* New York: Praeger. 1981.

Johnson, Kenneth, and Nia Ogle. *Illegal Mexicans in the United States.* Washington, DC: University Press of America. 1978

Knoll, Tricia. *Becoming Americans: Asian Sojourners, Immigrants, and Refugees in the Western United States.* Portland, OR: Coast to Coast Books. 1982.

Kritz, Mary M., ed. *U.S. Immigration and Refugee Policy: Global and Domestic Issues.* Lexington, MA: D.C. Heath. 1982.

Loescher, Gil, and John A. Scanlon. *Calculated Kindness: Refugees and America's Half-Open Door.* New York: Free Press. 1986.

Pozo, Susan, ed. *Essays on Legal and Illegal Immigration.* Kalamazoo, MI: W.E. Upjohn. 1980.

Siegel, Mark A., ed. *Immigration and Illegal Aliens—Burden or Blessing?* Wylie, TX: Information Plus. 1989.

Wittke, Carl. *Refugees of Revolution: The German Forty-Niners in America.* Philadelphia: University of Pennsylvania Press. 1952.

RELIGION AND CHURCHES

Alexander, June G. *The Immigrant Church and Community: Pittsburgh's Slovak Catholics and Lutherans.* Pittsburgh: University of Pittsburgh Press. 1987.

Andersen, Arlow W. *Salt of the Earth: A History of Norwegian-Danish Methodism in America*. Nashville, TN: Parthenon Press. 1962.

Anderson, Charles H. *White Protestant Americans: From National Origins to Religious Group*. Englewood Cliffs, NJ: Prentice-Hall. 1970.

Barry, Colman J. *The Catholic Church and German Americans*. Milwaukee, WI: Bruce Publishing. 1953.

Bobango, Gerald. *The Romanian Orthodox Episcopate of America: The First Half-Century, 1929–1979*. Jackson, MI: Romanian-American Heritage Center. 1979.

Butler, Jon. *The Huguenots in America*. Cambridge, MA: Harvard University Press. 1983.

Cada, Joseph. *Czech-American Catholics*. Chicago: Benedictine Abbey Press. 1964.

Dolan, Jay P. *The Immigrant Church: New York's Irish and German Catholics, 1815–1865*. Baltimore: Johns Hopkins University Press. 1975.

Douglas, Paul F. *The Story of German Methodism*. New York: Methodist Book Concern. 1939.

Elkholy, Abdo A. *The Arab Moslems in the United States: Religion and Assimilation*. New Haven, CT: College and University Press. 1960.

Kayal, Philip, and Joseph Kayal. *Syrian Lebanese in America: A Study in Religion and Assimilation*. Boston: Twayne. 1975.

Liptak, Dolores. *Immigrants and Their Church*. New York: Macmillan, 1988.

Miller, Randall M., and Thomas D. Marzik, eds. *Immigrants and Religion in Urban America*. Philadelphia: Temple University Press. 1977.

Mortensen, Enok. *The Danish Lutheran Church in America: The History and Heritage of the American Evangelical Lutheran Church*. Philadelphia: Board of Publication, Lutheran Church in America. 1967.

Nadel, Stanley. *Little Germany: Ethnicity, Religion and Class in New York City*. Urbana, IL: University of Illinois Press. 1990.

Nelson, Clifford, and Eugene L. Fevold. *The Lutheran Church among Norwegian-Americans: A History of the Evangelical Lutheran Church*. 2 vols. Minneapolis: Augsburg Publishing House. 1960.

Nyholm, Paul C. *The Americanization of the Danish Lutheran Churches in America*. Copenhagen, Denmark: Institute for Danish Church History. 1963.

Olson, James S. *Catholic Immigrants in America*. Chicago: Nelson-Hall. 1986.

Parot, Joseph J. *Polish Catholics in Chicago, 1850–1920*. DeKalb, IL: Northern Illinois University Press. 1981.

Pozzetta, George. *The Immigrant Religious Experience*. New York: Garland. 1991.

Stephenson, George M. *The Religious Aspects of Swedish Immigration: A Study of the Immigrant Churches*. Minneapolis: University of Minnesota Press. [1932] 1972.

Tarsar, Constance J., and John H. Erikson, eds. *Orthodox America, 1794–1976: Development of the Orthodox Church in America*. Syosset, NY: Orthodox Church in America. 1975.

Tomasi, Silvan M. *Piety and Power: The Role of Italian Parishes in the New York Metropolitian Area, 1830–1930*. Staten Island, NY: Center for Migration Studies. 1975.

Zwaanstra, Henry. *Reformed Thought and Experience in the New World: A Study of the Christian Reformed Church and Its American Environment, 1890–1918*. Kampen, Netherlands: J.H. Kok. 1973.

WOMEN

Cordasco, Francesco. *The Immigrant Woman in North America: An Annotated Bibliography of Selected References*. Metuchen, NJ: Scarecrow. 1985.

Dickinson, Joan Y. *The Role of Immigrant Women in the U.S. Labor Force, 1890–1980*. New York: Arno Press. 1980.

Diner, Hasia. *Erin's Daughters in America*. Baltimore: Johns Hopkins University Press. 1983.

Ewen, Elizabeth. *Immigrant Women in the Land of Dollars: Life and Culture on the Lower East Side, 1890–1925*. New York: Monthly Review Press. 1985.

Neidle, Cecyle S. *America's Immigrant Women*. Boston: Twayne. 1975.

Nolan, Janet A. *Ourselves Alone: Women's Immigration from Ireland, 1885–1920*. Lexington, KY: University Press of Kentucky. 1990.

Pozzetta, George. *Ethnicity and Gender: Immigrant Women*. New York: Garland. 1991.

Seller, Maxine, ed. *Immigrant Women*. Albany, NY: State University Press of New York. 1981.

Weinberg, Sydney S. *The World of Our Mothers: The Lives of Jewish Immigrant Women*. New York: Shocken. 1988.

IMMIGRANT GROUPS

Africans

Apraku, Kofi K. *African Emigres in the United States: A Missing Link in Africa's Social and Economic Development*. Westport, CT: Greenwood. 1991.

African-Americans

Aptheker, Herbert, ed. *A Documentary History of the Negro People in the United States*. 6 vols. New York: Carol Publishing Group. 1990.

Bennett, Lerone. *Before the Mayflower: A History of Black America.* 6th ed. New York: Penguin. 1993.

Foner, Philip Sheldon. *History of Black Americans.* 3 vols. Westport, CT: Greenwood Press. [1975] 1983.

Franklin, John Hope. *From Slavery to Freedom: A History of Negro Americans.* 6th ed. New York: McGraw-Hill. 1993.

*Meltzer, Milton, ed. *The Black Americans: A History in Their Own Words, 1619–1983.* New York: T.Y. Crowell. 1984.

*Smead, Howard. *The Afro-Americans.* New York: Chelsea House. 1989.

*Spangler, Earl. *The Blacks in America.* Minneapolis: Lerner. 1980.

Albanians

Demos, Constantine. *The Albanians in America: The First Arrivals.* Boston: Society of Katundi. 1960.

Arabs

Abraham, Sameer Y., and Habeel Abraham, eds. *Arabs in the New World: Studies on Arab-American Communities.* Detroit: Wayne State University Press. 1983.

Aswad, Barbara, ed. *Arab-Speaking Communities in American Cities.* Staten Island, NY: Center for Migration Studies. 1974.

Elkholy, Abado A. *The Arab Moslems in the United States: Religion and Assimilation.* New Haven, CT: Colleges and University Press. 1960.

Hagopian, Elaine C., and Ann Paden, eds. *The Arab-Americans: Studies in Assimilation.* Wilmette, IL: Medina University Press International. 1969.

Hooglund, Eric C., ed. *Crossing the Waters: Arabic-Speaking Immigrants to the United States before 1940.* Washington, DC: Smithsonian. 1987.

Naff, Alixa. *Becoming American: The Early Arab Immigrant Experience.* Carbondale, IL: South Illinois University Press. 1985.

Orfalea, Gregory. *Before the Flames: A Quest for the History of Arab Americans.* Austin, TX: University of Texas Press. 1988.

Armenians

Mirak, Robert. *Torn between Two Lands: Amermenians in America, 1890 to World War I.* Cambridge, MA: Harvard University Press. 1984.

Asian Indians

Chandraselchar, E., ed. *From India to America: A Brief History of Immigration, Admission, and Assimilation.* La Jolla, CA: Popular Review Books. 1982.

Daniels, Roger. *A History of Indian Immigration to the United States.* New York: Asia Society. 1989.

Dasgupta, Sathi S. *On the Trail of an Uncertain Dream: Indian Immigrant Experience in America*. New York: SMD Press. 1989.

Jensen, Joan M. *Passage from India: Asian Indian Immigrants in North America*. New Haven, CT: Yale University Press. 1988.

Lee, Joann F.J., ed. *Asian American Experiences in the United States: Oral Histories of the First to the Fourth Generation Americans from China, the Phillipines, Japan, India, the Pacific Islands, Vietnam, and Cambodia*. Jefferson, NC: McFarland. 1991.

Saran, Parmatma, and Edwin Eames, eds. *Asian-Indians in America*. New York: Praeger. 1980.

Asians

Chan, Sucheng. *Asian Americans: An Interpretive History*. Boston: Twayne. 1991.

Daniels, Roger. *Asian America: Chinese and Japanese in the United States since 1850*. Seattle, WA: University of Washington Press. 1988.

Daniels, Roger, and Harry H.L. Kitano. *Asian Americans: Emerging Minorities*. Englewood Cliffs, NJ: Prentice-Hall. 1988.

Gardner, Robert W., et al. *Asian Americans: Growth, Change, and Diversity*. Washington, DC: Population Reference Bureau. 1985.

Gee, Emma, ed. *Counterpoints: Perspectives on Asian America*. Los Angeles: 1976.

Hing, Bill O. *Making and Remaking Asian America through Immigration Policy, 1850–1990*. Palo Alto, CA: Stanford University Press. 1993.

Hirata, Lucie C., and Edna Bonacich, eds. *Labor Immigration under Capitalism: Asian Immigrant Workers in the United States before World War II*. Berkeley, CA: University of California Press. 1984.

Hong, Maria, ed. *Growing Up Asian-American: An Anthology*. New York: Morrow. 1993.

Hoyt, Edwin P. *Asians in the West*. Nashville, TN: Thomas Nelson. 1974.

Hundley, Norris, ed. *The Asian Americans*. Santa Barbara, CA: ABC-Clio. 1976.

Kim, Elaine H. *Asian Literature: An Introduction to the Writings and Their Social Context*. Philadelphia: Temple University Press. 1982.

Kim, Hyung-Chan, ed. *Dictionary of Asian American History*. Westport, CT: Greenwood. 1986.

Knoll, Tricia. *Becoming Americans: Asian Sojourners, Immigrants, and Refugees in the Western United States*. Portland, OR: Coast to Coast Books. 1982.

Lee, Joann F.J., ed. *Asian American Experiences in the United States: Oral Histories of the First to the Fourth Generation Americans from China, the Phillipines, Japan, India, the Pacific Islands, Vietnam, and Cambodia*. Jefferson, NC: McFarland. 1991.

Lyman, Sanford L. *The Asian in North America.* Santa Barbara, CA: ABC-Clio. 1977.

O'Hare, William P., and Judy C. Felt. *Asian Americans: America's Fastest Growing Minority Group.* Washington, DC: Population Reference Bureau. 1991.

*Perrin, Linda. *Coming to America: Immigrants from the Far East.* New York: Delacorte. 1980.

Takai, Ronald. *Strangers from a Different Shore: A History of Asian Americans.* Boston: Little, Brown. 1989.

Wei, William. *The Asian American Movement.* Philadelphia: Temple University Press. 1993.

Wong, Cynthia Sau-ling. *Reading Asian American Literature: From Necessity to Extravagance.* Princeton, NJ: Princeton University Press. 1993.

Australians

Bateson, Charles. *Gold Fleet for California: Forty-Niners from Australia and New Zealand.* Sydney, Australia: University Smith. 1963.

Austrians

Spaulding, Wilder. *The Quiet Invaders: The Story of the Austrian Impact upon America.* Vienna, Austria: Osterreicher Bundesverlag. 1968.

Basques

Douglass, William A., and Jon Bilbao. *Amerikanuak: Basques in the New World.* Reno, NV: University of Nevada Press. 1975.

Bulgarians

Altankov, Nikolay. *The Bulgarian-Americans.* San Carlos, CA: Ragusan Press. 1979.

Cambodians

Haines, David W., ed. *Refugees as Immigrants: Cambodians, Laotians, and Vietnamese in America.* Lanham, MD: Rowman. 1989.

Lee, Joann F.J., ed. *Asian American Experiences in the United States: Oral Histories of the First to the Fourth Generation Americans from China, the Phillipines, Japan, India, the Pacific Islands, Vietnam, and Cambodia.* Jefferson, NC: McFarland. 1991.

Chinese

Barth, Gunther. *Bitter Strength: A History of the Chinese in the United States, 1850–1870.* Cambridge, MA: Harvard University Press. 1964.

Brownstone, David M. *The Chinese-American Heritage*. New York: Facts on File. 1988.

Chan, Sucheng, ed. *Entry Denied: Exclusion and the Chinese Community in America, 1882–1943*. Philadelphia: Temple University Press. 1991.

———. *This Bittersweet Soil: The Chinese in California Agriculture, 1860–1910*. Berkeley, CA: University of California Press. 1986.

Chen, Jack. *The Chinese of America*. San Francisco: Harper & Row. 1980.

Daniels, Roger. *Asian America: Chinese and Japanese in the United States since 1850*. Seattle: University of Washington Press. 1988.

Jiobu, Robert. *Ethnicity and Assimilation: Blacks, Chinese, Filipinos, Koreans, Japanese, Mexicans, Vietnamese, and Whites*. Albany, NY: State University Press of New York. 1988.

Kinkead, Gwen. *Chinatown: A Portrait of a Closed City*. New York: Harper Perrenial. 1993.

Lee, Joann F.J., ed. *Asian American Experiences in the United States: Oral Histories of the First to the Fourth Generation Americans from China, the Phillipines, Japan, India, the Pacific Islands, Vietnam, and Cambodia*. Jefferson, NC: McFarland. 1991.

Lyman, Stanford M. *Chinese Americans*. New York: Random House. 1974.

Meltzer, Milton. *The Chinese Americans*. New York: Crowell. 1980.

Miller, Stuart C. *The Unwelcome Immigrant: The American Image of the Chinese, 1785–1882*. Berkeley, CA: University of California Press. 1969.

McKee, Delber. *Chinese Exclusion Versus the Open Door Policy*. Detroit: Wayne State University Press. 1977.

Steiner, Stan. *Fusang, The Chinese Who Built America*. New York: Harper & Row. 1978.

Sung, Betty Lee. *Mountain of Gold: The Story of the Chinese in America*. New York: Collier. 1967.

Tsai, Shih-Shan Henry. *The Chinese Experience in America*. Bloomington, IN: Indiana University Press. 1986.

Cornish

Rowse, A.L. *The Cousin Jacks: The Cornish in America*. New York: Scribner. 1969.

Croats

Prpic, George J. *The Croatian Immigrants in America*. New York: Philosophical Library. 1971.

Cubans

Garver, Susan and Paula McGuire. *Coming to North America from Mexico, Cuba, and Puerto Rico*. New York: Delacorte. 1981.

Masud-Piloto, Felix Roberto. *With Open Arms: Cuban Migration to the United States*. Totowa, NJ: Rowman & Littlefield. 1988.

Pedraza-Bailey, Silvia. *Political and Economic Migration in America: Cubans and Mexicans*. Austin, TX: University of Texas Press. 1984.

Portes, Alejandro, and Robert L. Bach. *Latin Journey: Cuban and Mexican Immigrants in the United States*. Berkeley, CA: University of California Press. 1985.

Prieto, Yolanda. *Cuban Migration of the 1960s in Perspective*. New York: New York University. 1984.

Riett, David. *The Exile: Cuba in the Heart of Miami*. New York: Simon and Schuster. 1993.

Rogg, Eleanor Meyer. *Assimilation of Cuban Exiles: The Role of Community and Class*. New York: Aberdeen. 1974.

Czechs

Cada, Joseph. *Czech-American Catholics*. Chicago: Benedictine Abbey Press. 1964.

Capek, Thomas. *Czechs (Bohemians) in America*. Boston: Houghton Mifflin. [1920] 1983.

Dvornik, Frances. *Czech Contributions to the Growth of the United States*. Chicago: Benedictine Abbey Press. 1962.

Jerabek, Esther. *Czechs and Slovaks in North America*. New York: Czechoslovak Society of Arts and Sciences in America. 1977.

Korytova-Magstadt, Stepanica. *To Reap a Bountiful Harvest: Czech Immigration beyond the Mississippi, 1850–1900*. Iowa City, IA: Rudi Publishing. 1993.

Laska, Vera. *The Czechs in America, 1633–1977*. Dobbs Ferry, NY: Oceana. 1977.

Danes

Christensen, Thomas P. *A History of the Danes in Iowa*. New York: Arno. [1952] 1979.

Hvidt, Kristian. *Danes Go West: A Book about the Emigration to America*. Copenhagen, Denmark: Rebuild National Park Society. 1976.

———. *Flight to America: The Social Background of 300,000 Danish Emigrants*. New York: Academic Press. 1975.

Knudsen, Johannes, and Enok Mortensen. *The Danish-American Immigrant*. Des Moines, IA: Published by the authors. 1950.

Mortensen, Enok. *Danish-American Life and Letters*. Des Moines, IA: Commission on Publications of the Danish Evangelical Lutheran Church. 1945.

————. *The Danish Lutheran Church in America: The History and Heritage of the American Evangelical Lutheran Church*. Philadelphia: Board of Publication of Lutheran Church in America. 1967.

Nyholm, Paul C. *The Americanization of the Danish Lutheran Churches in America*. Copenhagen, Denmark: Institute for Danish Church History. 1963.

Dominicans

Hendricks, Glenn. *The Dominican Diaspora: From the Dominican Republic to New York City—Villages in Transition*. New York: Teachers' College Press, Columbia University. 1974.

Dutch

De Jong, Gerald. *The Dutch in America, 1609–1974*. Boston: Twayne. 1975.

Krues, Rob, and Henk-Otto Neuschafer, eds. *The Dutch in North America: Their Immigration and Cultural Continuity*. Amsterdam: VU University Press. 1991.

Lucas, Henry S. *Netherlanders in America: Dutch Immigration to the United States and Canada, 1789–1950*. Ann Arbor, MI: University of Michigan Press. 1955.

Mulder, Arnold. *Americans from Holland*. New York: Lippincott. 1947.

Swierenga, Robert P. *The Dutch in America: Immigration, Settlement, and Cultural Change*. New Brunswick, NJ: Rutgers University Press. 1985.

English

Berthoff, Rowland T. *British Immigrants in Industrial America, 1790–1950*. Cambridge, MA: Harvard University Press. [1953] 1967.

Boston, Ray. *British Chartists in America, 1830–1900*. Totowa, NJ: Rowman & Littlefield. 1971.

Cressy, David. *Coming Over: Migration and Communication between England and New England in the Seventeenth Century*. Cambridge, United Kingdom: Cambridge University Press. 1987.

Ekrich, A. Roger. *Bound for America: The Transportation of British Convicts to the Colonies, 1718–1775*. New York: Oxford University Press. 1987.

Erickson, Charlotte. *Invisible Immigrants: The Adaptation of English and Scottish Immigrants in 19th Century America*. Ithaca, NY: Cornell University Press. [1972] 1990.

Fischer, David Hackett. *Albion's Seed: Four British Folkways in America*. New York: Oxford University Press. 1989.

Harnack, Curtis. *Gentlemen on the Prairie*. Ames, IA: Iowa State University Press. 1985.

Johnson, Stanley C. A History of Emigration from the United Kingdom to North America, 1762–1912. New York: E.P. Dutton. [1913] 1966.

Shepperson, Wilbur S. British Emigration to North America. Minneapolis: University of Minnesota Press. 1957.

Yearley, Clifton K. Britons in American Labor. Baltimore: Johns Hopkins Press. 1957.

Estonians

Parming, Tonu, and Imre Lipping, eds. Early History and the Emergence of an Organized Estonian-American Community. New York: Estonian Learned Society. 1979.

Pehnar, Jaan, Tonu Parming, and P. Peter Rebane, eds. The Estonians in America, 1627–1975: A Chronology and Fact Book. Dobbs Ferry, NY: Oceana. 1975.

Filipinos

Jiobu, Robert. Ethnicity and Assimilation: Blacks, Chinese, Filipinos, Koreans, Japanese, Mexicans, Vietnamese, and Whites. Albany, NY: State University of New York Press. 1988.

Lee, Joann F.J., ed. Asian American Experiences in the United States: Oral Histories of the First to the Fourth Generation Americans from China, the Phillipines, Japan, India, the Pacific Islands, Vietnam, and Cambodia. Jefferson, NC: McFarland. 1991.

Melendy, H. Brett. Asians in America: Filipinos, Koreans, and East Indians. New York: Hippocrene. [1977] 1981.

Saniel, J.M., ed. The Filipino Exclusion Movement, 1927–1935. Quezon City, Phillipines: University of Philippines Press. 1967.

Finns

Hoglund, William A. Finnish Immigrants in America, 1880–1920. Madison, WI: University of Wisconsin Press. 1960.

Jalkaner, Ralph J., ed. The Faith of the Finns: Historical Perspectives on the Finnish Lutheran Church in America. East Lansing, MI: Michigan State University Press. 1972.

Karni, Michael G., et al., eds. The Finns in North America: A Social Symposium. East Lansing, MI: Michigan State University Press. 1969.

Karni, Michael G., and Douglas J. Ollila, Jr., eds. For the Common Good: Finnish Immigrants and the Radical Response to Industrial America. Superior, WI: Tyomics Society. 1972.

French

Butler, Jon. *The Huguenots in America.* Cambridge, MA: Harvard University Press. 1983.

Eccles, W.J. *France in America.* East Lansing, MI: Michigan State University Press. [1973] 1990.

French Canadians

Brault, Gerard. *The French Canadian Heritage in New England.* Hanover, NH: University Press of New England. 1986.

Ducharme, Jacques. *The Shadows of the Trees: The Story of French Canadians in New England.* New York: Harper & Brothers. 1943.

Germans

Bayer, Ronald. *Neighbors in Conflict: The Irish, Germans, Jews and Italians of New York City, 1929–1941.* Baltimore: Johns Hopkins University Press. 1978.

Cunz, Dieter. *The Maryland Germans.* Princeton, NJ: Princeton University Press. 1948.

Dolan, Jay P. *The Immigrant Church: New York's Irish and German Catholics, 1815–1865.* Baltimore: Johns Hopkins Press. 1975.

Douglas, Paul F. *The Story of German Methodism.* New York: Methodist Book Concern. 1939.

Faust, Albert B. *The German Element in the United States.* 2 vols. New York: Houghton Mifflin. [1909] 1970.

Franck, Irene M. *The German-American Heritage.* New York: Facts on File. 1988.

Friesen, Gerhard K., and Walter Schatzberg, eds. *The German Contribution to the Building of the Americas.* Hanover, NH: Clark University Press. 1977.

Gleason, Philip. *The Conservative Reformers: German-American Catholics and the Social Order.* Notre Dame, IN: Notre Dame University Press. 1968.

Hartmut, Keil, and John J. Jentz, eds. *German Workers in Industrial Chicago, 1850–1910: A Comparative Perspective.* DeKalb, IL: Illinois State University Press. 1983.

Jordan, Terry G. *German Seed in Texas Soil.* Austin, TX: University of Texas Press. 1966.

Kamphoefner, Walter D. *The Westphalians: From Germany to Missouri.* Princeton, NJ: Princeton University Press. 1987.

Kamphoefner, Walter D., Wolfgang Helbich, and Ulrike Somme, eds. *News from the Land of Freedom: German Immigrants Write Home.* Ithaca, NY: Cornell University Press. 1991.

Luebke, Frederick C. *Bonds of Loyalty: German-Americans and World War I*. DeKalb, IL: Illinois State University Press. 1974.

Nadel, Stanley. *Little Germany: Ethnicity, Religion and Class in New York City*. Urbana, IL: University of Illinois Press. 1990.

O'Connor, Richard. *The German-Americans*. Boston: Little, Brown. 1968.

Olson, Audrey L. *St. Louis Germans, 1850–1920*. New York: Arno. 1980.

Rippley, LaVern J. *The German-Americans*. Laneham, MD: University Press of America. [1976] 1984.

Sallet, Richard. *German-Russian Settlement in the United States*. Fargo, ND: North Dakota Institute for Regional Studies. 1974.

Tolzmann, Don Heinrich. *German-Americana*. Metuchen, NJ: Scarecrow. 1975.

Walker, Mack. *Germany and Emigration, 1816–1865*. Cambridge, MA: Harvard University Press. 1964.

Wittke, Carl. *The German Language Press in America*. Lexington, KY: University Press of Kentucky. 1957.

———. *Refugees of Revolution: The German Forty-Niners in America*. Philadelphia: University of Pennsylvania. 1952.

Wust, Klaus. *The Virginia Germans*. Charlottesville, VA: University Press of Virginia. 1969.

Wyman, Mark. *Immigrants in the Valley: Irish, Germans, and Americans in the Upper Mississippi Country, 1830–1860*. Chicago: Nelson-Hall. 1984.

Greeks

Burgess, Thomas. *Greeks in America*. New York: Arno. [1913] 1970.

Moskos, Charles Jr. *Greek Americans: Struggle and Success*. Englewood Cliffs, NJ: Prentice-Hall. 1980.

Salutos, Theodore. *Greeks in the United States*. Cambridge, MA: Harvard University Press. 1964.

Gypsies

Brown, Irving. *Gypsy Fires in America*. New York: Harper & Brothers. 1923.

Sutherland, Anne. *Gypsies: The Hidden Americans*. New York: Free Press. 1975.

Haitians

Hunt, Alfred N. *Haiti's Influence on Antebellum America: Slumbering Volcano in the Caribbean*. Baton Rouge, LA: Louisiana State University Press. 1988.

Languerre, Michael S. *American Odyssey: Haitians in New York City*. Ithaca, NY: Cornell University Press. 1984.

Hispanics

Abalos, David. *Latinos in the United States: The Sacred and the Political.* Notre Dame: University of Notre Dame Press. 1986.

Bernal, Martha E., and George P. Knight, eds. *Ethnic Identity: Formation and Transmission among Hispanics and Other Minorities.* Albany: State University of New York Press. 1993.

Fernandez Florez, Dario. *The Spanish Heritage in the United States.* 3d ed. Madrid: Publicaciones Espanolas. 1971.

Gann, Lewis H. *The Hispanics in the United States: A History.* Boulder: Westview Press. 1986.

*Meltzer, Milton. *The Hispanic Americans.* New York: Crowell, 1982.

Shorris, Earl. *Latinos: A Biography of the People.* New York: W.W. Norton & Co. 1992.

Weyr, Thoma. *Hispanic U.S.A.: Breaking the Melting Pot.* New York: Harper & Row. 1988.

Hungarians

Gracza, Rezsoe, and Margaret Gracza. *The Hungarians in America.* Minneapolis: Lerner. 1969.

Lengyel, Emil. *Americans from Hungary.* New York: Lippincott. 1948.

Perlman, Robert. *Bridging Three Worlds: Hungarian-Jewish Americans, 1848–1914.* Amherst, MA: University Massachusetts Press. 1991.

Souders, David Aaron. *The Magyars in America.* San Francisco: George M. Dovan. [1922] 1969.

Szeplaki, Joseph, ed. *The Hungarians in America, 1583–1974: A Chronology and Fact Book.* Dobbs Ferry, NY: Oceana. 1975.

Icelanders

Walters, Thorstina J. *Modern Sagas: The Story of the Icelanders in North America.* Fargo, ND: North Dakota Institute for Regional Studies. 1953.

Irish

Adam, William F. *Ireland and Irish Migration to the New World from 1815 to the Famine.* New Haven, CT: Yale University Press. 1932.

Bayer, Ronald. *Neighbors in Conflict: The Irish, Germans, Jews and Italians of New York City, 1929–1941.* Baltimore: Johns Hopkins University Press. 1978.

Birchall, R.A. *The San Francisco Irish.* Berkeley, CA: University of California Press. 1980.

Brown, Thomas N. *Irish-American Nationalism, 1870–1890.* Philadelphia: Lippincott. 1966.

Diner, Hasia. *Erin's Daughters in America*. Baltimore: Johns Hopkins University Press. 1983.

Dolan, Jay P. *The Immigrant Church: New York's Irish and German Catholics, 1815–1865*. Baltimore: Johns Hopkins University Press. 1975.

Franck, Irene M. *The Irish-American Heritage*. New York: Facts on File. 1988.

Greeley, Andrew M. *That Most Distressful Nation*. Chicago: Quadrangle. 1973.

Kennedy, Robert W. *The Irish: Emigration, Marriage and Fertility*. Berkeley, CA: University of California Press. 1973.

Knobel, Dale. *Paddy and the Republic: Ethnicity and Nationality in Antebellum America*. Middletown, CT: Wesleyan University Press. 1986.

Levine, Edward M. *The Irish and Irish Politicians*. South Bend, IN: Purdue University Press. 1966.

Lockhardt, Audrey. *Some Aspects of Emigration from Ireland to the North American Colonies between 1660 and 1775*. New York: Arno. 1976.

Miller, Kerby. *Emigrants and Exiles: Ireland and the Irish Exodus to North America*. New York: Oxford University Press. 1986.

Miller, Kerby, and Paul Wagner. *Out of Ireland*. Washington, DC: Elliott & Clark. 1994.

Mitchell, Brian C. *The Paddy Camps: The Irish of Lowell, 1821–1861*. Urbana, IL: University of Illinois Press. 1988.

Niehaus, Earl. *The Irish in New Orleans, 1800–1860*. New York: Arno. [1965] 1976.

Nolan, Janet A. *Ourselves Alone: Women's Immigration from Ireland, 1885–1920*. Lexington, KY: University Press of Kentucky. 1990.

Perlmann, Joel. *Ethnic Differences: Schooling and Social Structure among the Irish, Italians, Jews, and Blacks in an American City*. New York: Cambridge University Press. 1988.

Schrier, Arnold. *Ireland and American Immigration*. Minneapolis: University of Minnesota Press. 1958.

Shannon, William V. *The American Irish*. Amherst, MA: University of Massachusetts Press. [1963] 1989.

Wittke, Carl. *The Irish in America*. Baton Rouge, LA: Louisiana State University Press. 1956.

Wyman, Mark. *Immigrants in the Valley: Irish, Germans, and Americans in the Upper Mississippi Country, 1830–1860*. Chicago: Nelson-Hall. 1984.

Italians

Barton, Josef. J. *Peasants and Strangers: Italians, Rumanians, and Slovaks in an American City, 1890–1950*. Cambridge, MA: Harvard University Press. 1975.

Bayer, Ronald, *Neighbors in Conflict: The Irish, Germans, Jews and Italians of New York City, 1929–1941*. Baltimore: Johns Hopkins University Press. 1978.

Bodnar, John, Roger Simon, and Michael P. Weber. *Lives of Their Own: Blacks, Italians, and Poles in Pittsburgh, 1900–1960*. Champaign, IL: University of Illinois Press. 1982.

Briggs, John W. *An Italian Passage: Immigrants to Three American Cities, 1890–1930*. New Haven, CT: Yale University Press. 1978.

Cordasco, Francesco, and Eugene Bucchioni, eds. *The Italians: Social Backgrounds of an American Group*. Clifton, NJ: A.M. Kelley. 1974.

De Conde, Alexander. *Half Bitter, Half Sweet: An Excursion into Italian-American History*. New York: Charles Scribner's Sons. 1971.

Fenton, Edwin. *Immigrants and Unions—A Case Study: Italians and American Labor*. New York: Arno. 1975.

Gabaccia, Donna R. *From Sicily to Elizabeth Street: Housing and Social Change among Italian Immigrants, 1880–1930*. Albany, NY: State University Press of New York. 1984.

———. *Militants and Migrants: Rural Sicilians Become American Workers*. New Brunswick, NJ: Rutgers University Press. 1988.

Gans, Herbert J. *The Urban Villagers: Group and Class in the Life of Italian Americans*. New York: Free Press. 1982.

Green, Rose Basile. *The Italian-American Novel*. Teaneck, NJ: Fairleigh Dickinson University Press. 1974.

Gumina, Deanna Paoli. *The Italians of San Francisco, 1850–1930*. New York: Center for Migration Studies. 1978.

Harney, Robert F., and J. Vincenza Scarpaci, eds. *Little Italies in North America*. Toronto, Canada: Multicultural History Society of Ontario. 1981.

Iorizzo, Luciano J., and Salvatore Mondello. *The Italian-Americans*. Boston: Twayne. [1971] 1980.

Kessner, Thomas. *The Golden Door: Italian and Jewish Immigrant Mobility in New York City, 1880–1915*. New York: Oxford University Press. 1977.

Managione, Jerre, and Ben Morreale. *La Storia: Five Centuries of the Italian-American Experience*. New York: HarperCollins. 1992.

Mormino, Gary R., and George E. Pozzetta. *The Immigrant World of Ybor City: Italians and Their Latin Neighbors in Tampa, 1885–1985*. Champaign, IL: University of Illinois Press. 1987.

———. *Immigrants on the Hill: Italian-Americans in St. Louis, 1882–1982*. Champaign, IL: University of Illinois Press. 1986.

Nelli, Humbert S. *The Business of Crime: Italians and Syndicate Crime in the United States*. New York: Oxford University Press. 1976.

———. *Italians in Chicago, 1880–1930: A Study in Ethnic Mobility*. New York: Oxford University Press. 1970.

Perlmann, Joel. *Ethnic Differences: Schooling and Social Structure among the Irish, Italians, Jews, and Blacks in an American City.* New York: Cambridge University Press. 1988.

Pozzetta, George. *Pane e Lavoro: The Italian American Working Class.* Toronto, Canada: Multicultural History Society of Ontario. 1980.

Rolle, Andrew F. *The Immigrant Upraised: Italian Adventurers and Colonists in an Expanding America.* Norman, OK: University of Oklahoma Press. 1968.

Tomasi, Silvano M., and M.H. Engel, eds. *The Italian Experience in the United States.* Staten Island, NY: Center for Migration Studies. 1970.

———. *Piety and Power: The Role of Italian Parishes in the New York Metropolitian Area, 1830–1930.* Staten Island, NY: Center for Migration Studies. 1975.

Vecoli, Rudolph J. *Italian Immigrants in Rural and Small Town America.* Staten Island, NY: Italian Historical Association. 1987.

Velikonja, Joseph, ed. *Italians in the United States.* Carbondale, IL: Southern Illinois University Press. 1963.

Yans-McLaughlin, Virginia. *Family and Community: Italian Immigrants in Buffalo, 1880–1930.* Ithaca, NY: Cornell University Press. 1977.

Japanese

Bonacich, Edna, and John Modell. *The Economic Basis of Ethnic Solidarity: Small Business in the Japanese-American Community.* Berkeley, CA: University of California Press. 1980.

Daniels, Roger. *Asian America: Chinese and Japanese in the United States since 1850.* Seattle, WA: University of Washington Press. 1988.

Hosokawa, Bill. *Nisei: The Quiet Americans.* Boulder, CO: University Press of Colorado. [1969] 1992.

Ichioka, Yuji. *The Issei: The World of the First Generation Japanese Immigrants, 1885–1924.* New York: Free Press. 1988.

Jiobu, Robert. *Ethnicity and Assimilation: Blacks, Chinese, Filipinos, Koreans, Japanese, Mexicans, Vietnamese, and Whites.* Albany, NY: State University Press of New York. 1988.

Kitano, Harry H.L. *Japanese Americans: The Evolution of a Subculture.* Englewood Cliffs, NJ: Prentice-Hall. 1969.

Lee, Joann F.J., ed. *Asian American Experiences in the United States: Oral Histories of the First to the Fourth Generation Americans from China, the Phillipines, Japan, India, the Pacific Islands, Vietnam, and Cambodia.* Jefferson, NC: McFarland. 1991.

Modell, John. *The Ecomonics and Politics of Racial Accomodation: The Japanese of Los Angeles, 1900–1977.* Urbana, IL: University of Illinois Press. 1977.

Petersen, William. *Japanese Americans.* New York: Random House. 1971.

Smith, Bradford. *Americans from Japan.* Westport, CT: Greenwood. [1948] 1974.

Jews

Bayer, Ronald. *Neighbors in Conflict: The Irish, Germans, Jews and Italians of New York City, 1929–1941*. Baltimore: Johns Hopkins University Press. 1978

Brandes, Joseph. *Immigration to Freedom: Jewish Communities in Rural New Jersey since 1882*. Westport, CT: Greenwood. [1971] 1975.

Brownstone, David M. *The Jewish-American Heritage*. New York: Facts on File. 1988.

Brauberg, Stephen F. *Going to America, Going to School: The Jewish Immigrant Public School Encounter in Turn-of-the-Century New York*. New York: Praeger. 1986.

Butwim, Frances. *The Jews in America*. Minneapolis: Lerner. 1980.

Dinnerstein, Leonard. *America and the Survivors of the Holocaust*. New York: Columbia University Press. 1982.

Feingold, Henry L. *The Politics of Rescue*. New Brunswick, NJ: Transaction. 1970.

———. *Zion in America*. New York: Hippocrene. 1974.

Friedman, Saul. *No Haven for the Oppressed: United States Policy toward Jewish Refugees, 1938–1945*. Detroit: Wayne State University Press. 1973.

Glazer, Nathan. *American Judaism*. 2d ed., Chicago: University of Chicago Press. 1972.

Goren, Arthur H. *New York Jews and the Quest for Community*. New York: Columbia University Press. 1970.

Helmreich, William B. *Against All Odds: Holocaust Survivors and the Successful Lives They Made in America*. New York: Simon and Schuster. 1992.

Hertzberg, Stephen. *Strangers within the Gate City: The Jews of Atlanta, 1845–1915*. Philadelphia: Jewish Publication Society. 1979.

Howe, Irving. *World of Our Fathers: The Journey of the East European Jews to America and the Life They Found and Made*. New York: Harcourt Brace Jovanovich. 1976.

Kessner, Thomas. *The Golden Door: Italian and Jewish Immigrant Mobility in New York City, 1880–1915*. New York: Oxford University Press. 1977.

Marcus, Jacob Rader. *The Colonial American Jew*. 3 vols. Detroit: Wayne State University Press. 1970.

Markowitz, Fran. *A Community in Spite of Itself: Soviet Jewish Emigres in New York*. Washington, DC: Smithsonian Institute. 1993.

Meltzer, Milton, ed. *The Jewish Americans: A History in Their Own Words*. New York: Crowell. 1982.

Metzker, Isaac, ed. *A Bintel Brief: Sixty Years of Letters from the Lower East Side to the Jewish Daily Forward*. New York: Schocken. [1971] 1990.

Moore, Deborah D. *At Home in America: Second Generation New York Jews*. New York: Columbia University Press. 1981.

Ornstein-Galicia, Jacob L. *The Jewish Farmer in America: The Unknown Chronicle.* Lewiston, NY: E. Mellen. 1993.

Perlman, Robert. *Bridging Three Worlds: Hungarian-Jewish Americans, 1848–1914.* Amherst, MA: University of Massachusetts Press. 1991.

Perlmann, Joel. *Ethnic Differences: Schooling and Social Structure among the Irish, Italians, Jews, and Blacks in an American City.* New York: Cambridge University Press. 1988.

Rischin, Moses. *The Promised City: New York's Jews, 1870–1914.* Cambridge, MA: Harper & Row. 1962.

Rosenberg, Stuart E. *The Jewish Community in Rochester, 1843–1925.* New York: American Jewish Historical Society. 1954.

Rubin, Steven J. *Writing Our Lives: Autobiographies of American Jews.* Philadelphia: JPS Philadelphia. 1991.

Sanders, Ronald. *The Downtown Jews: Portraits of an Immigrant Generation.* New York: Harper & Row. 1969.

Sherman, Charles B. *The Jew within American Society: A Study in Ethnic Individuality.* Detroit: Wayne State University Press. 1965.

Shokeid, Moshe. *Children of Circumstance: Israeli Emigrants in New York.* Ithaca, NY: Cornell University Press. 1988.

Sklare, Marshall. *America's Jews.* New York: Random House. 1971.

Vorspan, Max, and Lloyd P. Gartner. *History of the Jews of Los Angeles.* San Marino, CA: Jewish Publication Society of America. 1970.

Weinberg, Sydney S. *The World of Our Mothers: The Lives of Jewish Immigrant Women.* New York: Schocken. 1988.

Wyszkowski, Charles. *A Community in Conflict: American Jewry during the Great European Immigration.* Lanham, MD: University Press of America. 1991.

Zielonka, D., and R. Wechman. *The Eager Immigrants: A Survey of the Life and Americanization of Jewish Immigrants to the United States.* Champaign, IL: University of Illinois Press. 1972.

Koreans

Choy, Bong Youn. *Koreans in America.* Chicago: Nelson-Hall. 1979.

Jiobu, Robert. *Ethnicity and Assimilation: Blacks, Chinese, Filipinos, Koreans, Japanese, Mexicans, Vietnamese, and Whites.* Albany, NY: State University of New York Press. 1988.

Kim, Hyung-Chan, and Wayne Peterson, eds. *The Koreans in America, 1882–1974: A Chronology and Fact Book.* Dobbs Ferry, NY: Oceana. 1974.

———. *The Korean Diaspora: Historical and Sociological Studies of Korean Immigration and Assimilation in North America.* Santa Barbara, CA: ABC-Clio. 1977.

Melendy, H. Brett. *Asians in America: Filipinos, Koreans, and East Indians.* Boston: Hippocrene. 1977.

Patterson, Wayne. *Koreans in America.* Minneapolis: Lerner. 1992.

Laotians

Haines, David W., ed. *Refugees as Immigrants: Cambodians, Laotians, and Vietnamese in America.* Lanham, MD: Rowman. 1989.

Latvians

Akmentins, Osvalds. *Latvians in Bicentennial America.* Waverly, IA: Latvja Gramata. 1976.

Karklis, Maruta, Liga Streips, and Laimonis Streips. *The Latvians in America: A Chronology and Fact Book.* Dobbs Ferry, NY: Oceana. 1974.

Lebanese

Kayal, Philip, and Joseph Kayal. *Syrian Lebanese in America: A Study in Religion and Assimilation.* Boston: Twayne. 1975.

Lithuanians

Greene, Victor R. *For God and Country: The Rise of Polish and Lithuanian Ethnic Consciousness in America, 1860–1910.* Madison, WI: University of Wisconsin Press. 1975.

Mexicans

Camarillo, Albert. *Chicanos in a Changing Society: From Mexican Pueblos to American Barrios in Santa Barbara and Southern California, 1848–1930.* Cambridge, MA: Harvard University Press. 1979.

———, ed. *The Mexican American.* Multivolume. New York: 1974.

Davis, Marilyn P. *Mexican Voices/American Dreams: An Oral History of Mexican Immigration to the United States.* New York: Henry Holt. 1990.

Deutsch, Sarah. *No Separate Refuge: Culture, Class, and Gender on an Anglo-Hispanic Frontier in the American Southwest, 1880–1940.* New York: Oxford University Press. 1987.

Galarza, Ernesto. *Merchants of Labor: The Mexican Bracero Story.* Charlotte, NC: McNally and Loftin. 1969.

Garcia, Juan Ramon. *Operation Wetback: The Mass Deportation of Mexican Undocumented Workers in 1954.* Westport, CT: Greenwood. 1980.

Garcia, Mario T. *Desert Immigrants: The Mexicans of El Paso, 1880–1920.* New Haven, CT: Yale University Press. 1981.

———. *Mexican-Americans: Leadership, Ideology, and Identity, 1930–1960.* New Haven, CT: Yale University Press. 1989.

*Garver, Susan, and Paula McGuire. *Coming to America from Mexico, Cuba, and Puerto Rico.* New York: Delacorte. 1981.

Heer, David M. *Undocumented Mexicans in the United States.* New York: Cambridge University Press. 1990.

Jiobu, Robert. *Ethnicity and Assimilation: Blacks, Chinese, Filipinos, Koreans, Japanese, Mexicans, Vietnamese, and Whites.* Albany, NY: State University of New York Press. 1988.

Johnson, Kenneth, and Nia Ogle. *Illegal Mexicans in the United States.* Washington, DC: University Press of America. 1978

Langley, Lester D. *Mex America: Two Countries, One Future.* New York: Crown. 1988.

Lopez, Tiffany Ana, ed. *Growing Up Chicano: An Anthology.* New York: Morrow. 1993.

Meier, Matt S., and Feliciano Rivera. *The Chicanos: A History of Mexican-Americans.* New York: Hilland Wang. 1972.

Moore, Joan W., and Ralph C. Guzman. *The Mexican American People: The Nation's Second Largest Minority.* New York: Free Press. 1970.

Moore, Joan W., and Harry Pachon. *Mexican Americans.* Rev. ed. Englewood Cliffs, NJ: Prentice-Hall. 1976.

Moquin, Wayne, ed. *A Documentary History of the Mexican Americans.* New York: Praeger. 1971.

Pedraza-Bailey, Silvia. *Political and Economic Migration in America: Cubans and Mexicans.* Austin, TX: University of Texas Press. 1984.

Portes, Alejandro, and Robert L. Bach. *Latin Journey: Cuban and Mexican Immigrants in the United States.* Berkeley, CA: University of California Press. 1985.

Samora, Julian. *Los Mojados: The Wetback Story.* South Bend, IN: University of Notre Dame Press. 1971.

Stoddard, Ellwyn R. *Mexican Americans.* New York: University Press of America. 1973.

Weber, David J. *Foreigners in the Native Land: Historical Roots of the Mexican Americans.* Albuquerque, NM: University of New Mexico Press. 1973.

New Zealanders

Bateson, Charles. *Gold Fleet for California: Forty-Niners from Australia and New Zealand.* Sydney, Australia: University Smith. 1963.

Norwegians

Andersen, Arlow W. *The Immigrant Takes His Stand: The Norwegian American Press and Public Affairs, 1847–1872.* Northfield, MN: Norwegian-American Historical Association. 1953.

————. *The Norwegian-Americans*. Boston: Twayne. 1974.

Bjork, Kenneth O. *West of the Great Divide: Norwegian Migration to the Pacific Coast, 1847–1893*. Northfield, MN: Norwegian-American Historical Association. 1958.

Blegen, Theodore C. *Norwegian Migration to America*. 2 vols. Northfield, MN: Norwegian-American Historical Association. [1931] 1961.

Gjerde, Jon. *From Peasants to Farmers: The Migration from Balestrand, Norway, to the Upper Middle West*. Cambridge, United Kingdom: Cambridge University Press. 1985.

Lovoll, Odd S. *The Promise of America: A History of the Norwegian-American People*. Minneapolis: University of Minnesota Press. 1984.

Nelson, Clifford, and Eugene L. Fevold. *The Lutheran Church among Norwegian-Americans: A History of the Evangelical Lutheran Church*. 2 vols. Minneapolis: Augsburg Publishing House. 1960.

Norlie, Olaf M. *History of the Norwegian People in America*. New York: Haskell. [1925] 1973.

Qualey, Carlton C. *Norwegian Settlement in the United States*. Northfield, MN: Norwegian-American Historical Association. 1938.

Semmingsen, Ingrid. *Norway to America: A History of the Migration*. Minneapolis: University of Minnesota Press. 1978.

Wefald, Jon. *A Voice of Protest: Norwegians in American Politics, 1890–1917*. Northfield, MN: Norwegian-American Historical Association. 1971.

Pacific Islanders

*Ford, Douglas. *The Pacific Islanders*. New York: Chelsea House. 1989.

Lee, Joann F.J., ed. *Asian American Experiences in the United States: Oral Histories of the First to the Fourth Generation Americans from China, the Phillipines, Japan, India, the Pacific Islands, Vietnam, and Cambodia*. Jefferson, NC: McFarland. 1991.

Poles

Bodnar, John, Roger Simon, and Michael P. Weber. *Lives of Their Own: Blacks, Italians and Poles in Pittsburgh, 1900–1960*. Champaign, IL: University of Illinois Press. 1982.

Fox, Paul. *The Poles in America*. New York: George H. Doran. [1922] 1970.

Greene, Victor R. *For God and Country: The Rise of Polish and Lithuanian Ethnic Consciousness in America, 1860–1910*. Madison, WI: University of Wisconsin Press. 1975.

Grzelonski, Bogdan. *Poles in the United States of America, 1776–1865*. Warsaw, Poland: Interpress. 1976.

Kantowicz, Edward R. *Polish-American Politics in Chicago, 1888–1940*. Chicago: University of Chicago Press. 1975.

Parot, Joseph J. *Polish Catholics in Chicago, 1850–1920.* DeKalb, IL: Northern Illinois University Press. 1981.

Wytrwal, Joseph. *America's Polish Heritage.* Detroit: Endurance Press. 1961.

Zurawski, Joseph. *Polish American History and Culture.* Chicago: Polish Museum of America. 1975.

Portuguese

Brown, Walton John. *Portuguese in California.* San Francisco: R and E Research Associates. 1972.

Cardozo, Manoel da Silveira, ed. *The Portuguese in America, 590 B.C.–1974: A Chronology and Fact Book.* Dobbs Ferry, NY: Oceana. 1976.

Pap, Leo. *The Portuguese in the United States: A Bibliography.* Staten Island, NY: Center for Migration Studies. 1976.

Rogers, Francis Millet. *Americans of Portuguese Descent: A Lesson in Differentiation.* Beverly Hills, CA: Sage Publications. 1974.

Taft, Donal Reed. *Two Portuguese Communities in New England.* New York: AMS Press. 1967.

Puerto Ricans

Fitzpatrick, Joseph P. *Puerto Rican Americans: The Meaning of Migration to the Mainland.* Englewood Cliffs, NJ: Prentice-Hall. 1971.

*Garver, Susan and Paula McGuire. *Coming to North America from Mexico, Cuba, and Puerto Rico.* New York: Delacorte. 1981.

Larsen, Ronald J. *The Puerto Ricans in America.* Minneapolis: Lerner. 1989.

Senior, Clarence. *The Puerto-Ricans: Strangers—Then Neighbors.* Chicago: Quadrangle. 1965.

Romanians

Barton, Josef J. *Peasants and Strangers: Italians, Rumanians, and Slovaks in an American City, 1890–1950.* Cambridge, MA: Harvard University Press. 1975.

Bobango, Gerald. *The Romanian Orthodox Episcopate of America: The First Half-Century, 1929–1979.* Jackson, MI: Romanian-American Heritage Center. 1979.

Wertsman, Vladimir. *The Romanians in America, 1748–1974: A Fact Book and Chronology.* Dobbs Ferry, NY: Oceana. 1975.

Russians

Davis, Jerome. *The Russian Immigrant.* New York: Macmillan. [1922] 1969.

Markowitz, Fran. *A Community In Spite of Itself: Soviet Jewish Emigres in New York.* Washington, DC: Smithsonian Institute. 1993.

Sallet, Richard. *German-Russian Settlement in the United States.* Fargo, ND: North Dakota Institute for Regional Studies. 1974.

Smith, Henry C. *The Coming of the Russian Mennonites.* Berne, IN: Mennonite Book Concern. 1927.

Scandinavians

Franck, Irene M. *The Scandinavian-American Heritage.* New York: Facts on File. 1988.

Scotch-Irish

Dickson, Robert J. *Ulster Emigration to Colonial America, 1718–1775.* London: Routledge. 1966.

Green, E.E.R., ed. *Essays in Scotch-Irish History.* London: Routledge. 1969.

Leyburn, James G. *The Scotch-Irish: A Social History.* Raleigh, NC: University of North Carolina Press. 1962.

Scots

Black, George F. *Scotland's Mark on America.* San Francisco: R & E Research Associates. [1921] 1972.

Donaldson, Gordon. *The Scots Overseas.* London: Hale. 1966.

Erickson, Charlotte. *Invisible Immigrants: The Adaptation of English and Scottish Immigrants in 19th Century America.* Ithaca, NY: Cornell University Press. [1972] 1990.

Graham, Ian C.C. *Colonists from Scotland: Emigration to North America, 1707–1783.* Ithaca, NY: Cornell University Press. 1965.

Landsman, Ned. *Scotland and Its First American Colony.* Princeton, NJ: Princeton University Press. 1985.

Slavs

Prpic, George. *Southern Slavic Immigration in America.* Boston: Twayne. 1978.

Slovaks

Barton, Josef J. *Peasants and Strangers: Italians, Rumanians, and Slovaks in an American City, 1890–1950.* Cambridge, MA: Harvard University Press. 1975.

Jerabek, Esther. *Czechs and Slovaks in North America.* New York: Czechoslovak Society of Arts and Sciences in America. 1977.

Spaniards

Fernandez-Shaw, Carlos M. *The Hispanic Presence in North America.* New York: Facts on File. 1987.

Foster, George M. *Culture and Conquest: America's Spanish Heritage*. New York: Wenner-Gren Foundation. 1960.

Weber, David J. *The Spanish Frontier in North America*. New Haven, CT: Yale University Press. 1992.

Swedes

Ander, O. Fritiof. *The Cultural Heritage of the Swedish Immigrant*. Rock Island, IL: Augustana College. 1956.

Bartow, Arnold, ed. *Letters from the Promised Land: Swedes in America, 1840–1914*. Minneapolis: University of Minnesota Press. 1975.

Beibom, Ulf. *Swedes in Chicago*. Vajo, Sweden: Scandinavian University Books. 1971.

Capps, Finis H. *From Isolationism to Involvement: The Swedish Immigrant Press in America, 1914–1945*. Chicago: Swedish Pioneer Historical Society. 1966.

Kastrup, Allan. *The Swedish Heritage in America*. St. Paul, MN: Swedish Council of America. 1975.

Moberg, Vilhelm. *The Unknown Swedes: A Book about Swedes and America, Past and Present*. Carbondale, IL: Southern Illinois University Press. 1988.

Nelson, Helga. *The Swedes and Swedish Settlements in North America*. 2 vols. Lund, Sweden: C.W.K. Gleerup. 1943.

Ostergen, Robert C. *A Community Transplanted: The Trans-Atlantic Experience of a Swedish Immigrant Settlement in the Upper Middle West, 1835–1915*. Madison, WI: University of Wisconsin Press. 1988.

Runblom, Harald, and Hans Norman, eds. *From Sweden to America: A History of the Migration*. Minneapolis: University of Minnesota Press. 1976.

Stephenson, George M. *The Religious Aspects of Swedish Immigration: A Study of the Immigrant Churches*. Minneapolis: University of Minnesota Press. 1972.

Swiss

Grueningen, John P., ed. *The Swiss in the United States*. Madison, WI: Swiss-American Historical Society. 1940.

Schelbert, Leo. *Swiss in North America*. Philadelphia: Balch Institute. 1974.

Syrians

Hitti, Philip. *Syrians in America*. New York: George H. Doran. 1924.

Kayal, Philip, and Joseph Kayal. *Syrian Lebanese in America: A Study in Religion and Assimilation*. Boston: Twayne. 1975.

Ukranians

Halich, Wasyl. *Ukrainians in the United States.* New York: University of Chicago Press. [1937] 1970.

Kuropas, Myron B. *Ukrainians in America.* Minneapolis: Lerner. 1972.

Wertsman, Vladimir. *The Ukrainians in America, 1608–1975: A Chronology and Fact Book.* Dobbs Ferry, NY: Oceana. 1976.

Vietnamese

Haines, David W., ed. *Refugees as Immigrants: Cambodians, Laotians, and Vietnamese in America.* Lanham, MD: Rowman. 1989.

Hawthorne, Lesleyanne, ed. *Refugee: The Vietnamese Experience.* New York: Oxford University Press. 1982.

Jiobu, Robert. *Ethnicity and Assimilation: Blacks, Chinese, Filipinos, Koreans, Japanese, Mexicans, Vietnamese, and Whites.* Albany, NY: State University of New York Press. 1988.

Kelly, Gail P. *From Vietnam to America: A Chronicle of Vietnamese Immigration to the United States.* Boulder, CO: Westview. 1979.

Lee, Joann F.J., ed. *Asian American Experiences in the United States: Oral Histories of the First to the Fourth Generation Americans from China, the Phillipines, Japan, India, the Pacific Islands, Vietnam, and Cambodia.* Jefferson, NC: McFarland. 1991.

Liu, William T., M. Lamanna, and A. Murata. *Transition to Nowhere: Vietnamese Refugees in America.* Nashville, TN: Charter House. 1979.

Montero, Darrel, and Marsha I. Weber. *Vietnamese Americans: Patterns of Resettlement and Socioeconomic Adaptation in the United States.* Boulder, CO: Westview Press. 1979.

Welsh

Conway, Alan, ed. *The Welsh in America: Letters from the Immigrants.* Cardiff, United Kingdom: University of Wales Press. 1961.

Hartmann, Edward G. *Americans from Wales.* New York: Octagon. [1967] 1978.

Wends

Blasig, Anne. *The Wends of Texas.* San Antonio, TX: Naylor. 1954.

Nielson, George R. *In Search of a Home: The Wends (Sorbs) on the Australian and Texas Frontiers.* Birmingham, United Kingdom: University of Birmingham. 1977.

West Indians

Bryce-Laporte, Roy S., and Delores Mortimer, eds. *Caribbean Immigration to the United States*. Washington, DC: Smithsonian. 1976.

Foner, Nancy. *Jamaican Migrants: A Comparative Analysis of the New York and London Experience*. New York: Center for Latin and Carribean Studies. 1983.

Yugoslavs

Colakovic, Mita. *Yugoslav Migrations to America*. San Francisco: R&E Research. 1973.

Govorchin, George G. *Americans from Yugoslavia*. Gainesville, FL: University of Florida Press. 1961.

INDEX

• • • • • • • • •